HUMAN RIGHTS

HUMAN RIGHTS
Changing Perspectives

Dr I. Subramanyam

KALPAZ

Human Rights: Changing Perspectives

ISBN: 978-81-7835-920-5

Published in 2012 in India by
Kalpaz Publications
C-30, Satyawati Nagar,
Delhi-110052
E-mail: kalpaz@hotmail.com
Phone : 9212729499

Lasser Type Setting : Quick Media, Delhi
Printed at : G. Print Process,Delhi

Contents

Preface

The term "Human Rights" denotes all those rights which are inherent in our nature and without which we cannot live as human beings. In other words, human rights being eternal part of the nature of human beings. These are essential for individual to develop their personality, human qualities, their intelligence, talent and conscience to enable them to satisfy their spiritual and other higher needs. As such, the range of human rights is very wide. It covers variety of rights including traditional civil rights like the right to life, the right to personal liberty, the right to freedom of thought and expression, the right to work, the right to property and the right to freedom of religion. A number of political rights are recognized in modern states are the right to vote, the right to be elected, the right to hold public office, the right to criticism and the right to petition. And the newly developed economic, social and cultural rights. These are the right to work, right to education, right to health, right to adequate shelter and services, right to culture, right to family and right to marriage and the right to form and join trade union. In any state for ensuring economic and social justice to all the people these rights are necessary.

The general notion of human rights as such, has today penetrated into international convention national constitutions, legislations and even in the judicial pronouncements. According to protection of Human Rights Act, 1993, "Human Rights" means the rights relating to life, liberty, equality and dignity of the individual guaranteed by the Constitution or embodied in the International Covenants and enforceable by counts in India.

The growth of the concept of the "Human Rights", has been closely associated with the traditional natural law theories. As a matter of fact the notion of individual rights has never been projected as special feature in these theories. Law as such "Implies both duties and rights, and it is no doubt fair to say that the ancient and medieval theories of natural law were more connected with the foundation of moral, legal and political duty than with the foundation of rights.

Human Rights are neither derived from the social order nor confessed upon the individual by the society. They reside inherently in the individual human beings independent of and even prior to his participation in the society. As such, they are the result of recognition by the state but they are logically independent of the legal system for their existence.

Human Rights are said to be inalienable, natural and inherent. Human rights are inalienable in the sense that a holder of these rights cannot divert himself of them. The reason is simple. These rights are inherent in the very nature of human being.

All human beings are said to be essentially equal. Now it is established fact that human rights are derived directly or indirectly from the very nature of man. From this it may be argued that by virtue of being human, are inheres all those attributes which are inherent in human personality.

The decade starting from the year 1995 to 2004 has been declared by the United Nations as the decade of Human Rights Education. India has been a party to the Human Rights concerns eversince the Universal Declaration of Human Rights charter was adopted on 10th December, 1948. India was also a signatory to the two International Covenants viz., Civil and Political Rights and Socio-economic and Cultural Rights and several international instruments. In the same spirit India welcomed the United Nations decision on human rights education. As a part of this commitment, the National Human Rights Commission has been engaged in this task. Several institutions, research organization and universities evinced interest in this effort.

This book describes about various perspectives on Human Rights. It includes the role of state, media, violation of housing rights in the era of globalization. Impact of globalization on Human Rights in India. Right Housing, poverty and human rights, child labour and human rights in India. Empowerment of women and violation of women workers rights in rural areas. Violation of dalit rights in the era of globalization, constitutional safeguards for the protection of dalit rights in India, Dr. B.R. Ambedkar's ideology for protection of Dalit Rights, status of tribal development, right to health with special reference to vulnerable groups.

I hope this will be useful to all the Human Rights lovers and scholars.

Dr. I. Subramanyam

1

State, Human Rights and Globalisation

The state is the political organization of society. The term 'state' in a limited sense refers broadly to the administrative apparatus of the state, the instrumentalities of the state or the agencies of the state or the government. The legitimate functions of the state include not only the maintenance of internal peace and defence against external aggression, but also the administration of justice and the provision, whenever necessary, of various essential services and amenities for the people. The functions of the state being of an enduring nature, it is unrealistic to suppose that the state will wither away either now or at any time in the future.

A modern state has necessarily to look after people's requirements with regard to education, health and housing. It has also to provide for economic justice and promote healthy economic development. It must regulate currency, banking and international trade. The old maxim that government is the best which governs the least has still an element of truth, because the modern state has a tendency to expand beyond what is necessary in the public interest. It cannot, however, be denied that the state of today is required to discharge a larger number of functions than those which have formerly regarded as its legitimate domain. Today the state is accepted as a 'welfare' or 'social state' with new significance of functions it is required to perform. These are divided into three main categories, protective or police, welfare, economic and regulatory.

In the face of economic globalisation which is a complex trend, including globalisation of the production process, global capital mobility, neo-liberal development agendas and finally globalization of subcontracting and informal labour, it is difficult to limit the agenda of democracy and distributive justice within the state. The state is no longer the main framework for economic policy making and governments have been forced to accommodate outside pressure that adversely affect the living standards of ordinary citizens.

The debate on human rights suggests - undoubtedly and justifiably - that the state or the governments or the agencies of the state are the prime and foremost violators of human rights. Barring some exceptions, the role of the state in relation to human rights is widely perceived as being negative and the state as an institution turns out to be no respect for human rights more particularly so in relation to the poor, the downtrodden, the women, the suffering or any group agitating for their basic rights. Indeed, the state stands out as a repressive state or as an oppressor. The struggle for human rights thus seems to be mainly directed against the state and its agencies.

On the other hand, the major emphasis under the Universal Declaration of Human Rights as well as the pronouncements at the various conferences of the United Nations has been on the obligation of the member states to promote and protect human rights. Even the Vienna Declaration and Programme of Action adopted, on 25 June 1993 by the World Conference on Human Rights, reaffirmed the solemn commitment of all states to fulfill their obligations to promote universal respect for and observance and protection of all human rights. More specifically, it has been declared at the Vienna Conference that the protection and promotion of human rights is the first responsibility of the government. In other words, it would appear that those who regularly and consistently violate human rights are themselves expected to regulate their own behaviour to bring them in conformity with the requirements of a universal standard of human rights.

Indeed, the Indian Constitution itself has laid great stress on human rights and dignity of the individuals. Political and civil rights became the cornerstones in India's constitution with the rule of law and an independent judiciary occupying important position in the polity which combine political democracy with the ideas of social justice. The chapter on the Directive Principles of the Indian Constitution is an example of social and economic rights obtaining a constitutional sanction. Almost all the issues for which the people struggle in their daily lives, whether it is equality, freedom, human dignity, nondiscrimination, social and economic justice, right to work, right to livelihood, living wage or protection from exploitation find place in the Indian constitution in one form or the other. Subsequent to independence and the enactment of the constitution, the imperative need for economic and social justice was recognized through a number of public policy responses which had a direct bearing on the condition of masses in relation to the distribution of property and the means of livelihood. A series of social legislations emerged in line with the spirit of the constitution. A variety of institutions were also set up for the protection and promotion of values such as liberty, freedom and the rule of law. There is thus a long tradition of laws, legal prescriptions, institutional arrangements and administrative setup to accomplish the objectives of equality and social justice and to enable the protection of human rights. In a sense, the historical experience starting with the abolition of slavery by the Indian Slavery Act of 1843 down to the proscription of bonded labour about 130 years later by the Bonded Labour System (Abolition) Act 1976, highlight the potential positive role of the state and its institutions in the process of social transformation and upholding of human rights.

Leaving aside the state, free space guaranteed to the individual freedom and the safeguard for its nonviolation, along with the corresponding remedial measures, which could be termed as nonviolable rights to be enjoyed through noninterference by the state, there are a large number of positive human rights particularly those in favour of the poor, the disadvantaged and the underprivileged which have to be acted upon affirmatively by the state and its agencies. The constitutional provisions proclaiming the abolition of untouchability and the forbidding of forced and bonded labour, the Protection of Civil Rights Act 1955, the Bonded Labour System (Abolition) Act 1976, the Child Labour (Prohibition and Regulation) Act 1986, the whole series of land reform legislations, the land allotment rules and the myriad developmental programmes known as poverty alleviation programmes, the scheme of reservations in favour of the weaker sections not only in public services but in various other fields, including the allotment of land and housing - all these constitute positive rights intended to enhance human dignity and to mitigate human suffering. In other words, untouchability is a human right issue, bonded labour is a human right issue, poverty too is a human right issue. It would be interesting to note in this context that Article 11.2 of the International Covenant on Economic, Social and Cultural Rights recognizes the fundamental right to everyone to be free from hunger. All these rights are to be protected and promoted by the apparatus of the state.

The state and all the institutions of the state are bound by the constitution and the laws emanating from it. All the agents of the state owe allegiance to the constitution. The bureaucracy is bound by the constitution and the rule of law, even if this could lead to the criticism of its becoming 'rule bound' in the process. At the minimum, even if the state and its agencies adhere strictly to the constitution and the rule of law in their functioning, it will serve to enhance the human rights to a significant extent.

Globalization, Sovereignty and Nation-States

The phenomenon of globalization has seriously challenged the identity and sovereignty as well as the working of nation-states. If globalization means emergence of borderless states, then the very existence of the nation-state is questioned. Who controls the territory, population as well as the government in the globalized world? Not certainly the nation-states. Deterritorialization of the nation-states is taking place. Products and capital are moving with the least possible hindrance. As *Human Development Report* remarks "national borders are also breaking down in economic policy—as multilateral agreements and the pressures of staying competitive in global markets constrain the options for national policy, and as multinational corporations and global crime syndicates integrate their operations globally."

The states are in no capacity to take economic decisions such as what to produce, how to produce and, for whom and how much to produce. The process of liberalization and privatization has seriously weakened the control and functioning of bureaucracy considered to be the backbone of the states. What we are witnessing, today, is the emergence of "contracted and atrophied states".

As more and more countries belonging particularly to the "Third World" are taking recourse to free trade, the national and international economic policies are being taken not by the national governments but by powerful international economic and financial institutions like the International Monetary Fund, the World Bank and the World Trade Organization. These institutions are being ably supported by a new class of the people, called technocrats, who have taken over the role of the traditional bureaucrats. This process has gathered momentum in countries of Eastern Europe where a dramatic transition from centrally planned economic system to market democracies has taken place. This is equally true in case of the so-called socialist countries like China, Mongolia and Vietnam.

While commenting on the nature of global governance, the HDR points out that (a) intergovernmental policy-making in today's global economy is in the hands of the major industrial powers and the international institutions they control—the World Bank, the International Monetary Fund, the Bank for International Settlement, (b) ad hoc and self selected policy groups such as G-7 are making de facto global economic policy in which developing countries and G-15 have the least say, and (c) there is little participation of the poor countries in the formulation and implementation of the new rules that govern markets. This was very much obvious during the Uruguay round of GATT negotiations and this, is equally apparent in case of WTO negotiations where the poor countries have little capacity and skill to bargain with rich countries. Their weakness in the negotiating capacity has further been compounded due to the breakup of the common "South" position on global trade issues.

This highly skewed system and arrangement of global governance has adversely affected the notion of sovereign equality as propounded by the UN. As HDR remarks 'the rapidly increasing multilateral agreements—the new rules—are highly binding on the national governments and constrain domestic policy choices. The 'unbalanced' Trade Related Aspects of Intellectual Property Rights (TRIPS) has further eroded the sovereign decision making power of the poor countries as almost all knowledge-based production is now subject to tight intellectual property protection. Moreover the TRIPS agreement *provides an enabling environment for multinationals, tightening their dominant ownership of technology, impeding and increasing the cost of transfer to developing countries.* In sum we can say that in the age of globalization, the internal and the external behaviour of the nation-states is conditioned and governed by the multinational corporations as well as the multilateral institutions like the IMF, the World Bank and the WTO. Sovereignty belongs to those who are strong and powerful.

The establishment of globalized economic institutions like the IMF, the World Bank and the WTO has, on the one hand, been a symptom of and a stimulus for globalization and, on the other, it indicates the trend away from the dominance of the state as the exclusive unit of analysis in international affairs. The World Bank report observes that the "global events and international agreements are putting constraints on state's arbitrary action and are increasingly affecting its choices." Besides, as McCorquodale puts it "states no longer enjoy exclusive control over their economic, legal, political and sovereign affairs. Moreover, the current trend of globalization differs from past transnational influences on state sovereignty in the scale and speed of its operation."

The transnational flow of goods, capital, people, and ideas has equally affected the sovereign identity of the nation-states and so have the transnational corporations and intergovernmental institutions. The rise in popular participation at the grassroots level, emergence of civil-societies and the enhancement of non-governmental organizations have also influenced and limited the activities of the nation-states.

As one commentator points out, the globalization process has led to a corresponding decline in the role of the modern nation-state in regulating the nature of the growth of the political economy at the national level, as the multinational corporations driven by market forces have taken over. Economic reforms are being forced upon the nation-states so that national economies can be restructured in accordance with the external changes taking place at the level of the global economy. Globalization has also forced the nation-states to "retreat" from their welfare activities and become the promoter of the interests of the global capital/

capitalist class. The people are being left to the discipline and dictate of the market forces more and more brutally.

As Aijaz Ahmad observes, it is the state that is dismantling welfare and implementing liberalization in all the countries across the globe. In other words, the nation-state has become weaker in relation to capital, whose will it must implement most savagely, and weak in relation to labour, whom it treats with hateful contempt. In other words, the state is now not even pretending to be anything but the managing committee of the whole bourgeoisie—and this time, not the *whole* but also the *transnational* bourgeoisie. In the Third World, the state no longer even pretends to represent the people against imperialism. It represents imperial interest to the people.

Moreover, the retreat of the state from the realm of the popular entitlements, health, education, employment, preservation of natural resources, and so on has enabled the NGOs and social movements, to fill the vacuum. But the sad part of it is that they are always narrow and local in focus and frequently dependent on foreign funding agencies. Besides, in the name of performing the social responsibility of the state, they appear to supplant such historic forms of mass organizations as the trade union and the political party and, are funded from the imperial centres and have channels to such things as World Bank. They, thus, represent the interest of the imperial power and agencies instead of fulfilling the aspirations of the third world masses. However, in advanced countries, which hate the concept of too much government, such retreat of the state is celebrated as the triumph of "neo-liberal ideology" in the name of the "end of history". The "retreat of state", in other words, has signalled the doom for socialism and triumph of capitalism.

But, does all this mean that the state has become irrelevant and purposeless in the age of globalization? The answer is big 'No'. Only its nature and character has changed, particularly in the developing countries where the welfare function of the state has declined. As Aijaz Ahmad points out, "the mythology of globalization includes the sizeable myth that the nation-state is on way out. In reality, imperialism itself needs not the abolition of nation-states in the Third World but the strengthening of them for its own purposes."

First, a strong nation-state is required for the secure movement of capital. The US is the main capital exporting country, today, for the reason that the bearers of its capital could rely on the support, including the crucial military support, that their nation-state could provide them, anywhere in the world. Second, a strong nation-state is required as it creates space for the deep penetration of capital. Imperialism, capitalism aad nation-state are interrelated and they reinforce each other. Third, far from destroying the nation-state in its march toward globalization, capital indeed needs the state for the enforcement of the contract law, internationalized legal systems and other instruments that are necessary to ensure linkages between national and transnational market forces. The US is not averse to the Chinese communism as it protects the interest of its big corporate houses. Fourth, a strong nation-state is required to protect the interest of the bourgeoisie from the jungle aspects of economic globalization, particularly in the wake of the rising trends of anti-globalization movements and the phenomenon of terrorism.

Role of the State

The obvious starting point is to consider the role in globalization of the nation-state. Although market liberalization often carries with it an anti-state ideology, and globalization has reduced the power of many instruments of state action in the economic field, national governments still retain, to varying degrees, the capability to promote and articulate the values and goals of people in the process of globalization, including in social domains such as health, security, labour and education, all of them essential foundations for a market economy, whether national or global.

There are two dimensions to the state's role in relation to the social dimension of globalization. The first lies within countries. Domestic policies have a great deal of influence over whether countries benefit from globalization, and the nature and distribution of those benefits. Many states engage in strategic investment to take advantage of globalization, notably investment in education, skill and capabilities, investment in key productive sectors, or investment in research, science and technology aimed at generating a longer-term comparative advantage. Of course, the extent to which states can take advantage of this potential depends on their resources and capabilities, which in many countries are extremely limited. A second aspect concerns the ability of states to control or regulate the actions of its citizens or enterprises beyond its borders. Thus the border-free internet has in the end turned out to be responsive to at least a degree of state regulation (because internet services providers have to be located somewhere), and the legal frameworks which have developed at the national level retain a degree of effectiveness even in the global economy, for ultimately even global enterprises must operate within countries.

The second dimension relates to coordination between countries. The interdependence of states implies that the gains from coordination are large. Many international pacts and conventions concern agreements between states to either apply similar domestic policies, thereby avoiding socially undesirable competition, to operate under a common set of rules, to extend reciprocal advantages or - like OPEC, for example - to act as a cartel in global markets. The most developed form of this coordination presently lies in mechanisms such as trade rules or international labour standards, but a much wider agenda is possible. In particular, the development of better international frameworks for the fair, efficient and predictable regulation of markets for capital, goods and services would be in the general interest.

There are in practice many difficulties in achieving coordinating action on social policies between states. These include problems of monitoring and enforcement, democratic deficits in the reaching of agreements and the inevitable tendency for power relations to trample on real needs. International coordination requires states to act responsibly in respecting the legitimate goals and rights of other countries, which is of course far from the case since domestic agendas dominate. The policy agenda is, in practice, dominated by the interests of the most powerful states. Therefore, the importance and role of state undermined in the era of globalization.

Globalization and Poverty Alleviation in India

Globalization leads to higher rate of growth which, in turn, leads to reduction in poverty. Indeed it is true that the rate of growth has increased substantially in few countries like India after they have embraced globalization. But that does not prove that poverty has been reduced.

Globalization leads to more poverty because it promotes capital intensive production. For example, about 20 years ago, 10 tons of goods were carried in a truck. Nowadays three-axle trucks carry 30 tons of goods, courtesy globalization. Previously three drivers and three cleaners were required to transport 30 tons of goods. Now only one each is needed. The share of labour in the income from transportation has declined while that of capital has increased.

Another argument is that globalization and economic growth leads to higher revenues for the government and enables it to run welfare programmes which benefit the poor. The Government of India has launched the Employment Guarantee Programme across the country because it has huge revenues flowing in from the taxes paid by big companies. But such increase in welfare expenditures is unreal. According to the *Economic Survey*, the share of social services in the budget of Union Government was 28.8 per cent in 2003, it declined to 27.2 per cent in 2007 even though in absolute numbers it increased from Rs 145,000 crore to Rs 247,000 crore. In other words, the increase in social services is less than that in the revenues of the government. This is a negative impact of globalization. Furthermore, increase in government expenditures on social services should not be equated with increase in incomes or welfare of the poor. Most of the government money is consumed in paying salaries of the welfare bureaucracy. Secondly, the recipient develops a dependent mentality. Instead of encouraging the people to find self-employment through business, welfare does create the tendency to demand ever more reliefs from the government. One can see this most starkly in the competition between castes to have them declared backward. This race to the bottom, courtesy welfare expenditures, is made from higher revenues obtained from globalization.

The Issue of Democracy

In theory, IMF says that it stands to strengthen democracy. But in practice, its policies subtly violate all the democratic processes. As parts of globalization, different countries are adopting themselves to the free movement of the international investment but not to meet the necessities of their people. As a result, democracy in these countries is destroyed. On the other hand, these countries have no chance of enjoying profits and on the other hand, these face economic, social and political crisis. Further, globalization takes away their deciding powers and hand over them to undemocratic and non-transparent companies like the World Bank and the World Trade Organisation. In democratic system, people themselves elect governments. They entrust them responsibilities to discharge certain duties. But bodies like the WTO are not responsible to anybody. These bodies reduce the role of state in their decision making process.

Unimproved Development

Globalization totally failed in improving the development in practice. According to Hazoon Chang, globalization increased poverty, unemployment and inequalities. During 1960-80, the income annual rate per head was three per cent in the world. But during the past twenty years, where globalization process was speeded up, it was recorded as two per cent. In developed nations, it fell from 3.25 to 2.2 per cent. India and China are exceptions.

Corporate Ruling

Ruling in globalization is totally centralized in the corporate bodies. According to Ruchi Tripati, globalization means the ruling by certain companies and cultures. In reality, we are seeing only the corporate globalization. It has three defects:

- It is looking at both rich and poor countries as equals and asking them to freely open the doors of their economic systems.
- It is growing itself with several economic failures. That is why, we are experiencing marketing failures, increasing inequalities, concentration of wealth in certain corporate companies etc.
- It is giving importance to new capitalistic methods, ignoring local problems, national goals, human rights, environment protection and weaker sections welfare in developing countries like India.

Poor People's Plight

Poor and weaker sections are the worst sufferers due to globalization. As an international project, it is destroying the agriculture of small and poor farmers. It is evolved to destroy village units. In 1997, the finance globalization destroyed the economic systems of the East Asian countries. In the same year, it drowned two crores of Indonesians in poverty. On the other side, the brands like Coca Cola and McDonald are smashing local cultures. Because of these, people are kept away from resources like earth, water, seeds, technology etc. so, there is increase in hunger due to lack of food protection.

Inequal Opportunities

In practice, globalization is not providing equal opportunities to all countries and to all people. Multinational companies are well trained to use all the resources in small countries for their selfish ends. Because of this, crores of craftsmen, small farmers, fishermen are losing their daily livelihood. Traditionally prepared village products are unable to compete and stand before factory made goods. Hence, there is an urgent need to look into their problems from ethical stand-point.

The Welfare State Approach

The Preamble and Directive Principles of State Policy of the Indian constitution make it very clear that the framers of the constitution wanted India to move towards building a welfare state for the people, and made provisions in it to harness it. The Preamble has envisaged "justice social, economic and political" for all people, and wanted the state to work for the well-being of all. It wanted India to become a society based on equality and justice. Accordingly, many provisions have been made in the Fundamental Rights and Directive Principles of State Policy to take the country towards it. Equality of opportunity, right to freedom, right against exploitation, are all parts of it. More distinctly, the Directive Principles of State Policy have pointed the way for India to develop into a welfare state. Article 38 of the Constitution says: "The State shall strive to promote the welfare of the people by securing and protecting as effectively as it may a social order in which justice, social, economic and political shall inform all the institutions of the national life." Article 39 speaks about the right of all people for adequate means of livelihood, equal pay for equal work, healthy work environment, protection of children against exploitation and material abandonment, and made it incumbent on the state to assure that "the ownership and control of the material resources of the community are so distributed as best to subserve the common good." Article 41 makes the state responsible to make "effective provision for securing the right to work, to education and to public assistance in case of unemployment, old age, sickness and disablement, and in other cases of undeserved want." Similarly, Articles 42 and 43 have made the state responsible for provision of maternity relief, and for securing all workers jobs, "a living wage, conditions of work ensuring a decent standard of life and full enjoyment of leisure and social and cultural opportunities." Article 45 provides for free and compulsory education for all children upto 14 years. Similarly, there are also provisions which stipulate that children should be provided with opportunities and facilities to grow and develop in a healthy manner and in conditions of freedom and dignity. Despite the presence of these provisions in the Indian Constitution, the progress India made in the direction of becoming a welfare state has been negligible. During the last 15 years, even limited, rudiment welfare state measures havs been undermined to promote market forces and private companies in the country due to globalization. As part of globalization, government hospitals are starved of funds, staff and medicines. Funding of children's education has been systematically transferred from public funds to the shoulders of parents or of children themselves, who are being asked to go to banks, to take loans from there for the purpose and prematurely become debtors, even as students. This is unacceptable. In addition, a new category of self-financing colleges has sprung up everywhere, where taking huge bribes in the form of capitation fee or donations for admissions is legitimate business. There should be no doubt that such institutions can only corrupt our system beyond repair. When will we recognize that our children are the asset of the nation (and not of parents alone) who have a right to full development of their talents and faculties, regardless of their social background and parental income? That understanding is essential when we strive for building a welfare state.

However, under the present dispensation, child care, care of the old, infirm and the handicapped, are only marginal concerns of the Indian state. A recent survey has shown that two per cent of Indian children, under six years, are undernourished. The budget allocation for public welfare in India has been kept around four per cent of the national budget, compared to 37 per cent in the national budget of a welfare state like Sweden. However, cumulatively, the welfare state content in India has been steadily shrinking during the last 15 years. Labour welfare, gender justice, child welfare, education, health care, and so on are less and less a state responsibility. The public health care services have been weakened to such a point that even poor people are forced to approach the new extortionist private hospitals for simple ailments. This present trend needs to be reversed.

Globalization and Human Rights

The widespread anti-globalization movements from Seattle to Geneva and the cry for globalization with humane face indicate that everything that globalization does is not uniformly good and acceptable. While globalization has worked well for a few, it has marginalized, dispossessed, deprived and, destroyed many. While the rich and the powerful have benefited, the poor and the weak have been excluded and subjugated. Globalization in this sense is not an inclusive phenomenon but an exclusive one. There are many, particularly in the Third World, who are questioning the impact of globalization not only on the nation-states but primarily on the human beings and their rights. Globalization has resulted in loss of jobs, cultural identity, democratic rights, clean air and water. It has not only created social and cultural divide but also economic, technological, and digital divide between and within nations. Studies are being conducted to find out the impact of globalization and its agents particularly that of MNCs and WTO on economic, environmental and developmental rights of the people.

As Professor Jagdish Bhagwati has remarked, globalization a focal point of hostile passions and sometimes - violent protests - has become a phenomenon doomed to unending controversy. Advocates cite its virtues and its inevitability. Central to many of the protests against it is the trilogy of discontents about the idea of capitalism, the process of globalization, and the behaviour of corporations. And all three of these discontents have become interlinked in the minds of the many protesters. Globalization's enemies see it as the worldwide extension of capitalism, with multinational corporations.

It is in this perspective that discourse on relationship between globalization and human rights becomes important and inevitable. Today, there is no divergence of opinion that globalization has resulted in widespread social and economic inequality. It has increased the incidence of poverty, hunger, and disease. As Vandana Shiva has pointed out "starvation is the inevitable result of policies of globalization which are transforming food from a basic need, to which everyone has a right, to a globally traded-commodity." The denial of right to food is the most important violation of human rights.

Economic inequality and income disparities between and within the nations have contributed to a rise in social strife and ethnic conflicts at an unprecedented scale, particularly in Asia and Africa. As *HDR*, 1999, observes "uneven globalization is not only bringing integration but also fragmentation—dividing communities, nations and regions into those that are included and those that are excluded." The extreme inequality between the marginal and the powerful are igniting social tensions and conflicts. The 'retreat of state' from social and welfare responsibilities has deepened the problem of economic inequality and human insecurity. The 'horizontal inequalities' between groups—whether ethnic, religious or social—are major cause of the current wave of civil conflicts. The shrinking job and economic opportunities has further compounded the problem.

Farewell to the Welfare State

Globalization and 'Glocalization' obviously, are undermining the sovereign nation-state from without and also from within. This does not mean, the state has become impotent or its demise is imminent. However, in the wake of the post-cold war capitalist economic integration, the conceptions of the nature and the role of the state have undergone and are undergoing radical transformation. While farewell to the state is not in the works (as claimed by some early champions of globalization), India is going through the political and economic fall-out of bidding farewell to the 'welfare state'! Business is not the business of the government it is asserted. National and state governments should get out of the business of producing and marketing of goods and services. Governments should confine themselves to governing, maintaining law and order, and providing the basic amenities like food, shelter, sanitation, drinking water, primary education etc. to the people. It is argued that the state should go back to the role of being the regulator. It should do all it can to ensure a level playing field for all entrepreneurs.

Globalization sets out to frame policies and programmes that imply a drastic reduction in the government's role in economic and social governance, framing of policies and programmes. Certain policies of the 1980s that were devised keeping in view the interests of dalits and other poor, socially downtrodden classes have been revised. This can be seen from the following developments.

1. Land reform measures are now put on hold.
2. Ceiling and land holdings have been selectively relaxed.
3. Private players have been granted entry into the field of education, particularly technical and vocational education, which makes such education costly, without provisions for affirmative action for discriminated groups.
4. Entry has been promoted for private insurance companies without making them pro-poor.
5. Industry, banking and insurance sectors are being privatized, which again means that these private players are not bound by any affirmative action policy.
6. Expenditure reduction has been introduced for many anti-poverty schemes like integrated Rural Development Programme etc.
7. Labour reforms are being planned without taking into consideration adequate social security and other protective measures.

In a welfare state, health and education are the two most important areas of government intervention. This is enshrined in the Constitution of India. But in the era of globalization, liberalization and privatization, the major impact of economic reforms in India is the reduction of government spending on public health and the withdrawal of government responsibility for the fulfillment of the people's basic health needs.

Conclusion

It is axiomatic that if market forces and private contractors establish a dominant grip on the public welfare sector, the democratic state as a political entity will lose its centrality in organizing a welfare state for the benefit of the whole people. That will be detrimental to the poorer sections of our society as they simply cannot afford to buy services from the private market. Therefore, the centrality for the state to provide such poor people with quality services by the state institutions, should be kept in tact at all costs. Needless to say that richer the state, better will be the conditions of the poor, and vice-versa. Therefore, it is imperative to keep the Indian state strong, resourceful, and sovereign. Anyone who undermines its resource base is not only anti-poor, but anti-welfare state as well.

In the construction of a welfare state in India, it is necessary to adopt a full employment policy. The state should assume the responsibility of ensuring full employment, so that all socio-economic and technology policies in the country would remain job-friendly all the time. Every employable person must be provided with opportunities to produce something useful for the society. It will take India to new heights of prosperity, greatness and social peace. So we must maximize employment opportunities for our people. There is another reason too why India should follow a full employment policy, accompanied by a steeply progressive income tax system. This will ensure a steady flow of resources required for the upkeep of the welfare state system in the country. It can bring down the income disparity between people and families and promote mutual respect among the people. It will free people from greed and acquisitiveness, and unnecessary customs and ceremonies. A welfare state can change the perception, attitude and behaviour pattern of the people spectacularly. It will create a new, healthy and harmonious atmosphere in society. In addition, India should position the public sector as a strong pillar of Indian welfare state, especially in the spheres of public utilities. As public utilities are part of public welfare, they should be delinked from purely profit seeking private concerns.

The imperatives of globalization never contribute to the proper development of any nation-state in the world. Globalization of the capital and commodities is incompatible with the real growth and development of both the developing and the under-developed nation-states. Further, the worldwide expansion of capitalism curtails the growth of every national and permanently makes it a slave to the helping unit or organization. That is why, today, the capitalist expansion needs to be challenged with suitable policy guidelines, which may take the shape of appropriate parameters with managerial capabilities. Only thing is that a realistic and pragmatic trail has to be attempted by the interested nation-states to implement them, without smashing humanness in humankind.

REFERENCES

Anbalagan, T. 2007. "Globalization of Higher Education." *Third Concept*, Vol. 21, No. 248, October: 53-55.

Babu Ramesh. 2006. "Globalization, Glocalization and South Asian Insecurity." The ICFAI *Journal of Governance and Public Policy*, Vol. 1, No. 1, June: 54-74.

Jhunjhunwala, Bharat. 2007. "Globalization Fails in Poverty Alleviation." *Third Concept*, Vol. 21, No. 248, October, New Delhi.

Kannabiran, M. 2007. "Globalization and Governance." *Third Concept*, Vol. 21, No. 249, November: 25-28.

Kumar, Pankaj. 2007. "Globalization and Tribal Society." *Third Concept* Vol. 20, No. 239, January: 43-46.

Rodgers, Gerry. 2005. "The Pattern of Globalization and Some Implications for the Pursuit of Social Goals." *The Indian Journal of Labour Economics*, Vol. 48, No. 1, Jan-Mar.

Sakya, Agya Ram. 2007. "Youth Suicide and Globalization." *Third Concept*, Vol. 20, No. 240, February:45-47.

Sankaran, S.R. 1997. "Bureaucracy and Human Rights: Repressive State or Responsive State." *Indian Journal of Human Rights*, Vol. 1, No. 2:38-52.

Sankaran, S.R. 2002. "Globalization and Marginalized Sections." *Indian Journal of Human Rights*, Vol. 6, No. 1 and 2:1-15.

2

Impact of Globalization on Human Rights in India*

The term globalization is defined differently in different contexts. According to Robert McCorquodale "globalization is a contested term and there is no one accepted definition of it". In a broader sense it includes two things—integration of the world and interdependence of the sovereign nation-states. The term is all encompassing is defined and understood in both 'economic and non-economic contexts which broadly include socio-cultural, historical and political'.

Globalization refers to the process of the intensification of economic, political, social and cultural relations across international boundaries. It is principally aimed at the transcendental homogenization of political and socio-economic theory across the globe. It is equally aimed at 'making global being present worldwide at the world stage or global arena" [S.T. Kindle: 2002:12]

It deals with the 'increasing breakdown of trade barriers and the increasing integration of world market'.

Globalization is further seen in the context of ascendancy and dominance of capitalism; market forces and liberal democracy particularly in the aftermath of the collapse of the Eastern bloc in the late 80s and 90s. "Globalization" as quoted in S.T. Kindle means the "broadening and deepening linkages of national economies into a worldwide market for goods and services, especially capital". It aims at "removing all national barriers to the free movement of international capital" reinforced by the

*Paper presented at Andhra Pradesh Sociological Society, VIIth All India Conference on "Globalization: Opportunities and Challenges" on 5th and 6th April 2007, organized by the Dept. of Sociology, S.V. University, Tirupati.

"supersonic transformation in information technology. It is principally aimed at the universal homogenization of ideas, cultures, values, and even life styles as well as at the de-territorialization and villagization of the world". This paper will discusses the impact of globalisation on human rights with reference to developing countries like India.

Globalization has substantially contributed to the intensification of debt, poverty and economic crisis in the developing world. The structural Adjustment programmes (SAP) designed and imposed by the global creditor institutions is a typical instrument to create a favourable atmosphere for globalization, which ultimately affects developing countries. In order to meet the mandates set by the SAP, a country spends less by cutting back government expenditures, social services, and economic investments so that resources can be placed elsewhere. More money is being spent on export orientation. Which results in local economies becoming dependent on the integration with the world economy. The international lenders demand poor economics to divert substantial resources away from sectors serving domestic needs: withdraw all subsidies for poor people, privatize the state sector, deregulate the market, and decrease wages. In effect, this process opens up countries to globalization. Thus structural adjustment programmes and import-export-led strategies of industrialization were part of a political and economic restricting process, a prelude to globalization. The advocates of globalization give philosophical justifications to accept export-led growth, lower wages and living standards for workers, shrinking government budgets, and extremely high interest rates. They say "There Is No Alternative" - TINA, the phrase coined by British Prime Minister Margaret Thatcher in 1980s. Powerful institutions like the international Monetary Fund, the World Bank and the World Trade Organization raise the TINA, argument to persuade the developing nations to qualify themselves to borrow money. The developing countries are left into no option but to accept the liberalization and market-oriented reforms. Under this liberalization policy production tends to be export-oriented. Meeting the basic needs of the people becomes less important. State-run factories or enterprises are often privatized to suit the needs of foreign investors. Free trade and liberalization lead to competition and local producers, like farmers, have to suffer the consequences.

Globalization has created a situation where the role and importance of nation-state is becoming irrelevant. Kenichi Ohmae, widely recognized as one of today's top business gurus, asks, in a world where economic borders are disappearing and money flows around the globe beyond the reach of governments, "who, indeed needs the nation, State?" He argues that 4 'I's-Investment, Industry, Information technology and Individual consumers - make the traditional middleman function of nation-states, and of their governments, largely unnecessary. Because, the global markets for all the 'I's work just fine on their own, nation- states no longer have to play a market-making role. In this situation multinational corporations are becoming the actors even in international politics. A growing trend to promote the idea of recapturing the capitalist frontier and its lost values is more visible through the globalization and market liberalization in the developing countries.

"Globalization requires the humiliation of hundreds of millions of people keeping them in constant insecurity, pitting them against one another in a competitive struggle for survival". The Human Development Report of 1997 says; Globalization can also shift patterns of consumption. Luxury cars and soft drinks can rapidly become a part of daily life, heightening relative deprivation. The pattern can increase absolute poverty by undermining the production of goods on which poor people rely. A flood of imported wheat can shift consumption away from sorghum or cassava, making them scarcer in local markets.

Roberto Verzola, a Social activist of the Philippines, comments that in the same way that colonization was the trend one hundred years ago, globalization is, today. Today global corporations have replaced the colonial powers. In developing countries, global corporations are allowed to feast on natural resources, human resources and national wealth. They displace farmers from their land, workers from their jobs, and communities from their roots. They are responsible for the breaking up of communities and the destruction of the environment to serve the human and raw material requirements of global production for the global market. The consequence is the collapse of food security and the emergence of global environmental crises, which in the end may turn out to be even worse than colonization. Even the peoples of developed countries suffer from the profit-hungry rules of global corporations today. Which virtually rule the world. Globalization and market-oriented economic reforms have been designed for the benefit of these groups. In reality, globalization means the rule of global corporations. It means decision about lives are being made in corporate boardrooms in the USA, Europe and Japan, instead of in local community councils or at the national level. National governments are becoming the implementers of orders received from the international actors. This has created a situation of powerlessness and suffering for many in developing countries, which results in violation of human rights of millions of people.

Globalization, Development and Human Rights

The relation between globalization, development and human rights raises policy and legal questions. One such question is whether globalization of market-oriented economic system is essential for development and protection of human rights? While searching for an answer to this question we should analyze how we perceive the concept of development and human rights, especially in the context of developing countries. Human rights have become an integral part of the process of globalization in many ways. The Western countries are increasingly using their view of human rights concept as a yardstick to judge developing countries and to deal with economic and trade relations to extend development assistance. At the same time globalization intensifies impoverishment by increasing the poverty, insecurity, fragmentation of society and thus violates human rights and human dignity of millions of people.

Development or economic development is widely perceived as a historical process that takes place in almost all societies characterized by economic growth and increased production and consumption of goods and services. Development is also often used in a normative sense as a multi-valued social goal covering such diverse spheres as better material well-being, living standards, education, health care, wider opportunities for work and leisure and in essence the whole gamut of desirable social and material welfare. But, in today's globalization, the concept of development itself is interpreted differently and the concept of right to development is not taken seriously.

The Preamble of the Declaration of the Right to Development, adopted by the UN General Assembly in 1986, describes "development as a comprehensive economic, social, cultural and political process that aims at the constant improvement of the well-being of the entire population and of all individuals on the basis of their active, free and meaningful participation in development and in the fair distribution of resulting benefits". The 1990 UN Global consultation on the Right to Development as a Human Right, stated that the right to development is an inalienable human right with the human being as the central subject to the right and that all the aspects of the right to development set forth in the Declaration of the Right to Development are indivisible and interdependent, and these include civil, political, economic, social, and cultural rights. It was further maintained that the right to development is the right of individuals, groups and peoples to participate in, contribute to, and enjoy continuous economic, social, cultural and political development, in which all human rights and fundamental freedoms can be fully realized. A development strategy that disregards or interferes with human rights is the very negation of development.

The aims and objectives of the so-called development models promoted by different governments or international development agencies are not compatible with human rights standards. A new model of development ideology is being promoted that is based on the market and its logic. Several decades of discussion on alternative development model is withering away and a dominant model of market-oriented development taking roots in that place. As a result of the globalization process, more negative effects are visible now. Global integration of the structures, processes, and ideologies produce injustice, oppression, exploitation and Mal development in society. The systematic integration of the forces that are dominant in the globalization process intensifies human rights violations.

The TNCs which have gained; strength in the post-globalization era is the main actor in several developed countries in formulating new foreign policies to shape a new global order.

This trend has been highlighted in a recent study that the emerging global order is spearheaded by a few hundred corporate giants, many of them bigger than most sovereign nations. By acquiring earth-spanning technologies, by developing products that can be produced anywhere and sold everywhere, by spreading credit around the world, and by connecting global channels of communication that can penetrate any village or neighbourhood, these institutions we normally think of as economic rather than political, private rather than public, are becoming the world empires of the twenty-first century.

The impact of these global giant's operations have negative impact on Human Rights. Virtually all developing countries at the present time seek private foreign investment for development. Such investment now greatly exceeds loans or grants from official sources. The growth of Transnational corporations-now numbering about 35,000 with 1,50,000 foreign affiliates - is evidence of the increased role of the private sector and of market economies in developing countries. New technologies have transformed the nature of production and facilitated relocation of firms. Nationalization, once the centre of debate, has now virtually disappeared from the agenda of developing countries.

The Human rights implications of these trends are outlined by an economist, David Korten in the following terms:

Today the most intense competition in the globally integrated market is not between the gigantic Transnational Corporations, but it is between governments that find themselves competing with one another for investors by offering the cheapest and most compliant labour; the weakest environmental, health, and safety standards, the lowest taxes; and the most fully developed infrastructure. Often governments must borrow to finance the social and physical infrastructure needed to attract private investors. Having pushed almost the entire social and environmental costs of production onto the community, many firms are able to turn a handsome profit. Having bargained away their tax base and accepted low wages for their labour, many communities reap relatively few benefits from the foreign investment, however, and are left which no evident way to repay the loans contracted on the firms behalf.

Impact of Globalization on Human Rights

Globalization has its winners and losers. With the expansion of trade, market, foreign investment, developing countries have seen the gaps among themselves widen. The imperative to liberalize has demanded a shrinking of state involvement in national life, producing a wave of privatization, cutting jobs slashing health, education and food subsidies, etc. affecting the poor people in society. In many cases, liberalization has been accompanied by greater inequality and people are left trapped in utter poverty. Meanwhile, in many industrialized countries unemployment has soared to levels not seen for many years and income disparity to levels not recorded since last century. The collapse of the economies of the Asian Tigers are examples of this. The Human Development Report of 1997 revealed that poor countries and poor people too often find their interests neglected as a result of globalization. Although globalization of the economy has been characterized as a locomotive for productivity, opportunity, technological progress, and uniting the world, it ultimately causes increased impoverishment, social disparities and violations of human rights. That is what we see today.

Among the serious watchers of globalization, we find two groups arguing for against globalization. The former points out the benefits of globalization. Globalization helps inflow of surplus capital of developed countries to underdeveloped countries. Modern technology and managerial services are made available to enterprises established in different parts of the globe by the multinational corporations. Globalisation promotes competition. Due to lack of competition, the big business houses were selling average products at high prices. But liberalization and globalization has increased the scales and allocative efficiency of markets for goods and capital. It is also agrued by the supporters of globalization that it has helped in the expansion of liberal democracy by strengthening accountability and transparency of power. It has created global electronic communication systems.

As a result of globalisation, India's share of world exports has been increasing slowly from 0.55 per cent in 1990s to 0.65 per cent in 2000-2001. As a result of globalization, India has been able to gain in respect of trade in services, especially in respect of information technology industry. Indian software professionals have created a brand image in the global market. Globalisation has been creating an improved condition of trade for agricultural commodities and textiles, especially cotton textiles produced in India. The current account deficit which peaked to 3.2 per cent of GDP in 1990 has been declining and is remaining around only one per cent of GDP in the last few years. The foreign exchange reserves of the country has been increasing and stands today at $129 billion.

The second group argues that this so-called development is not development at all because it negatively affects the poorer sections and helps the richer sections, blocking a balanced national development with social justice. There has been a cut in welfare measures, reduction in subsidies of goods of mass consumption and decline in real wages. In the wake of globalization there is substantial increase in unemployment. It has greatly circumscribed the power of nation-state under pressure from multinational companies. There also is a process of cultural imposition and domination. Through cable TV and Internet, the multinational corporations are successfully promoting consumerism and western values. The human rights like the right to food, the rights of farmers, the right to work, the rights of dalits, the right to environment and Bio-diversity and the right to education are seriously affected by globalization.

India has spent the last more than a decade in restructuring its socio economic links with the world. But the package of economic reforms has not triggered progress and prosperity, as expected. To substantiate, India has slipped three places (from 124 to 127) in the human development ranking of the United Nations in the year 2004. Besides, unemployment is growing at an alarming rate, more people without job and, are still living below poverty line. As a result of globalization', Indian companies started to face growing competition, from free flow of products produced by multi-national companies (MNCs). Unequal competition between the domestic companies and mighty MNCs has resulted closure of weak industrial units both under large, medium and small-scale categories. There is greater increase in imports than increase in exports. This shows how the access to foreign markets by Indians is growing slowly as compared to the entry of foreigners in our domestic market.

Conclusion

But whatever may be the drawbacks, demerits and discontents of globalisation, it has to be acknowledged that it has now become a part of contemporary times and current history. In other words, globalization has become a permanent guest whether we like it or not. Therefore what we can do is only to curb and control its negative fallout.

So long as the paradigms of globalization remains elitist in nature and nuance, there would be enough voices of discontent and disturbance. Undoubtedly, opening doors to foreign capital and expertise does hold several advantages as the world economy integrates. But the fact remains that there are still vulnerable sections of society that need handholding, even to enjoy the fruits of globalization. Some kind of a global fund for providing social security to the vulnerable workers and aid to the needy should be created, if necessary by taxing the international traders and finance capitalists who are the main beneficiaries of the globalisation process. It is well known that one such mechanism for creating a global fund to fight poverty by imposing tax on international speculative investment (Known as Tobin Tax) has been widely acclaimed by the global civil society.

As an African statesman has observed to us, the fact that the world is a global village does not mean that it will be run by one village headman. In this age of democracy it will be headed by a panchayat. For us the United Nations is the global Panchayat, and that is why we want it to be democratized and sustained.

REFERENCES

Mathews George Chunakara, "Globalization and its impact on Human Rights", Institute of Human Rights, Vigil India movement, 2000, Bangalore.

Siddartha Dash, "Globalization and India", *Vision*, Vol. XXIV, No. 3-4, Jan-June 2005, Journal of the Jayaprakash Narayan Institute of Social and Economic Study Bhubaneswar.

Gerry Rodgers, "The Pattern of Globalization and some implications for the pursuit of social goals", *The Indian Journal of Labour Economics*, Vol. 48, No. 1, Jan- March 2005, New Delhi.

Anwar Alam, "Globalization and Nation - State", *Third Concept*, Vol. 12, No. 140, October 1998, New Delhi.

Dr. L.P. Singh, "Globalization, multinationals and the Indian corporate sector", *Yojana*, Vol. 47, No. 12, Dec. 2003, Publications division, New Delhi.

Dr. A.K. Ojha, "Globalization and liberalization - prospects of new world order", *Third Concept*, Vol. 16, No. 186, August 2002, New Delhi.

3

Globalization, Role of Media : A Human Rights Perspective

Media known as the fourth pillar of the state is increasing its potential through modern technologies and becoming synonymous with mass media with its identification with the masses, their rights, their values and culture. Due to its association with human rights and their causes it is becoming more universal. It has become the widest democratic front where people can fight for their rights and their concerns. As a result of the communication revolution it has made the world a global village. Though media with development in technology has revolutionised communication. Where it can reach to masses within very-few time with case and is very much synonymous with mass media. But media besides covering news papers, magazines, radio, television, cinema, internet, etc. too covers stage shows, street plays, ballads, puppet shows, folk arts etc. these have played a very significant role in arousing energies in the minds of the masses to rise against exploitation.

Key words : Globalization, media, information, human rights, women in mass media, government, TV, newspapers, radio.

Media in its broad canvas is giving space to human rights, promotion and protection. With the spread of industrialization and urbanization violence, disorder and inhuman activities are growing in a pace. Awareness about the events concerning human rights violation is the most important role that is played by the media. Exposure in the media and more liberalization in civil, political and economic sphere is making people confident where illegitimate authority becomes unbearable.

The world of late, is moving to global village where state's sphere of influence is eroding. Media in this situation is playing a major role in guiding and checking the activities of MNCs, NGOs when they go against the interests of individuals living in a society. In addition to these media is exposing the lacuna of legislature, executive and to some extent judiciary before the public so that the rights of masses remain safe. Sensitizing public servants and security forces of their duties media plays a grand role in safeguarding the rights of the people.

Media exposing issues such as unavailability of food, shelter for the poor masses, inequality of men and women, injustice to Scheduled Castes, Tribes, other Backward Castes and classes, atrocities by government and administration, exploitation of majority community over minority community, domination of elites over weaker sections of society etc. Media, as the store house of information both on news and views makes it the most powerful instrument to unveil the evils perpetrated on the masses. It can instill confidence in their head and heart to make themselves the protectors of their own rights.

Behind the statistical claims of growth and productivity in numerous development projects in official reports, lies heaps of unofficial, unpublished reports on the plight of thousands of people rendered homeless, unemployed, even physically maimed for their lives as a result of construction and functioning of projects like Hirakud Dam (displacement of people), Union Carbide Corporation (Bhopal Gas Tragedy) and Rajaji National Park in Haridwar in UP (Deprived people who survived by the forest produce of the area). Media, in this regard, has protested against these lopsided aspects of development, acting as the voice of the people as well as the leader of the society. It supported, people in their cause by adding pressure on the government to take measures to get solution of these problems. In suggesting measures to be followed by the government it becomes the standard setter of the plans, policies and programmes. The role of the media in safeguarding human rights by creating a human rights cell and reporting, profusely about human rights is indeed laudable.

Apart from reporting the stories, media's support and struggle for disarmament is worth praising. It has played a major role by disseminating knowledge about the real danger of nuclear holocaust facing the world. It has brought into focus global problems of terrorism, war and the havoc played in certain parts of the world. By focussing these conflicts areas, media has brought the public opinion to the desks of the politicians and policy makers.

Securing the right to peace and international security at a time of nuclear world is the same as right to preserving the mankind itself.

Media has a powerful impact upon the human mentality and behaviour. So the media shall constantly keep in mind that the basic rights of the people have priority over its own interests. It should not strive for profit as an industry, no manipulation of information be made since violence comes out of dis-information. Not commercialization but concern should be the motto of media.

Blackmailing, sensationalism, obscenity, violence, vulgarism should not become the buzzwords of media because when media subverts the cases related to human rights it commits the worst offence against humanity. The mysterious deception against humanity at the time of bombing of Hiroshima and Nagasaki by US, media deception by BBC while reporting on Falkland War and deceptive reporting on trouble spots like Kashmir keeps the treacherous atrocities in shadow. Media as the fountainhead of democracy and as an empowering instrument serve the competence and consciousness of each individual, to articulate their human needs and human existence. It acts as the intermediary between the people and different authorities at various levels and different spheres of administration. It shows the path to government by identifying the neglected areas and needy sections of society. By exposing the failure, shortcomings of the system, it becomes the harbinger of a new national and international socio-economic order which will guarantee individual and group rights to all.

Media promotes value-based civil society, based on equality, justice, tolerance, which is the guarantee of safeguarding human rights. A culture of prevention should be created so as the evils to be nipped in the bud. Virtues like social harmony, peaceful coexistence should be given upper-hand by media in pluralistic societies. Through investigative journalism, media gives information in drug related crimes, racket of illegal procedures and traffickers. It searches the polluting factors and ecology destructive activities and agents and highlights the hazards posed by these activities.

Through processes of alternative communications involve practices in different media like folk songs, puppet shows, street theatres, local newspapers, they are invariably directed at the creation of public sphere, a socio-cultural commons which is autonomous of the institutions of state and market. By contextualising the issues of human rights, sub-altern roots come to the forefront. The mainstream media catch these glimpses of local essence, since serious and sensitive journalists had gravitated to mainstream media after years of activism. Movements like Narmada Bachao Andolon, Chhatisgarh Movement, Chipko Movement, Movements against Enron, Silent Valley Project, Bhopal Gas Tragedy and killings by Ranvir Sena found spaces within the dominant media where it brought local elements in addressing social issues of the moment. Other instances of media playing a tremendous role like during Emergency of 1977 when many journalists went to jails. Journals like Social Action, Other India, Gandhi Marg, Manushi, Marxism Today, Down to Earth and Ecologist have given space to human rights issues. So, dominant media with non-dominant media have unitedly focussed these issues. Big dominant media need to extend its protective umbrella to small ones by ensuring security for them, highlighting their precarious conditions and pressures exhorted on them. Both should, therefore, fight unitedly for, the cause of human rights.

Freedom of media flows from one of the fundamental rights, so rights of human beings get due place in media's coverage. Freedom of the media is not licence. It means greater responsibility and greater self-restraint. The freedom of media, therefore, to be harnessed for the benefit of people as a whole. United Nations and the subsidiary organisations like UNESCO and some NGOs and their activities are highlighted by media. Many people have said in a survey that mass media is an instrument of human intervention, which reports the human rights observance and violation. So, Media has safeguarded human rights by establishing peace by reducing tension through pressure of public opinion, pressurizing for disarmament action as an empowerment instrument, standing as the grand pillar of democracy, creating a culture of prevention of conflicts, and setting the standard for the government as well as the society as a whole.

Indian Media : Role and Function

Media have been the reflector of dominant values and work as an active agency in reinforcing and strengthening dominant value structure. A platform where various interests can be brought together exists in the form of media in today's democratic society while the role of media in early liberal thought was defined mainly in terms of a watchdog. The expectations from this medium widened with development of mass society.

Generally speaking, mass media do not mean the media of the masses, it is only the media, which report to the masses the trivialities, fads, problems and foibles of the elite. Impact of mass media on women is only a matter of conjecture and in fact it is really distressing. For unlike conjecture and in fact it is really distressing. For unlike other marginalized groups women are always pitted simultaneously against many powerful agencies like the state, society, caste and religion all of which represent patriarchy in an institutionalized form. Naturally, therefore, advancing the cause of women means a comprehensive interrogation of the existing power relations. Media are a 'power resource' in terms of exerting influence in society, they are played out, they are source of varied definitions of social reality, changing culture and values and most importantly they are a source of the public meaning system. Media are the carrier of public opinion and play a crucial role in giving voice to the people.

All the contents of the media are important to our national life not just what frankly and directly relate to public affairs. To some extent, it sounds true that the TV reflects the reality; somehow, it does not stop at the depiction of reality but tries to step forward. It constantly evaluates the reality and point out the ideal picture of the world. On the other hand, the groups of people controlling any media constantly try to influence the reality by presenting their own ideal situations. There are enough evidences and researches to suggest that any medium is a powerful medium which can have positive as well as negative effects.

Women in Mass Media

The presentation of concise and accurate picture of how the media portrays women around the world poses enormous problems of compression and synthesis. Overall, media treatment of women can best be described as narrow. On film, in the press and the broadcast media, women's activities and interests typically go no further than the confines of home and family. Both as characters in fictional media material and as newsmakers in the press and broadcasting, women are numerically under-represented, an absence which underlines their marginal and inferior status in many spheres of social, economic and cultural life. Prevalent news values define most women's problems, as unworthy, admitting women to coverage primarily as the wives, mothers or daughters of men in the news, in their own right, they make the headlines usually only as fashionable or entertainment figures. Much media advertising directed at women as consumers is condescending in tone and manipulative. In products that are advertised, women are exploited in terms of their sexuality and physical appearance.

Media without women does not exist because in general, films, advertisements, songs, TV signboards and drama they portray women as a lustful thing. Women are portrayed as self sacrificing persons with no self respect or as jealous cats. Most of the films and TV shows, women as a weaker sex, second class roles and most of the time, females are shown as sex objects. In the battle for equal status and fair treatment of women, important role is generally attributed to the mass media and in particular to television because it has become a significant part of life, in a developing country like ours. In different countries, after searching the role of women depicted be the media that the image of women as it is shown in the films and television in either of a housewife, a mother or as a sexual object. Women are shown as dependent foolishly inclusive deceitful incompetent and so on.

The situation of women working within television or films reflects the fact that these segments of work are male-dominated. It has been estimated that there are approximately twenty eight per cent of women in broadcasting in India. The serials shown on the TV from the early 80s were noted for their homogenous construction of womanhood and gender stereotyping. Gender was often viewed as an overarching category which by itself defined the interest, tastes and value premises of women discounting cross-cutting class, caste, religion and regional variations existing among them. This always gave the women characters, depicted in the serials, a unity of purpose and solidarity which are actually conspicuous by their absence in real life situation.

In print media also portrayal of women deals with the treatment of women in pictorial, textual and linguistic contents of various newspaper sections. The presentation of concise and accurate picture of how the media portrays women around the world poses enormous problems of compression and synthesis. Both as characters in fictional media material and as newsmakers in the press and broadcasting, women are numerically under represented, an absence which underlines their marginal and inferior status in many spheres of social, economic and cultural life. Prevalent news values define most women's problem, as unworthy, admitting women to coverage primarily as the wives, mothers or daughters or men in the news, in their own right, they make the headlines usually only as fashionable or entertainment figures. Mass media advertising directed at women as consumers is condescending in tone and manipulative.

Media, Violence and Vulgarity

The influential nature of media could have really done a miracle by inculcating right thinking, encouraging positive process of development and shaping and guiding the fruitful ideals of peace, harmony and justice. But unfortunately it has become irresponsible because of petty politicking, commercialization and negligence of the authority who control and regulate it. There could be hardly any argument over the point that the hands which control the media also control the minds of the people directly or indirectly. Presently these are the hands of the business class, which is having policies. They have made the media a powerful instrument of opinion-making, merely business and entertainment oriented. However, combining information and entertainment they have coined a new nomenclature 'infotainment'. But in real sense information has taken a back seat and entertainment has surged ahead. In the name of entertainment the artificial desires of the people are aroused and they are motivated to purchase their products as can be seen in the cheap and vulgar programmes and advertisements presented on various means of mass communication. The newspapers and magazines are made attractive with the help of nude and vulgar photographs. The image of modern women are presented in a commoditified sexual object. It will affects the human rights, decency, dignity and modesty of women.

Modern media is increasingly becoming the silent advocate of the violence too. It has strong potential to change the likes, dislikes and preferences of the people particularly of the youth. Films which are shown on the big as well as screen convey the message that evils can be removed from the society through the 'hinsatmak' or the violent means only.

The newspapers and magazines give undue coverage to violence. The numerous items telling about murder, rape, dacoity, adultery, frauds, scandals are printed on front pages of national dailies. This practice influences the tender minds of the youth deeply, which is the future of any country. The children who are like the 'plain-paper' are not equipped for using their logic to draw the result.

They enjoy violence and vulgarity because of their immature mind. They imitate what is projected and wrongly glorified by the media. Cases of murder are reported by the tiny-todds of their younger brothers or friends following the line of action witnessed on the screen.

With the advent of innumerable channels in the television, it has become the most popular mass medium. It has reached the remotest corner of the country and is being watched by the young and old alike watching so much violence and vulgarity on television passively accept the behaviour pattern. They don't find any guilt in it, but they treat it as a way of life. Due to the social acceptance of sex and violence of which the media has been the greatest instrument, this behaviour-pattern has reached from road to the drawing room. It is a common sight that the physically strong boys identify themselves with the villain or the aggressive hero in their day to day life. They take them as their ideals or models. It shows the cause and effect relationship between observing violence on media and the actual aggressive behaviour to the viewer. It definitely affects the atmosphere of the home, the school discipline, social relations, overall personality and the value system of the society.

If this trend is not stopped now, we would not be able to save our culture from the brink of extinction. Every society has its own history, norms and values. We are having our own well-defined value-system. There is no sense in getting infected with the miseries of Western life styles. Free flow of information without moral restrictions would lead to the destruction of centuries old cultural ethos. Father of the nation, Mahatma Gandhi had said almost half a century ago, that 'I want the cultures of all lands to blow as freely as ppssible in India. But I refuse to be swept off my feet by any one of them'.

One American researcher Hary J. Scorniya, while studying the detrimental effects of media has put forth forcefully a wonderful theory. He says that 'Gone are the days to bring turmoil and unrest in neighbouring nation through sword or gun point. If you allow me I'll grasp their mind and shall inject a heavy dose of violence, vulgarity, corruption, brutality and hatred in such an entertaining way that they would accept it as their way of living. Once I am able to imbibe this culture in their day to day life, the chain reaction would automatically go on'. Let us hope, he is not referring to India.

Various researches reveal that in all media categories, but particularly on broadcast television and radio and in newspapers, women are grossly under represented and occupy less central roles than men.

Suggestions

The role of all agencies is very important and effective in uplifting the images of women presented by media. Improvement can be brought by using following guidelines -

1. Developing mass media material which portray women in a positive and constructive manner and in a wide variety of roles.
2. The adoption of non-sexist guidelines by advertisers, broadcasters, film makers, journalists and publishers.
3. Creating positive attitude among mass communicators towards the integration of women in the mainstream of social life.
4. Allowing for their increased commitment to bringing information for and about women to the public's attention.

5. Making those who control media, aware of the need for a balanced workforce for both sexes.
6. Publicity campaign sponsored by these organizations to expose discrimination against women in the media, to notify women about their legal rights and highlight the public awareness of media images which are insulting and demeaning to women.
7. Spontaneous as well as organized action on the part of consumers to protest against sex-stereotyped portrayals in mass media via letter writing, campaigns, product boycotts, etc.

REFERENCES

Anuradha Mathu, "Women and Media where do we stand?", *Social Welfare*, Vol. 51, No. 1, April 2004, Central Social Welfare Board, New Delhi.

Behera and Banchhanidhi Pani, "Role of Media in Safeguarding Human Rights", *Third Concept*, April-May 1999, New Delhi.

F.R. Gauhar, "Media: Violence and Vulgarity", *Third Concept*, Vol. 12, No. 134-35, April-May 1998, New Delhi.

Satyanarayana Pattnaik, "Mass Media in Population Education", *Third Concept*, Vol. 11, No. 122-23, April-May 1997, New Delhi.

K.S. Chandrasekar, "Broadcast Media and The Indian Middle Class", *Third Concept*, Vol. 11, No. 126, August 1997, New Delhi.

Janaki Chundi and Dr. Alka Srivastava, "Role of Media in Rural Areas", *Kurukshetra*, Vol. 48, No. 10, July 2000, Ministry of Rural Development, New Delhi.

Dr. Shivali Agarwal, "Media and Crimes against Women", *Third Concept*, Vol. 21, No. 242, April, 2007, New Delhi.

4
Globalization and Violation of Housing Rights

Globalization, is defined as the freeing of market forces, reducing economic regulation and the increased inter-connections in the world economy. It is invariably more detrimental than supportive to the enjoyment of housing rights to the one-quarter of humanity that do not yet have their housing rights met. For as markets become less regulated, as public expenditures decline and as the trade of goods and services across national borders becomes increasingly unfettered. The natural assumption is that the implementation of rights requiring some form of governmental intervention will suffer as a result of the renewed dominance of profit over people.

However, we define globalization not purely in economic terms, but view this process within additional political, social and legal contexts. The negative impact of globalization on housing rights is by no means comprehensive. It is true that the economic dimensions of globalization can and clearly yield negative socio-economic results for the most vulnerable groups throughout the world. Due to increases in housing costs, forced evictions to acquire prime land, reductions in social housing construction, privatization of the housing stock, exclusion of the poor from policy consideration and so forth. However, great strides have been made during the globalization era relating to the recognition, enforceability and seriousness accorded to housing rights. Granted this may have come about in response to the overall decline or stagnation in housing and living conditions. But arguably the advancements that have been made with respect to the law relating to housing rights can, at least in part, be attributable to the increased openness and access by popular groups, civil society and individuals to institutions that were previously the exclusive domain of states.

Recent Developments

While the number of people living inadequate housing or no housing at all appears to have increased during the era of contemporary globalization, paradoxically, the legal prominence of the "Human Right to Housing" has improved dramatically. Housing rights in law have certainly advanced, even if housing rights in practice have surely not. In this light, globalization is an ambiguous influence with respect to the human right to adequate housing.

The emergence of civil society is an influential political force, whether implicitly or explicitly as a side-effect of globalization. It has manifested in ways that are favourable to changing laws, policies and procedures to strengthen rather than undermine economic, social and cultural rights, including housing rights. While the past two decades have been correctly criticized as a period of declining housing and living standards for many, this same historical period was witness to unparalleled advances with respect to the treatment of housing as a human right. It is now widely accepted that housing rights provide clear and consistent criteria against which the actions, policies, practices and legislation of states can be judged.

Housing rights are also an important means of providing citizens with legal procedures and mechanisms designed to ensure the implementation of the right to adequate housing and the receipt of compensation in the event of violations. Further, viewing through the looking glass of human rights creates a systematic, common and universally applicable frame work for developing appropriate legal and other measures leading to the full realization of housing rights. Most actions have now understood that the pursuit of housing rights as human rights promotes good governance, governmental accountability, transparency, democratic decision making, popular participation and international co-operation.

During the 1990s, many important, advances were made with respect to housing rights. The work of the United Nations Special Rapporteur on Housing Rights (1992-1995), the publication of Human Rights Strategy by the UNCHS (Habitat) in April 1995, the United Nations Housing Rights Programme (UNHRP), a joint programme between UNCHS (Habitat) and the United Nations

Office of the High Commissioner for Human Rights that will seek to provide overall United Nations wide guidance on housing rights issues, the launching by UNCHS (Habitat) of the Global Campaign for Secure Tenure in 2000 and the appointment by the United Nations Commission on Human Rights of a Special Rapporteur on Housing Rights in 2000 - all the above represent key strides forward.

These and positive developments are noteworthy in many respects, not the least of which is the recognition of the important role played by the law as a means of securing adequate housing for all. The relative permanency of legislation provides a valuable assurance that the acceptance of housing as a human right will not be subject to the whims of differing political administrations. Enshrining housing rights standards in national legal frameworks may be the only manner of ensuring equitable access to adequate housing resources by disadvantaged groups and protecting the rights of economically marginalised populations. The incorporation of housing rights provisions in law encourages governmental accountability to citizens and provides tangible substance to what are often vague international commitments by a particular state. Housing rights laws can be important determinants for equality of treatment. It is on this basis that Committee on Economic, Social and Cultural Rights have emphasised that "policies and legislation should not be designed to benefit already advantaged social groups at the expense of others".

Forced Evictions

Forced eviction is defined as the permanent or temporary removal against their will or individuals, families or communities from the homes and the land which they occupy, without the provision of, and access to appropriate forms of legal or other protection. (Evictions carried out by force in accordance with the law and in conformity with the provisions of the International Human Rights Covenants do not however come under this category).

Forced evictions are, prima facie, incompatible with the requirements of the Covenant. Forced eviction, while in itself is a violation of rights, is also related to the violation of other rights like civil and political rights, right to life, the right to the security of the person, the right to non-interference with privacy, family and home and the right to peaceful enjoyment of possessions.

International standards addressing the practice of forced evictions grew in scope in the 1990s, and began consistently to equate forced evictions with violation of human rights, in particular housing rights. The United Nations Commission on Human Rights has declared forced evictions as "gross violation of human rights, in particular the human right to adequate housing" (Res. 1993/77); a perspective echoed on numerous occasions by various United Nations human rights bodies and other human rights institutions. In one of the first of what have become regular pronouncements on forced evictions, the United Nations Committee on Economic, Social and Cultural Rights declared in General Comment No. 4 (1991) that : "Instances of forced evictions are prima facie incompatible with the requirements of the Covenant (on Economic, Social, and Cultural Rights) and can only be justified in the most exceptional circumstances, and in accordance with the relevant principles of international law".

UN Committee on Economic, Social and Cultural Rights

In 1997 the United Nations Committee adopted what is now widely seen to be the most comprehensive decision yet under international law on forced evictions and human rights. General comment No. 7 on forced evictions significantly expands the protection afforded to dwellers against eviction, and goes considerably further than most previous pronouncements in detailing what governments, landlords and institutions such as the World Bank must do to preclude forced evictions, and by inference, to prevent violations of human rights.

General comment No. 7 arrests "the state itself must refrain from forced evictions and ensure that the law is enforced against its agents or third parties who carry out forced evictions". And requires countries to "ensure that legislature and other measures are adequate to prevent and, if appropriate, punish forced evictions carried out, without appropriate safeguards by private persons or bodies". Thus in addition to governments, private landlords, developers and international institutions such as the World Bank and any other third parties or non-state actors are subject to the relevant legal obligations and can anticipate the enforcement of law against them if they "carry out forced evictions".

The role of an appropriate domestic legal framework as a means of securing protection for people against forced evictions is a pervasive theme throughout General comment No. 7, which notes that "legislation is an essential basis upon which to build a system of effective protection". Governments that wish to act in good faith with their housing rights obligations and comply with the sentiments expressed in the comment, therefore, should consider adopting laws expressly prohibiting forced evictions and developing proper legal procedures that can be drawn upon by evictees to secure the prosecution and punishment of "persons or bodies" who may carried out illegal evictions.

While extending protection to all persons, the comment gives special consideration to groups that suffer disproportionately from forced evictions, including women, children, youth, older persons, indigenous people and ethnic and other minorities, with respect to the rights of women, the text asserts that: "Women in all groups are especially vulnerable given the extent of statutory rights (including home ownership) or rights of access to property or accommodation and their particular vulnerability to acts of violence and sexual abuse when they are rendered homeless."

General comment No. 7 declares that "evictions should not result in rendering individuals homeless or vulnerable to the violation of other human rights". Thus making it incumbent on government to guarantee that people who are evicted—whether illegally or in accordance with the law—are to be ensured some form of alternative housing.

Marginalization and Denial of Basic Rights

Imagine that a women staying at a place for the last 10 to 15 years. This is the place that she calls her home. Forget the fact that she has to stay in a small hutment, that she go to the mobile toilet that charges her Re 1 for each usage, that her children are called slum children, that it takes two hours daily to fetch water, that her husband's work gets a very meager and irregular amount but it is still her home.

A bulldozer comes to your area and announces that you are given a few hours notice or may be a day's notice to vacate your home. The trauma that you will undergo that time be immense. The situation of the people of the slums is as such that they are helpless. This is so because they are ignorant of the multiplicity of the authorities in their city. Their president who has been negotiating with the authorities has been promised a corner plot at the site of relocation. He is absent on the day of the eviction from the slum.

Left alone are the women with their younger siblings. Elder ones have gone to school and husbands are off to work. It is solely the plight of the women on that day that makes them the vulnerable and the marginalised. The women feel so insecure and helpless that it is difficult to put those feelings here in word. She sees her home go down in front of her eyes. The pain that is caused by these happening is irreparable. She is sent to an unknown area and given a plot of land. Although she and her family has paid for the land but somehow it is not home. The basic right of the family to procure livelihood is encroached when they are relocated to far off corners of the city. The first thing that is affected is their means of livelihood. Most of them are daily wage earners, lose their work and the market that they developed over the years for themselves. They are relocated without any prior knowledge of the area where they are going. The community is given one-day notice that they are being shifted to 'unknown' or 'xyz' area. This is denial of their basic right to information and denial of their rights as a human being.

As the South Africa authors Mamphela Rampher and Francis Wilson wrote, 'in using metaphor uprooting poverty, we wish to emphasize need for radical action'. They believed that the society is an organisation that grows, rather than a structure that can be dismantled and reassembled, thus demanding a paradigm shift from engineering to growth. However, this is not the way the city planners think or execute their decision. They have to follow orders that come from the top and fulfill target. What is the plight of the women, the effect on their lives and livelihood is not their concern.

The facilities in the relocated area speak volumes of the marginalisation of the people. They have no roof over their heads when they arrive. Due to loss of means of livelihood the construction of a pucca house is delayed and they are forced to stay in the makeshift arrangements (*jhuggies*). There is no proper drinking water facility, sanitation or health facilities. They are just sent to wilderness and given one plot of land to dwell on. There are no schools in the area; no health facilities are there in the area. They are just given a plot of land. This land is given on a lease for 10 to 15 years.

Security of Tenure

Of all elements of the right to housing, it is the right to security of tenure (and increasingly the 'right to security of place') that forms the most indispensable core element. When security of tenure—the right to feel safe in one's own home, to control one's own housing environment and the right not to be arbitrarily forcibly evicted—is threatened or simply non-existent, it jeopardises the full enjoyment of housing rights. Security of tenure derives from a justiciable right of access to and use of land and property, underwritten by a known set of rules that may be anchored in constitutional and legal frame-works, social norms or cultural values.

While it is true that all human rights are premised on principles of equality and non-discrimination, treating security of tenure as a human right (rather than as an exclusive by-product of ownership or the comparatively rare cases of strong protection for private tenants). It expands the legal protection afforded by human rights not merely to all who can afford to buy a home, but to all people of all incomes and in all housing sectors. In this regard, it is important to note that securing tenure for a household does not necessarily secure tenure for women and children; gender equality is a fundamental principle underpinning the global campaign for Secure Tenure. Considering security of tenure in terms of human rights allows an approach to housing that treats all persons on the basis of equality.

In general, the rights associated which ownership of housing offer considerably more security of tenure protection against eviction or other violations of housing rights than those afforded to renting tenants or those residing in informal settlements (where perhaps one-quarter of humanity resides). Therefore, the right to security of tenure raises the base line or minimum core entitlement guaranteed to all persons who posses housing rights based on international human rights standards, irrespective of housing tenure. In recognition of the central place of security of tenure to the rights of dwellers (just as every one is a citizen, so too is every one a dweller) as well as to the important role it can play in promoting individual and family investments in the improvement of their own homes. International human rights standards increasingly approach security of tenure in terms of human rights.

This right is also inexpensive to confer and is viable in all countries regardless of overall levels of human development. The conferral of secure tenure is particularly important to slum dwellers, squatters, residents of housing owned or controlled by exploitative landlords. And others threatened by insecure housing situation and most likely to be evicted. When security of tenure is squarely in place, people are legally protected from most forms of forced eviction. And consequently will begin investing in their own homes. In the process augmenting the enjoyment of housing rights through personal efforts. While there are obvious distinctions between the systems and structures in which tenure security is generated. The universal importance of secure tenure is clear. Its significance is recognised by the Global Campaign for Secure Tenure, an important new partnership initiative launched by UNCHS (Habitat) in 2000. The campaign is aimed at furthering the realization of the right to housing as part of a more encompassing strategy to provide all people with access to adequate shelter. It spearheads a new, more pragmatic and affordable approach to implementing the Istanbul Declaration and the Habitat Agenda, adopted at the City Summit of 1996, with less emphasis on conferences, meetings of experts and ritual reporting of progress by national bureaucracies and with more emphasis on partnership and decentralization.

Conclusion

It is abundantly obvious that despite the many legal gains made during the initial phases of globalisation, much more needs to be done to ensure the implementation of housing rights. The bulk of such activity needs to take place at the national and local level. In terms of international actions, however, several undertakings would be particularly timely and potentially effective in securing housing rights for all, including reappraising housing rights standards; creating a global property registry; developing housing rights indicators; and improving complaint mechanisms.

REFERENCES

Urban voices: Supporting the realisation of housing rights. UNDP, Shelter, Vol. 4(3), Hudco-hsmi Publication New Delhi, Oct. 2001.

Sood, Rewa and Priyanka Awasthy. Shelter: A right or a misnomer.

5
Right to Housing for Social Development

Introduction

House is the place where people cater for most of their bodily needs. They can seek protection of their children with quiet and privacy. Physical and mental health, working efficiency, security and social status are all likely to be influenced by housing conditions. A suitable house is vital to the modern family.

House can be defined as any structure built for human habitation. Housing is one of the most ancient and primordial activities in which man consistently and zealously engaged himself. Street sleeping permits no family life, no privacy, no relief from heat, no escape from cold or rain and decent means for disposing of human waste. Housing is also of direct significance to the community and the nation. It also has its own importance to the individual family.

At the national level, housing is important not only because it affects health and welfare and is closely related to such political principles as "equal opportunity" and "minimum standards", but also because it is a vital factor in the national economy. A large number of workers depend on residential construction for employment directly or indirectly. And house construction in turn depends on most of complex factors, including physical resources, technical developments, population mobility, manufacturing and building enterprises, finance and general economic conditions.

Housing as Basic Human Right

As shelter is primary need, it should be considered as a basic human right. Habitation necessarily postulates residential space and family can survive only if there are homely circumstances provisions enough to promote the faculties and personality of every member. This is habitational justice, a facet of social justice.

However only a few countries of the world have so far recognized shelter as basic human right. The United Nations is promoting this concept. To arouse public consciousness and help formulate national policies for shelter, the United Nations General Assembly has declared 1987 as International Year of Shelter for the Homeless" (IYSH-1987). The United Nations Centre for Human Settlement (UNCHS), Nairobi is the principal agency of the U.N., which is organizing a wide range of international activities to build up meaningful national programmes of realization of shelter as a basic human right.

The global hope of the human family necessarily compels the actualization of a right to reside and that is why the international covenant on social, economic and cultural rights provides for a right to residence as a human right. It reads: "The states, parties to the present covenant, recognize the right of everyone to an adequate standard of living for himself and his family, including food, clothing and housing and to the continuous improvement of living conditions. The State parties will take appropriate steps to ensure the realization of this right, recognizing to this effect the essential importance of international cooperation based on free consent."

The Family, Shelter and Livelihood

The new world human order will remain a promise of unreality and project of verbalism unless the basic conditions of personhood with its pluralist implications are adequately met. We have, therefore, to examine the right to life and its inseparable ancillaries the world over, particularly the populous and deprived regions of south Asia. Here again, the lens looks not at the peaks of opulence of a few but on the dark valleys of dismal privation of the people as a whole, especially the have-nots. Indeed, the conditions of the homeless and the hungry are appalling, although five-star luxury and affluent consumerism confined to small but dominant sector may give a misleading picture of the system.

If social justice were to be the aim of stable progress and balanced development, there is no doubt that the eradication of the enormity of handicaps like shelterless life, starving conditions and juvenile injustice are a must. The dialectic of ground realities and the logic of life's aspirations desiderate a radical change in the existing extortionist system. The categorical imperative of a reasonably happy family in a decent environment-friendly accommodation can be attained only if material and moral values humanize the harrowing South Asian situation. This fighting faith is the locomotive of the New Humanist order of work, wealth and weal.

Housing under the Constitution

Every member of the polity, if constitutional diction is not fiction, has a certain claim to the habitational resources of the nation on an equitable basis, and yet it is a tragic truth that urban slums, expansively ugly, exist side by side with five-star edifices and affluent residences. There are shanties and *juggies* in many cities and towns which deny human conditions of life to substantial numbers. A slum is an ugly name for a place in which to live sans sanitation, privacy and decency. It is the final phase of a neighbourhood sickness that attacks our urban centers. It is a social malady rather than an urban misfortune.

The homelessness of the vast number of humans, despite the International Year of Shelter for the Homeless have come and gone, persists die-hard fashion, with no solace of a roof nor a spot to sit, eat, sleep or die. If only one sees with empathy the miserable families on our city pavements, slimy shanties and cesspool *juggies*, remembering simultaneously that a substantial part of our city population live in such circumstances, we can feel the shock and shame of mass violation of human rights.

The Indian constitution has created a socialist republic and in several places repeats the right to social justice, including the right to life in its widest amplitude and the right to an adequate means to livelihood plus opportunities and facilities for children for to develop in healthy manner and in conditions of freedom and dignity and interdiction of moral and material abandonment.

The foremost human right is indubitably the right to life itself (Art. 3) The Universal Declaration of Human Rights further recognizes the dignity and worth of personhood (Art. 23). The right to a reasonable standard of living includes "food, clothing, housing and medical care (Art. 25). Art. 11 of the International

Covenant on Economic, Social and Cultural Rights recognizes the right of every one" to an adequate standard of living for himself and his family, including adequate food, clothing and housing. The state parties will take appropriate steps to ensure the realization of this right. It follows that the right to housing or shelter is part of International Human rights jurisprudence. The right to shelter is not state charity or condescending grace but basic share, as of right, in the happiness of humanity.

The Seoul Declaration has demanded a home in a community for every one and given reasons for the demand. The very words of the declaration are as follows:

"Rural people come to the cities by the millions because there is no future for them in the country side. In the cities they are forced to settle illegally on government or private land because they cannot afford to pay the rents charged in available legal housing or purchase a house and lot of their own.

The migrants to the cities are poorly educated, unskilled so the work they find pays very little. They work hard, but they can barely feed and clothe their families and their children to school, overall their days hangs the threat they will be evicted from their homes when governments or private landowners care to develop the land. Often their evictions are very brutal. They destroy not only homes but damage people, especially the young, for life.

Government policies, laws and programmes favour the rich. Many countries have no realistic housing programmes of their poor citizens. Governments do not know how to tell the poor what plans there are, and more seriously, do not listen to the people when they draw up the plans.

However, over the time people have learned on their own how to solve their problems. The key to these solutions is forming community organizations that bring the people together and give them an effective voice on the issues that affect their lives.

Government must listen to the people. Permanent solutions to the housing problems of countries can only be when poor people participate and initiate in the policy planning and implementation of projects. This requires "Governments be truly democratic, or the voices of the people can't be heard".

A determined and untired struggle, the poor being conscious that they are the majority in eyery country, will awaken governments reprioritizes their agenda of action. But solidarity of the squalid majorities in misery across South Asia, preceded by activist dialogues and collective strategies, and finally taking to political action to actualize human rights from dead print to vibrant operations is the route to shelter for all. We must share our ideas, exchange our experiences, create organizations which work in co-ordination with leaders and cadres, spell out short-term goals and long-terms objectives and use pressure on the administration, seek to enforce rights through the judicial process and ultimately form a Coalition of the Houseless to battle for a place to sit, sleep and live.

The problem of urban poor and the menace of the forced evictions aggravate their housing situation. The people in the promulgation of new housing legislation and towards the development of fair and equitable and policies and legislation, and accordingly to reject new laws adopted without such participation by affected groups.

Enforcement of urban ceiling laws which already exists in the statute book is an urgency if humanism and compassion are constitutional fundamentals. The right to life includes the right to housing and therefore we have to be serious in implementing laws national and international.

Housing Helps Socio-economic Development

The impact of appropriate housing technologies on the eradication of rural poverty can best be judged by assessing the extent of economic gains and social uplift of the rural poor families, which could be achieved in the following manner.

The following economic gains accrue when programmes for improvement of housing and environmental conditions are taken up by application of appropriate technologies.

1. Employment Generation

Local employment in housing construction is enhanced to the extent of 50 per cent of the total expenditure on construction. The bulk of employment is for unskilled labour and traditionally skilled and semi-skilled labour which includes women.

Employment guarantee can be achieved by undertaking massive housing programmes, through National Rural Employment Programme (NREP), Rural Land-less Labourers Employment Guarantee Programme (RLEGP) and Food for work programme. Rural Youth could be provided employment in housing construction by training them in construction skills as *in the* TRYSEM. The skill of local building artisans can be upgraded and also new skills can be imparted to unskilled and semi-skilled rural labour by promoting centers for building material programmes and training.

2. Development of Indigenous Resources

The optimum use of locally available building materials entails development of wide variety of cottage and small scale rural industries and handicrafts which provide economic gains by boosting production and increasing productivity. Such activities could also be pursued by women to supplement income.

3. Skill Formation and Upgradation

Unskilled labour is trained in various building trades and new skills are imparted to the traditionally skilled labour. They provide new and additional employment opportunities and income to rural poor. Effecting improvement in housing and environmental conditions helps in eradication of rural poverty and social betterment in several ways:

(i) **House Ownership:** The lot of homeless rural poor families are dramatically changed when they become house owners. The acquisition of tangible real assets brings social status as well as human dignity which are important motivating factors in development.

(ii) **Rural Roots:** House ownership deepens and strengthens the rural roots, thus reduces the incidence of migration from rural to urban areas and prevents denudation of rural areas especially by younger able-bodied people.

(iii) **More Habitable Villages:** By making villages more habitable, the local population is able to enjoy the benefits of over all economic and social development and poor families are drawn into the process of development, thereby contributing their share as well as obtaining their rightful due. This has special relevance in the case of Scheduled Caste, Scheduled Tribe and other vulnerable group families of the society.

Housing Statistics

Table 1 presents the total population, total number of households and housing stock in both rural and urban areas. When compare to 1951, the population in 1991 increased by 235 per cent. The increase in the number of household has been 206 per cent and that of occupied residences 229 per cent. The increase in the number of houses has not been in commensurate with the increase in population.

Between 1981 and 1991, the proportion of houseless households in rural areas of India has declined from 0.47 per cent 0.28 per cent as shown in Table 2. In 1981, Andhra Pradesh, Gujarat, Haryana, Himachal Pradesh, Maharashtra, Madhya Pradesh and Rajasthan had a higher proportion of houseless households (over 0.5 per cent). In 1991, Gujarat and Maharashtra had a houseless proportion of more than one per cent. For the country as a whole, the proportion in the urban areas declined from 0.73 per cent to 0.55 per cent during the period, Andhra Pradesh, Gujarat, Himachal Pradesh, Karnataka, Maharashtra and Orissa having a high proportion. In contrast to rural areas, there was an increase in the absolute number of the households in the urban areas.

Table 3 presents the proportion of households, having access to safe drinking water and also in rural areas. In 1981 the proportion was lower in Andhra Pradesh, Karnataka, Madhya Pradesh, Maharashtra, Orissa, Rajasthan and Uttar Pradesh and very high in Kerala, Punjab, Tamil Nadu and West Bengal. This clearly shows that during 1981-1991 there has been vigorous action programme to provide safe drinking water and all the states have achieved a high level though still much has to be done. However, when the water quality problem is considered the problem becomes intensive. If 63 per cent of rural households have access to safe drinking water in the country, the proportion is 90 per cent in urban areas. The table also highlights the proportion of households having toilet facilities which is a mere 9 per cent in rural areas (and 64 per cent in urban areas). State-wise Assam,

Gujarat, Kerala, Punjab and West Bengal have shown a higher proportion of households' toilet facilities. The proportion of households having electricity in rural areas was only 14.3 per cent in 1981 increasing to 31 per cent in 1991. Gujarat, Haryana, Maharashtra and Punjab have higher rate of electricity households. In urban areas, the proportion is 76 per cent in 1991. Sundaram and Tendulkar (1996) have constructed an index of amenities deprivation and according to them about 28 per cent of the rural households did not have even one of these basic amenities in 1991; while less than six per cent of the households lacking access to only one of the three amenities, one per cent of the households were deprived of water, while two per cent were deprived of electricity, in contrast to about 17 per cent lacking toilet facilities. Amongst the states, Orissa has the highest proportion (about 46 per cent) in the category of having none of the three amenities, while the proportion in Punjab is only three per cent. Kerala has the highest proportion of households having all the three amenities (31 per cent), followed by Punjab (14.3 per cent) and Gujarat (9.9 per cent). In Karnataka, the proportion was 5.16 per cent. In this State, none of the three amenities is reported in 17.2 per cent of households, neither electricity in 17.4 per cent; and neither electricity nor toilet in 57.4 per cent. The percentage of households not having any two amenities is 46.8 per cent for the country, 49 per cent in Karnataka and lower in Haryana, Himachal Pradesh, Kerala and Punjab. The percentage of not having water is less than that of electricity, higher in Assam and Haryana and then for toilet the deprivation was very high in many states. In urban areas, the deprivation has been 8.14 per cent for all the three, 2.13 per cent in water, 3.97 per cent in electricity and 14.3 per cent in toilet facilities. About 57.2 per cent of households had all the three amenities, the proportion being higher in Assam, Gujarat, Haryana, Kerala, Maharashtra, Punjab and West Bengal.

The extent of deprivation with respect to quality of structure is lower in urban areas, (10.3 per cent) than in rural areas where it has been 15.3 per cent. The proportion was higher in Assam, Bihar, Haryana and West Bengal. The proportion of households having non-serviceable *kutcha* houses is greater in rural areas, Assam, Bihar and West Bengal has a higher proportion.

The proportion of non-serviceable *kutcha* houses is 9.24 per cent, bad condition houses 6.03 per cent and slums 6.25 per cent in rural and 14.7 per cent in urban areas. The proportion of non-serviceable *kutcha* houses is very high in Assam, Bihar and West Bengal that of bad condition houses in Gujarat, Haryana, Maharashtra and that of slum houses in Assam and Maharashtra. In Karnataka 5.6 per cent of houses are non-serviceable *kuthca* houses, 7.6 per cent *pucca* and semi-pucca in bad condition and 7.38 per cent slums. In urban areas the proportion of slum households is 14.7 percent, higher in Maharashtra, Orissa, West Bengal and Andhra Pradesh; non-serviceable *kutcha* houses 2.88 per cent (higher Assam, Andhra Pradesh, Kerala and Madhya Pradesh) and 7.41 per cent pucca and semi-pucca houses in bad condition (higher in West Bengal Bihar and Haryana).

Table 4 presents the percentage and types of rural households in India during 1991. The proportion of pucca or permanent houses has been 30.6 per cent, higher in Goa, Gujarat, Haryana, Himachal Pradesh, Kerala, Punjab, Rajasthan, Delhi and West Bengal. The proportion of semi-pucca houses has been 24.02 per cent, higher in Bihar, Goa, Gujarat, Haryana, Himachal Pradesh, Karnataka, Madhya Pradesh, Maharashtra, Sikkim and other States. The proportion of temporary thatched houses is higher at 33.76 per cent, Andhra Pradesh, Arunachal Pradesh, Assam, Manipur, Meghalaya, Mizoram, Nagaland, Orissa, Tripura and West Bengal having a very high proportion.

Regarding over crowding rural population there has been a decline in 1991 except in Bihar and Uttar Pradesh. The percentage of over-crowding has been 52.23 per cent in 1981, slightly declining to 47.24 per cent in 1981 and Andhra Pradesh, Assam, Bihar, Gujarat, Karnataka, Maharashtra, and West Bengal in 1991 have a high proportion of over-crowding.

According to Sundaram and Tendulkar the shelter deprivation index in rural area in 1991 is 13.41 per cent, which includes houseless, amenities deprivation, poor quality structure and over-crowding (both locality level and big house). The index is higher in Assam and Bihar, Maharashtra, Orissa, Rajasthan, West Bengal and lower in others. In Karnataka, the percentage of rural households affected with houselessness has been 0.29, that of amenities deprivation 22.68 per cent, poor quality structure 13.11

per cent, locality level over-crowding 7.38 percent, over-crowding within a house 50.6 per cent and index of shelter deprivation 12.56 per cent. For the country as a whole, the proportion has been 0.28 per cent houselessness, 26.83 per cent amenities deprivation 15.27 per cent poor quality structure, 6.23 per cent locality level over-crowding and 13.41 deprived in shelter.

Conclusion

Improvement in housing conditions in rural as well as urban areas had manifold advantage. It raises the level of living, provides greater opportunities for work and is vital for transformation of rural life. Yet, because of the magnitude of the problem and its inherent difficulties, the task of improving conditions in the villages has to be viewed, not as an isolated objective, but as a part of the larger scheme of rural development. Consequently, rural housing is intrinsically a part of community development and village planning. The specific programme for rural housing as such, is intended to supplement the resources of the community development movement at the block level and the village by way of assistance. In the form of technical advice, demonstration, provision of finance. Its essential object is to help create healthy environmental conditions for sections of the village population and for balanced development of rural life as a whole. To achieve this objective the Government of India has set up six "Rural Housing Wings" in various parts of the country, under the agencies of National Building Organization as long as 1959. In order to broad base their activities to include Urban Housing also in their ambit of work programme the "Regional Housing Wings" have been renamed as "Regional Housing Development Centres". So far 15 of such centers have been set up in different parts of the country. These centers have been providing technical assistance and guidance to state government departments etc., in evolving appropriate economical designs of housing, making use of locally available building materials and construction technology limited to the area. To educate the people in different aspects of construction, to adopt cost effective and eco-friendly technologies, exhibits are organized in villages and also at places of large gatherings of rural folk. A number of large-scale rural housing schemes have also been implemented in different states in which technical guidance and assistance have been provided by these centers. By providing all these to the people the right to housing is protected and it will promote the social development.

Table 5.1 : Population, Households and Housing Stock in India (in Lakhs)

Census Year	Population			Households			Occupied Residences		
	Rural	Urban	Total	Rural	Urban	Total	Rural	Urban	Total
1951	2985	624	3609	606	128	734	541	103	644
1961	3601	791	4392	686	149	835	651	141	791
1971	4383	1089	5472	780	192	971	727	181	908
1981	5255	1597	6852	935	291	1226	872	272	1144
1991	6291	2172	8463	1116	395	1511	1085	387	1472

Source: Census of India, Various years.

Table 5.2 : Population of Houseless Households in India

State	% of Houseless H/H (Rural Areas)		% of Houseless H/H (Urban Areas)	
	1981	1991	1981	1991
Andhra Pradesh	0.52	0.26	1.03	0.80
Assam	N.A.	0.02	N.A.	0.15
Bihar	0.07	0.06	0.49	0.39
Gujarat	1.41	1.03	0.60	0.63
Haryana	0.51	0.21	0.43	0.27
Himachal Pradesh	0.60	0.23	0.52	0.90
Jammu and Kashmir	0.27	N.A.	0.10	N.A.
Karnataka	0.46	0.29	0.84	0.60
Kerala	0.17	0.12	0.51	0.29
Madhya Pradesh	0.98	0.39	0.91	0.58
Maharashtra	1.47	1.08	1.03	0.66
Orissa	0.28	0.15	0.77	0.85
Punjab	0.36	0.25	0.62	0.39
Rajasthan	0.68	0.30	0.66	0.46
Tamil Nadu	0.13	0.07	0.25	0.20
Uttar Pradesh	0.08	0.07	0.47	0.51
West Bengal	0.20	0.07	0.93	0.58
All India	0.47	0.28	0.73	0.55

N.A: Not available

Source: K. Sundaram and S.D.Tendulkar (1995), 'Measuring Shelter Deprivation in India', *Indian Economic Review*, Vol. XXX, No. 2, pp. 134-135.

Table 5.3 : Population Growth Rate and Provision of Drinking Water and Toilet Facilities (1991)

State	*% of H/H having safe drinking water*	*Toilets*	*% of National growth rate (rural)*
Andhra Pradesh	48.98	6.62	1.51
Assam	43.28	30.53	2.25
Bihar	56.55	4.96	2.27
Gujarat	60.04	11.16	1.89
Haryana	67.14	6.53	2.40
Himachal Pradesh	75.51	6.42	1.80
Karnataka	67.31	6.64	1.67
Kerala*	21.00	44.07	1.40
Madhya Pradesh	45.56	3.64	2.24
Maharashtra	54.02	6.64	1.76
Orissa	35.32	3.58	1.71
Punjab	92.09	15.79	1.80
Rajasthan	50.62	6.65	2.59
Tamil Nadu	64.28	7.17	1.06
Uttar Pradesh	56.62	6.44	2.50
West Bengal	80.26	12.31	1.93
All India	55.54	9.48	—

* In Kerala, inside Wells Proportion is very high.

Source: D. Lahiri, (1996), "Rural Housing : Policies and problems in Rural India", *Kurukshetra*, May-June, p. 85.

Table 5.4 : Percentage and Types of Rural Households in India (1991)

State/U.T.	*No. of H/H (mil)*	*No. of Rural H/H (mil)*	*%*	*Types of houses occupied (%)*		
Andhra Pradesh	13.71	10.34	75.4	29.77	25.24	44.99
Arunachal Pradesh	0.17	0.15	88.2	9.76	10.53	79.71
Assam	3.80	3.33	87.6	10.53	30.37	76.09

Bihar	14.11	12.25	86.8	24.07	38.33	37.56
Goa	0.22	0.13	59.0	41.58	52.36	6.06
Gujarat	7.47	4.79	64.1	43.42	51.61	4.97
Haryana	2.65	1.92	72.5	41.46	41.32	17.32
Himachal Pradesh	0.99	0.88	88.9	49.75	43.86	6.39
Karnataka	8.02	5.53	69.0	30.45	49.34	20.21
Kerala	5.39	4.03	74.8	51.56	20.55	27.89
Madhya Pradesh	11.77	9.05	76.8	20.93	73.79	5.28
Maharashtra	14.90	8.99	68.3	35.37	47.36	17.27
Manipur	0.30	0.22	73.3	2.46	35.90	61.46
Meghalaya	0.33	0.26	78.8	9.33	28.17	62.50
Mizoram	0.12	0.06	50.0	2.86	35.68	61.45
Nagaland	0.08	0.05	62.5	12.35	31.00	56.65
Orissa	5.98	5.17	86.3	13.00	22.63	64.37
Punjab	3.38	2.36	69.8	72.14	12.26	15.60
Rajasthan	7.37	1.66	76.8	47.04	27.46	25.50
Sikkim	0.08	0.07	87.5	22.13	40.43	37.43
Tamil Nadu	12.34	8.43	68.3	34.60	19.63	45.77
Tripura	0.52	0.40	76.9	1.91	17.35	80.74
Uttar Pradesh	22.41	18.09	80.7	32.70	33.60	33.70
West Bengal	12.50	8.89	71.1	50.74	34.17	50.10
Delhi	1.86	0.16	8.6	86.63	5.87	7.50
Union Territories	0.40	0.15	37.5	43.98	24.02	32.00
All India	151.03	111.53	73.8	30.59	35.65	33.76

Source: Census of India, Housing and Amenities - A Data Based on Housing in Districts, Cities and Towns, Occasional Paper No. 5, 1994.

REFERENCES

Encyclopedia Britannica, Vol. II, 1968, London.

Charles, Abraham, *Housing in the Modern World*, London.

Luther H. Fides and Others, *The Decade of Development-Problems and Issues.*

Justice V.R. Krishna Iyer, *Housing as a Human Right and its Constitutional Parameters.*

G.C. Mathur, (1987), 'Appropriate Technology for Shelter for the Homeless', *Journal of the National Buildings Organization*, Vol . XXXII, No. 1, April, New Delhi.

G.C. Mathur, (1989), 'Rural Housing Tech and Poverty Eradication', *Kurukshetra*, September, New Delhi.

S. Giriappa, (1998), *Housing Finance and Development in India*, Mohit Publications, New Delhi.

6

Poverty and Human Rights : A Rights based Approach to Development

Poverty is probably the most serious human rights and development challenge faced by both advanced and developing countries. The recognition of poverty as a human rights issue is a recent development. It coincides with the greater acceptance of economic, social, and cultural rights as enforceable human rights rather than mere policy objectives. In the Indian situation, this transition is indeed telling given that an integral understanding of the chapters on fundamental rights and directive principles of state policy of the Constitution of India has been elaborated over time through a progressive interpretation by the Indian judiciary, in particular, the Supreme Court.

In September 2000, at the United Nations Millennium Summit, world leaders agreed to a set of time-bound measurable goals and targets for combating poverty, hunger, disease, illiteracy, environmental degradation, and discrimination against women. Among these objectives, which are now called the UN Millennium Development Goals (MDGs), the first is to eradicate extreme poverty and hunger. Specifically, the goal is to reduce by half the proportion of people living on less than a dollar a day and the proportion of people who suffer from hunger. All 191 U.N. member states have pledged to meet these goals by the year 2015. It is very unlikely that these targets will be met. However, human rights-based approaches focus on the empowerment of the people as a core strategy in ensuring thrat the system of governance is reformed to respond to issues that affect their lives, including poverty.

One of the important proposals that a report by the U.N.'s independent expert on human rights and extreme poverty, Arjun Sengupta, makes is to recognize the removal of the conditions of poverty as a "core" obligation, which should be realized immediately and not progressively. To overcome possible objections from many developing countries to this proposal, Professor Sengupta, has argued, "The idea is to identify as extremely poor any group whose number is limited so that the society does not find it unmanageable to deal with their problems. Once .... Identified, the removal of their conditions of extreme poverty must be taken as an obligation corresponding to the fulfilment of human rights norms".

It is in this context that the legal frame work and the notion of legal empowerment of the poor through law and institutional reforms become significant. In countries where there is a functioning and effective legal system based on the rule of law, the courts and other democratic institutions would inevitably play an important role in determining what constitutes legal entitlements and how they can be enforced.

The focus of rights based approaches to development is to ensure that governments are constantly evaluated and made accountable to citizens and the international community on the basis of their progress. A rights-based approach would integrate the norms, standards, and principles of the international human rights system into the plans, policies, and processes of development including anti-poverty policies in the domestic context. Another important aspect of such an approach is that it defines human rights goals and objectives specifically by providing for timelines, indicators, and measurements to monitor progress in the realization of specific development objectives such as those dealing with food, shelter, drinking water, education and health. Extreme poverty impedes social and economic development, and threatens the rule of law and social fabric of any society.

If poverty is recognized as a violation of human rights, it is possible that the judiciary may be empowered to intervene when situations of poverty are consequences of failures in governance. A wrongful act, when understood to be a human rights violation, would provide for valuable judicial space and ensure mandatory enforcement of its directions for possible relief measures. Judicial empowerment, through an expanded-interpretation of rights, would necessitate an attitudinal change in government to facilitate the development of anti-poverty mechanism while recognizing that abolishing poverty is no longer merely a public policy goal, but a constitutional and human rights imperative. Institutions like the national human rights commission will also have an important role to play.

Role of Civil Society

Active and sustained involvement of civil society is necessary for tackling any social problem, including poverty. If poverty is recognized as a human rights issue, both domestic and international civil society would need to taken an active part in promoting it as such, and in resisting any policy that loses sight of the need to constantly keep poverty in check. The human rights activism that is typically generated through the work of civil actors can be useful for the various departments of governments that engage in formulating and implementing policies relating to fighting poverty. A human rights approach creates an empowering dimension in the work of civil society in ensuring transparency of the government. Poverty recognised only as an economic and public policy issue invites official responses from government bodies. But the human rights aspects of the discussion will receive a wider community of responses. This empowering dimension of the human rights discourse is useful in sustaining poverty-free governance as a basic principle of administration.

When poverty is recognized as a human rights issue, it is possible to achieve political consensus on the ways and means of fighting it. Further, it can ensure that objectively is maintained in the implementation of policies relating to fighting poverty so that resource allocation and targeting of the areas and people who are suffering from extreme poverty is not based on any biases or prejudices. This is important as it is possible that the resources that are allocated to fight poverty may not reach the true and deserving beneficiaries because of corruption or other abuses of power. To avoid this problem, the recognition of poverty as a human rights issue broadens the scope for engagement and political consensus can be developed to ensure that violations are uniformly recognized, without any form of discrimination. Maintaining political consensus on issues relating to poverty can then in time result in the broader application of internationally developed good governance principles.

Poverty is Complex and Multifaceted

Poverty is a complex, multi-faceted, world that requires clear understanding in all its dimensions. That it exists, and affects us is known. Yet, the way it is created and perpetuated and the way it affects us are still being explored. The phenomenon of poverty is widespread and has defied a solution for ages, because poverty is seen as a condition of deprivation, and also as a condition, which deprives. It is a concept, which could be understood in terms of perceptions and interpretations. The poor face multiple and interlinked hardships, each of which makes it difficult to escape from the other-poverty, hunger, disease, oppression, conflict, pollution and depletion of natural resources. Development, in this context means enabling people to escape from this vicious circle.

The human right, to be free from poverty is the right of everyone. Everyone has the right to a standard of living, adequate health and well-being, including food, clothing, housing and necessary social services. The human right to live in dignity, free from want, is spelt out in most human rights documents, as it is an essential part of the realization of all other human rights - rights that can't be separated or denied because of one's race, gender, age, class, immigration status, country, sexual orientation, physical abilities or religion.

The Fight against poverty a moral one

To fight against poverty is a moral imperative, especially due to the paradox of widespread poverty co-existing with scientific and social progress capable of eliminating it. The relationship between human rights and poverty is a two-way one. Poverty itself is a denial of human rights, but also a shortfall of human rights makes it difficult to achieve poverty reduction objectives. Kofi Annan's declaration of all human rights for all' is meant to focus specifically on this part. It clearly links the Economic, Cultural and Social Rights to the Civil and Political rights, and also links it to poverty reduction. It envisages a scenario where human rights are the lens through which reality is perceived. He has rightly pointed out that like the struggle for independence from colonial rule, the struggle for development too has to be carried on mainly in the developing countries by their people.

Out of the estimated 1000 million people in the world who live in extreme poverty, about 50 per cent live in India, Bangladesh, Pakistan, Indonesia and Nigeria. India alone accounts for one-third of such people. By the government's own admission, 3000 children become blind in India due to deficiency of vitamin-A every year. According to the National Institute of Nutrition, Hyderabad, 63 per cent of children below three years, and 45 per cent of the children between 3-5 years, suffer from severe anaemia, due to iron deficiency.

Is poverty simply about the level of income obtained by individuals or households? Is it about a lack of access to social services? Or is it more correctly understood as inability to participate in society, economically, culturally, or politically? Perhaps all of these and more. The indicators that have evolved over a period of time could range from income poverty, human development, and sustainable livelihood to social inclusion, current consumption and future security. Complexity of measurement mirrors complexity of definition. This proliferation of concepts and indicators would matter less if the same individuals were being identified by all the measures. However, there is often a limited correlation. Yet to gauge poverty we often need universal measures like the international poverty line of US $ one a day. This is a useful tool to raise awareness as well as to generate political momentum.

It is important to note here that measuring poverty is not the same as why it occurs. Interventions need to tackle causes and not the symptoms.

Empowerment Hurdles

Empowerment is the link between rights-based approach and development of political systems. However, the course of empowerment is fraught with formidable hurdles. For example, a provision giving the poor a 'voice' could directly infringe upon the privilege of the rich. It is anybody's guess how this class would react to such a trespass. There is also the question of who is the duty holder-government, NGO's, MNCs, civil society, private sector-or do all of them have to carry out their share of responsibility as a section of society?

In all this it may be noticed that co-operation, flexibility, and imagination play a far larger role than financial assistance.

An ethic of equality must be integrated with the ethic of solidarity. The whole human family should share scientific progress and social development equitably.

A multi dimensional approach to poverty

The issue of tackling poverty requires a multi-dimensional approach. Sustained economic growth always remains a necessary condition. However, growth alone cannot ensure the eradication of poverty unless it is coupled with an enabling environment where the benefits of growth could be equitably distributed amongst the poor. A targeted and bottom-up approach involving the poor through their social mobilization, addressing the following issues remains critical for a successful poverty alleviation strategy.

- Defining the economic content of social mobilization processes at the micro level and indicating how these will be linked at the national level;
- Ensuring meeting the basic needs, including minimum food, shelter, clothing, healthcare and education entitlements, of all the poor;
- Providing income-generating opportunities through an enabling legal, financial and market environment;
- Given the success of micro credit in empowering the poor, up-scaling and replicating such best practices throughout the region;
- Ensuring adequate investment on children through programmes like food for education;
- Paying special attention to women in poverty with a view to freeing them from their perpetual entrapment;
- Mobilizing unemployed youth through various skill development and vocational training programmes;
- Taking special care of the disabled, aged and socially disadvantaged people through various social welfare benefit schemes;

- Emphasizing the need for rapid and sustainable economic development without degrading the environment and creating special safety nets for people living in ecologically vulnerable areas;
- Making affordable and sustainable technologies available for the poor so that they can reap the maximum benefits through better farming practices as well as from off farm activities;
- Attaching greater emphasis on rural poverty eradication programmes given the fact that majority of the poor still live in the rural areas;
- Resorting to Information and Communication Technology (ICT) for various poverty alleviation programmes;
- Encouraging more interaction amongst the government agencies and the NGOs, research institutions and civil society representatives at the regional level for better coordination and dissemi-nation of ideas and information;
- Encouraging private sector to get directly involved in poverty alleviation efforts by offering tax rebates and other incentives;
- Emphasizing on decentralization and devolution of power at the grass roots level involving the poor in local level decision-making, which will also bring about more transparency, accountability and good governance at the local level;
- Ensuring, as far as feasible, a pro-poor element in national development planning in individual states with maximum provisions of investment of Human Resources Development.

REFERENCES

Bibu Mohapatra & S. Usha, " Poverty and Human Rights", *Liberal Times*, Vol. X, No. 2, 2002, New Delhi.

Q. A.M.A. Rahim, "Poverty Alleviation in South Asia; The SAARC experience", *Liberal Times*, Ibid.

C. Rajkumar, "Poverty Human Rights and development", *The Hindu*, Vol. 130, No. 45, February 22, 2007, Chennai.

Muhammad Yunus, "Poverty is a threat to peace", *Janata,* Vol. 62, No. 1, January 28, 2007, Mumbai.

Dr Partha J. Shah, "Economic Freedom: The forgotten human right". *Liberal Times,* Vol. VII, No. 3, 2000, New Delhi.

7

Child Labour in India : A Human Rights Perspective

Introduction

Children are the blooming flowers in the garden of society. They are the most valuable assets of the nation and their importance in nation building process cannot be undermined. Children of today are the potential citizens of tomorrow. The quality of life, they enjoy today would ultimately determine the quality of future population of the nation. The children have rights like other human beings, to be respected with regard to their integrity, dignity, interest and opinions. But significantly enough, children in India are deprived of even the basic human rights due to them, as they ought to be in any civilized society.

'Child' defined by the Constitution of India (Article 24) as anyone below the age of 14 years.

According to the United Nations Convention on the Rights of the Child (Article 1) it is below the age of 18 years.

The child labour (prohibition and regulation) Act was enacted in 1986. As per Child Labour (Prohibition and Regulation) Act, 1986 "Child means a person who has not completed 14 years of age".

Child labour is an economic practice and a social evil. In the first context it signified employment of children in gainful occupations with a view to addition of income to the family. In the second context, in assessing the nature and extent of social evil, it is necessary to take into account the character of the jobs in which they are engaged, the dangers to which they are exposed and the opportunity for development, which they have been denied (V.V. GIRI).

Work may become a serious burden and risk to children while their social and educational role is neglected. In such case; work predominates and places children under severe stress, becomes a danger to their healthy development and future prospects. It is in this context that child work is exploitative and abusive. In other words, work that impinges on children's right to education, play, leisure, mental, physical, spiritual and psychological development is child labour.

Most of the developing countries facing the child labour problem, India being one among these countries has the specific features of child labour.

The Problem and Forms of Child Labour in India

The problem is more acute in developing countries, given the changes that they undergo in their societies. Industrialization and urbanization have brought with it qualitative changes in the nature of children's work in developing countries. India being one of the developing countries has the specific features of child labour. Its forms differ in rural to urban areas. Rural areas constitute more of child labour activities than in urban areas, hence magnitude of problem is more in rural areas than in urban areas.

The form of child labour in agricultural sector in rural areas includes farm labour, which constitutes seventy percent of labour force. In urban areas its form changes which includes activities in different sectors such as domestic servants, match and fireworks industries of Sivakasi in Tamil Nadu, the diamond polishing industry in Surat (Gujarat), the precious stone polishing industry in Jaipur (Rajasthan), the brassware industry in Moradabad (UP), glass industry of Firozabad, a town in Agra district (UP), Aligarh's Lock industry (UP), carpet making industry in Jammu and Kashmir and UP, Beedi making industry in Madhya Pradesh, Pottery industry in Khurja (UP), Coir industry in Kerala, Zari industry in Banaras, Brick kiln industry in West Bengal, Slate industry in Markapur (AP) Kiln industry of Dhone (AP), which constitutes thirty per cent of the urban labour force.

Causes of the Child Labour

Children are sent to work due to sheer necessity in the family. Whenever literacy levels are low, the size of the family is large and a family is compelled to send their children to work. Poverty forces the parents to send their children to seek employment because augmentation of their income is essential for the survival of the families, which are invariably large. However, the burgeoning population growth, increasing rural to urban migration, family disintegration, inadequate measures of social security, lack of avenues for education, social choices, social policies and shortcomings in institutional arrangements and ineffective law enforcement machinery are some of the contributory factors for the increase in number of child workers in India.

Why Child Labour (Children) are Preferred ?

Children's employment in all possible sectors is preferred because of the following reasons, they work for less remuneration than adult labourers, they are more flexible mentally as well as physically and can be moulded and pressurized easily into the exploitative tactics of the employers, child labour is not only very cheap to the employers, but also trouble free since they can't organize by themselves, children cannot demand any overtime, nor the medical and other similar benefits, employers find children more amenable to discipline and control.

Multi-Rights of Children

The convention on the rights of the child contains 54 articles, each of which details a different type of rights. These can be classified into four broad categories.

1. **Survival Rights:** It covers child's rights to life and the needs that are most basic to existence; these include an adequate living standard, shelter, nutrition and access to medical services.

2. **Development Rights:** It includes those things that are required by children in order to reach their fullest potential. Examples are the right to education, play and leisure, cultural activities, access to information, freedom of thought, conscience and religion.

3. **Protection Rights:** It requires that children be safeguard against all forms of abuse, neglect and exploitation. They cover issues such as special care for refugee children,

torture, abuses in the criminal justice system, involvement in armed conflict, child labour, street children, drug abuse and sexual exploitation.

4. **Participation Rights:** It allows children to take an active role in the communities and nations. It encompasses the freedom to express opinions, to have a say in matters affecting their own lives, to join associations and to assemble peacefully. As their abilities develop, children are to have increasing opportunities to participate in the activities of their society in preparation for responsible adulthood.

The categories of child rights reveals that the convention recognizes the exceptional vulnerability of children, which proclaims the childhood, is entitled to special care and assistance. It obligates state of respect and ensures that children get a fair and equitable deal in society. It advocates the concerted action on the part of individuals, government and non-governmental organizations to promote and protect the rights of the children.

Constitutional Provisions Relating to Child Labour

India being a welfare state follows a proactive policy in the matter of tackling the problem of child labour. The Constitution of India has adopted the following articles which reflects the nation's concern for children in general and child labour in particular.

Article-23 : Prohibition of traffic in human being and forced labour

Traffic in human being and beggars and other similar forms of forced labour are prohibited and any contravention of this provision shall be an offence punishable in accordance with law.

Article-24 : Prohibition of employment of children in factories etc

No child below the age of fourteen years shall be employed to work in any factory or mines or engaged in any other hazardous employment.

Article-39 (e&f) : Certain principles of policy to be followed by the state

The state shall, in particular direct its policy, securing : (e) that the health and strength of the worker, men and women and the tender age of children are not abused and that citizens are not forced by economic necessities to enter a vocation unsuited to their age or strength, (f) that children are given opportunities and facilities to develop in a healthy manner and in a condition of freedom and dignity and that childhood and youth are protected against exploitation and moral and material amendment.

Article-45 : Provision for free and compulsory education for children

That the state shall endeavour to provide within a period of ten years from the commencement of this constitution for free and compulsory education for all children until they complete the age of fourteen years.

Child Labour (Prohibition and Regulation) Act, 1986 - Salient Features

(a) Ban on the employment of the children i.e. those who have not completed their fourteen year in specified occupations and processes.

(b) Regulate the working condition of children in occupations where they are not prohibited for working.

(c) Lays down penalties for employment of children in violation of the provision of this act and other acts which forbid the employment of children.

(d) Except in the process of family based work or recognized school based activities, children are not permitted to work in occupations connected with :

  (i) Transport of passengers, goods or mail by railway.

  (ii) Cinder picking, cleaning of ash pit or building operations in the railway premises.

  (iii) Work in catering establishment at railway stations.

  (iv) In works relating to the construction of a railway station or any other work done in close proximity to or between the railway lines.

  (v) Work relating to selling of crackers and fireworks in a shop with temporary license.

(vi) Handling of toxic substances, inflammable or explosive.

(vii) Beedi making.

(viii) Mica Cutting, Spiting.

(ix) Hazardous process and dangerous operations as defined in the Factory Act 1948.

(x) Soldering process in electronic industries.

(xi) Colour printing dyeing, weaving etc.

General Development Programme for Benefit of Child Labour

To successfully rehabilitate child labour withdrawn from employment and to reduce the incidence of child labour progressively the focus in is the environment of the child (a) By providing better and readily accessible education through formal and non-formal system of education, (b) By providing healthy conditions for child labour, (c) By providing nutrition through schemes like the Integrated Child Development Services, (d) By intensifying the anti-poverty programmes such as Integrated Rural Development Programme, National Rural Employment Programme etc. (e) Area specific project to be undertaken, to focus on an area, to know the concentration of child labour, and to adopt a project approach for identification, withdrawal and rehabilitation of working children.

Suggestions for Elimination of Child Labour in Indian Society

— Providing non-formal education and vocational skills training programmes for out of school children particularly for working children.

— Inform and educate the families, employers and working children about labour laws and the impact of work on children.

— Improve the understanding and expand the responsibilities of labour inspectors.

— The problems of child labour has drawn little media attention. It should have good media coverage.

— Steps should be made to improve the understand of the parents and children on the negative impact of the child labour on health.

— Encourage and assist in providing educational opportunities to children.

— There should be effective co-ordination between government and non-governmental organizations regarding the action plan for the welfare of working children.

— The elimination of child labour and the universalization of elementary education both deal with that no child should work and all children should be in schools.

— Empower the children, and caring an environment in which all children are able to live happily and realize their potential leading to balance and sustainable social development.

Conclusion

The goal of elimination of child labour cannot be achieved in one stroke in developing and very large country like India. The real solution therefore lies in identifying the root cause of child labour, social and economic. Total economic development coupled with social justice is a long-term measure. It seems the joy of childhood reserved only for some privileged children. Ongoing support from all sections of the people is very essential for the removal of child labour in India. Every child in India need social protection, economic support for the fullest enjoyment of their human rights without violations at all the levels of society. The abolition of child labour is not practicable, so long as every citizen is not made free from the bondage of poverty and is assured of a minimum standard of living. A strategy for rehabilitation of child labour is necessary, failing which all the policies and acts will prove a day dream.

REFERENCES

Gouri Kumar Nanda and Chinmayee Nanda (2007) "Child labour and rights of children", *Third concept*, Vol. 21, No. 250, December 2007, New Delhi.

Manjulika Gautam (2006), "Child development in India', *Yojana*, November 2006, Vol. 50, Publications Division, New Delhi.

Dr. Narayana S.C. (2006) "Child Labour in India, Is it a curse?", *Kuruskshetra* (Monthly) November 2006, Vol. 55, No. 1, Publications Division, New Delhi.

Neela Dabir & Mohua Nigudkar (2007), "Child Abuse confronting reality", Economic and Political Weekly, July 14, 2007, Vol. XLII, No. 27 & 28, A Sameeksha trust publication, Mumbai.

Dr. Srivastava R.C. (2004) "Child labour is a disgrace to mankind", Employment News (Weekly), 1-7 May 2004, New Delhi.

Dr. Subramanyam I (2006), "Child labour - A human rights perspective", *The PRP Journal of Human Rights*, July - September 2006, Vol. 10, No. 3, New Delhi.

Vivekanandan B (2007), "Relevance of Democratic Socialism", *Janata*, Vol. 62, No. 36, September 30, 2007, Mumbai.

Yojana, November 2007 "Leave No Child Behind" Vol. 51, Publications Division, New Delhi.

Ritu Saraswat, "Child Labour", *Yojana*, Vol. 50, November 2006, Publication Division, New Delhi.

Dr. R.C. Srivastava, "Child Labour is a Disgrace to Mankind", *Employment News*, 1 -7 May 2004, New Delhi.

8
Child Labour: A Human Rights Perspective*

Introduction

To understand the phenomenon of child labour, it is necessary to begin with the meaning of the child work. The concepts of child labour and child work are usually used interchangeably in the literature of the subject, in fact, child labour is sub-set of child work denoting that work, which is exploitative of the child. Child work become child labour when it threatens the health and development of the children it is child labour not the child-work but that one has to be concerned with. Child work becomes exploitative when one starts full-time work at too early an age. This happened historically in the earlier stages of industrialization in Europe where child began work in factories from nine, eight or even five years. This is still the case today in many developing countries. Working too long within or outside of the family so that children are unable to attend school, where it is available, or to make the most of school due to fatigue or lack of time. In some cases children still work 12-16 hours a day. Work resulting in excessive physical, social and psychological strains upon the child as in the case of sexual exploitation in prostitution and pornography work in sweatshops, as well as such dangerous work as military service and mining. Work and life on the street is unhealthy and dangerous.

Inadequate remuneration for working outside of the family as in the case of child workers in carpet weaving who are paid U.S. $ 3.00 per a sixty hours a week. Too much responsibility at

*Paper presented at "South India Regional Consultation on "Children at Risk: Focus to Child Labour and Street Children", organized by Vigil India Movement, Bangalore at RCPDS, Madurai.

early stage as in the domestic situation where children under ten years may have to look after young brothers and sisters for a whole day thereby preventing school attendance. Work that does not facilitate the psychological and social development of the child as in dull and repetitive tasks associated with industries like handicrafts. Work that inhibits the child's self-esteem as in bonded labour and prostitution and in a less extreme case the negative perception of street children (UNICEF, 1986). Thus, child labour refers to the employment of children in gainful occupations or a material contribution to the income of the family. It is both an economic and social evil, in that it leads to serious health hazards and denies them opportunity for physical and mental development. Hence any work by children that interfere with their full physical and mental developments, their opportunities for a desirable minimum of education or their needed recreation (Homer Folks). Hence, Child Labour is an economic practice and a social evil. In the first context, it signified employment of children in gainful occupations with a view to addition of income to the family. In the second context, in assessing the nature and extent of social evil, it is necessary to take into account the character of the jobs in which they are engaged, the dangers to which they are exposed and the opportunity for development, which they have been denied (V.V. Giri).

The problem is more acute in developing countries, given the changes that they undergo in their societies. Industrialization and urbanization have brought with it qualitative changes in the nature of children's work in developing countries. India being one of the developing countries has the specific features of child labour. Its forms differ in rural to urban areas. Rural areas constitute more of child labour activities than in urban areas, hence magnitude of problem is more in rural areas than in urban areas. The form of child labour in agricultural sector in rural areas includes farm labour, which constitutes seventy per cent of labour force. In urban areas its form changes which includes activities in different sectors such as match and fire industry of Sivakasi in Tamil Nadu, glass industry of Firozabad, a town in Agra district (U.P.) Aligarh's lock industry (U.P.), carpet making industry in Jammu and Kashmir and U.P., Beedi making industry in Madhya Pradesh, pottery industry in Khurja (U.P.), coir industry in Kerala, zari industry in Banaras, brick kiln industry of West Bengal, slate industry in Markapur (A.P.), kiln industry of Dhone (A.P.), which constitutes thirty per cent of the urban labour force.

Types of Child Labour

Normally there are three categories of children involved in child labour. They were broadly classified under the categories of street children, bonded children and working children. The street children are living in the streets without the protection of permanent shelter, love and affection. They work as shoeshine boys, newspaper-vendors, rag pickers and at times do begging. The problem of this group is more acute in comparison to that of children working in factories and workshops. At least those children can have home to go back in the evening. But the street children are completely alone and are at the mercy of their employers night and day. They live on the pavements, in the bus stands, railway platforms and in small eating places. They are being exposed to the agencies. Due to their complex problem normally they are on the run are deprived of education and childhood.

The project-based plan of action identified 10 areas with high incidence of child labor in hazardous industries. The areas identified were:

(i) The match industry in Sivakasi, Tamil Nadu.
(ii) The diamond polishing industry in Surat, Gujarat.
(iii) The precious stone polishing industry in Jaipur (Rajasthan).
(iv) The glass industry in Ferozabad (U.P.).
(v) The brassware industry in Moradabad (U.P.).
(vi) The handmade carpet industry in Mirzapur-Bhadohi (U.P.).
(vii) The Lock-making industry in Aligarh (U.P.).
(viii) The handmade Carpet industry in Jammu and Kashmir.
(ix) The slate industry in Mandsaur (M.P.).
(x) The slate industry in Markapur (A.P.).

The strategy in these industrial areas will have to evolve a package comprising the following elements:

(a) Stepping up the enforcement of Factories Act 1948, the Mines Act, 1952, and CLA, 1986. If necessary special enforcement staff will be created for this purpose.

(b) Coverage of families with child labour to be covered under/employment-generating programmes.

(c) Scheduled Caste (SC), Scheduled Tribe (ST) families with child labour to be covered under special component and tribal sub-plans.

(d) Provision of formal and non-formal education to all children engaged in hazardous employment, the setting up of special schools providing vocational training and supplementary nutrition for - child workers, and a programme of adult education for the parents of working children. The policy also anticipates a stipend for children withdrawn from prohibited employment. Health care for all children attending special school.

(e) Co-ordination of different departments, ministries of the central and state Governments to benefit child labour.

Causes of Child Labour

Children are sent to work due to sheer necessity in the family. Wherever literacy levels are low, the size of the family is large and a family is compelled to send their children to work. Poverty forces the parents to send their children to seek employment because augmentation of their income is essential for the survival of the families, which are invariably large. However, the burgeoning population growth, increasing rural migration, family disintegration, inadequate measures of social security, lack of avenues for education, social choices, social policies and shortcomings in institutional arrangements and ineffective law enforcement machinery are some of the contributory factors for the increase in number of child workers in India.

The wage structure of the adult workmen has a direct bearing on the occurrence of child labour. If the adult workmen could get a real living wage, they are likely to desist from sending their children to work. Sometime children go to work because of the compelling circumstances in the event of loss of the bread winner is also fallacious to some degree because it is usually the head of the family who forces children to go the labour market. Sociological factors, too have their share of this scourge. The tradition of family occupation often motivates the child to become a bread winner. The educational system adds yet another dimension to the prevalence of the child labour problem. In many places the school presents a drab and dismal picture and holds little attraction for the child. Moreover, the increasing volume of unemployment among educated youth undermines the faith of the poor in the efficacy and pay-off of education.

Why Children are Preferred?

Children's employment in all possible sectors is preferred because of the following reasons:

(i) they work for less remuneration than adult labourers.

(ii) they are more flexible mentally as well as physically and can be moulded and pressurized easily into the exploitative tactics of the employers.

(iii) child labour is not only very cheap to the employers, but also trouble-free since they can't organize by themselves.

(iv) being minors, the membership of trade unions is not open to child labour and hence it is advantage to the employer.

(v) children cannot demand any overtime, nor the medical and other similar benefits.

(vi) Employers find children more amenable to discipline and control, and

(vii) They can be coaxed, admonished, pulled up and punished for default without jeopardizing relationship.

Multi-Rights of Children

The convention on the Rights of the Child contains 54 Articles, each of which details a different type of rights. These can be classified into four broad categories:

1. **Survival Rights**: It covers child's rights to life and the needs that are most basic to existence; these include an adequate living standard, shelter, nutrition and access to medical services.

2. **Development Rights**: It includes those things that are required by children in order to reach their fullest potential. Examples are the right to education, play and leisure, cultural activities, access to information, and freedom of thought, conscience and religion.

3. **Protection Rights:** It requires that children be safeguard against all forms of abuse, neglect and exploitation. They cover issues such as special care for refugee children, torture, abuses in the criminal justice system, involvement in armed conflict, child labour, street children, drug abuse and sexual exploitation.
4. **Participation Rights:** It allows children to take an active role in the communities and nations. It encompasses the freedom to express opinions, to have a say in matters affecting their own lives, to join associations and to assemble peacefully. As their abilities develop, children are to have increasing opportunities to participate in the activities of their society and in preparation for responsible adulthood.

The categorization of Child Rights reveals that the Convention recognizes the exceptional vulnerability of children, which proclaims the childhood, is entitled to special care and assistance. It is guided by the principle of a 'first call children' - a principle that the essential needs of children should be given highest priority in the allocation of resources.

It obligates the State of respect and ensures that children get a fair and equitable deal in society. It emphasizes the importance of family and the need to create an environment that is conducive to the healthy growth and development of children. It advocates concerted action on the part of individuals, Government and Non-Governmental Organi-zations to promote the Rights of the Child. To put it in short, it is a means of empowering children, and caring an environment in which all children are able to live happily and realize their potential leading to balance and sustainable Social Development.

Conclusion

An integrated approach is the only basis for elimination of child labour. There has to be convergence of various services in order to make a dent in child labour situation. Panchayats and urban local bodies at local level charged with the responsibility of ensuring development and social justice and implementation of various programmes can ensure this convergence. Panchayats and urban local bodies could build linkages with the following in the process of convergences. Health department to cover medical inspection of all working children to ensure that people are aware of various concerns; Education department to ensure access, enrolment and retention of children; Labour department to ensure that various provisions of Child Labour Act and national policy on child labour are followed, Rural development to ensure that Child Labour families have priority in both welfare and developmental programmes. Agriculture to ensure proper storage of food items, marketing, information and transportation and so on. Since the rural sector absorbs 80 per cent of child labour, panchayats have to pay special attention to this department and ensure effective implementation of programmes like crop insurance, cheap credit, subsidized fertilizers and seed. Along with convergences of services, there has to be convergences of attitude among law enforcement agencies, parents, panchayat leadership, and the civil society. Last, but no way the least, unless there is an ethical shift in favour to total elimination of child labour. On the other hand with a strong will and sound package the problem of child labour may decrease over the years.

REFERENCES

L. Mishra, "Government of India's Stand on Child Labour", *Management in Government*, Vol. XXXI, No. 4, January-March 2000, New Delhi.

U. News, monthly newsletter of the UN Information Centre, Vol. 60. No. 6, June 2005, New Delhi.

K. Suriyan & P. Anandharajakumar, "Convention on the Rights of the Child an Overview". *Third concept*. Vol. 12, No. 139, September 1998, New Delhi.

Rekha Pande, "Girl child Rights and Labour Exploitation in the Beedi Industry". *Indian Journal of Human Rights*, Vol. 7, Nos. 1 & 2, January-December 2003, University of Hyderabad, Hyderabad.

K. Mohana Sundaram, "Human Rights and Child Labour", *Third concept*, Vol. 14, No. 157, March 2000, New Delhi.

P. Anandharaja Kumar, "Child Labour Issues and Solutions", *Kurukshetra*, Vol. 47, No. 10, July 1999, Publication Division, New Delhi.

Om Raj Singh, "Child Labour Eradication", *Yojana*, Vol. 47, No. 11, November 2003, Publication Division, New Delhi.

D.K. Giri, "Panchayati and Child Labour", *Kurukshetra*, Vol. 49. No. 7, April 2001, Publication Division, New Delhi.

9
Empowerment of Women and Protection of their Rights

Introduction

In 20th century the terms 'Women Empowerment', 'Women Welfare', 'Gender Justice' have come in lime light in the social, economic and political development analysis both in developed and developing nations.

Traditionally women in almost every society have remained second grade citizen. Neither they were allowed to get themselves educated nor they were given legal rights in the property, government and in administration. Their freedom and status were exploited by marrying them in tender age and keeping them inside the house, exploiting their labour and dignity to maximum possible extent and at last force them to get themselves burn alive with the dead body of their husbands.

The situation took turn with the spread of liberal ideas of the west among the Indian people as well as in other third world countries. The new intelligentsia were convinced that the new society could politically, culturally, and economically develop only on the basis of liberal principles, such as the recognition of individual liberty, freedom of unfettered expression of human personality and social equity. The newly educated persons increasingly revolted against social conventions and outdated customs. They could no longer tolerate irrational and dehumanizing social practices. In their revolt they were inspired by the humanistic ideals of social equality and the equal worth of all individuals. This class of Indian society had taken lead during the nineteenth century in the religious and social reforms, which gave birth to the empowerment of various segments of the society.

Meaning of Empowerment

Empowerment means giving legal and moral power to an individual in all spheres of life social, economic, political, psychological, religious and spiritual, which are essential for the survival and overall development of the mankind. Every society has known racism, Xenophobia depriving men and women of their dignity and freedom in broader terms empowerment is nothing but a religious, cultural and legal struggle against oppression, injustice and discrimination. Empowerment expresses the bold idea that all people have claims to social arrangements that protect them from the worst abuses and deprivations and secure the freedom for a life of dignity. It is also a process of enhancing human capabilities to expand choices and opportunities so that each person can lead a life of respect and value.

According to Pramila Kapur, "Women's empowerment could be considered as a process in which women gain greater share of control over resources, material, human and intellectual like knowledge, information, ideas and financial resources like money and access to money and control over decision-making in the home, community society and nation, and to gain power." "The term women's empowerment has come to be associated with women's struggle for social justice and equality".

Empowerment lends moral legitimacy and the principle of social justice to the objectives of human development. The process of empowerment helps shift the priority to the most deprived and excluded, especially to deprivations because of discrimination. It also directs attention to the need for information and political voice for all people as a development issue and to civil and political rights as integral parts of the development process.

Empowerment of Rural Women

Women constitute half of the world's population, worshipped as a 'Lakshmi' and 'Saraswathi' on one hand, tortured and exploited in many ways on the other hand also are kept systematically away from the awareness of human needs and human benefits. During the peace time it is the women and girl children who are sexually harassed at home and work place and forced into prostitution due to economic insecurity and hunger. At the wartime, she becomes victim of rape, brutal atrocities in the hands of protector of society, the so called police and armed personnel. Position of the women can be observed from the figures mentioned below:

- Women are 1/2 of the world's population, work 2/3rd of the world's working hours.
- Earn 1/10 of the world's income, and own less than 1/10 of the world's property.
- Women make up 70 per cent of the world's one billion absolute poor.
- Women make up two third of the world's illiterates.
- One half of women in Asia and Africa are malnourished.
- One third of the women in the developing world are subject daily to domestic violence.

Female Mortality

Approximately a quarter of our population of 846 million comprises of girls upto the age of 19 years of which 3,00,000 girls die annually. Large number of little girls are allowed to die on account of malnutrition and diseases which are either not treated or treated inadequately.

Every year about 12 million girls are born in India of which 25 per cent do not survive to see their fifteenth birthday. One third of these death takes place in the first year of life.

Sex Ratio

Around 105 males are born for every 100 female births. The sex ratio (females per 1000 males) for children up to the age of six is 945. Despite improvement in the economy and provision of basic services in India, the sex ratio has been deteriorating from 972 in 1901 to 929 in 1991.

Rural women constitute 75 per cent of the total female population of the country (1991). On any given indicator of development, the rural women are disadvantaged compared to her urban counterpart. The profile of rural women is that of a poor, ignorant, illiterate, superstitious and suppressed being with low level of skills. Her access to information, assets, and opportunities is also low. She is unorganised and under represented. She is over worked but a producer and a homemaker. Hence she needs to be trained, organized so that she is empowered.

Economic Empowerment

Economic development is the key and may lead to all kinds of development. This is true in the context of women. Economically, rural women are in a dire state of poverty. Rural families are considered as consumers and not producers with no occupation, property, education or skills. They are however, a major work force in informal sector. Skill development, income generation and credit availability are the main planks of economic empowerment of women. The major thrust of the sixth plan was "economic upliftment of women" through greater opportunities for employment and imparting new skills. As a result, today there are 27 programmes involving 6 ministries and 8 departments, which focus on women upliftment and income generating activities.

Integrated Rural Development Programme (IRDP) which is the main plan of poverty alleviation provides 40 per cent beneficiaries as women. The Programme of Training of Rural Youth for Self Employment (TRYSEM) again provides 40 per cent trainees as women. Wage employment programmes such as Jawahar Rozgar Yojana (JRY) and Employment Assurance Scheme (EAS) have also provided wage employment to women to the extent of 40 per cent. Then the programme of Development of Women and Children in Rural Areas (DWCRA) provides income-generating activities to women. However, on the performance, the implementation of these provisions varies widely across the country. The level of self-employment among women is also low. Some steps have been taken to ensure accessibility of women to credit through schemes like 'financing of self help groups' and institutions like Rashtriya Mahila Kosh. The Government is also promoting local women's self help groups in a big way in the name of Indira Mahila Yojana (IMY) and Mahila Samriddhi Yojana (MSY).

Inspite of these interventions, the basic problems that effect women's role and opportunities which spring from their dependence, illiteracy, limited skills restricted mobility and lack of autonomous status, remain to be talked in a big way.

The problems are known likewise, the solutions are also known. But the question is how to accelerate the pace of development of women, particularly the rural poor. To make women, stand on equal footing with their male counterparts they should be empowered, and further to realize the benefits of improvement they should have adequate awareness which can be brought about by education. And this could be realized only when their economic base is strengthened. If the economic condition of women improves, it directly affects the living standard of the whole family.

Social Empowerment

Social Empowerment is by far the most difficult and long-term goal to attain, because social equality includes equality of treatment, equality of respect, equality of opportunity, equality of recognition and above all equality of status. Social legislation in this regard may do very little except providing a legal sanctity to a social equality measure. The Constitution of India grants equality to women and the Fundamental Rights ensure equality before law, equal protection of law, prohibits discrimination against any citizen on grounds of religion, race, sex, caste, creed or place of birth and guarantees equality of opportunity to all in matters related to employment. Articles 14, 15, 15(3), 16, 39(A), 39(B), 39(C) and 42 of the Constitution of Specific significance in this regard. Secured important social legislation is also enacted which aim at social empowerment of women like:

- Widow Remarriage Act 1856;
- The Factories Act, 1948 (provision relating to creches);
- The Child Marriage Restraint Act, 1929;
- The Hindu Marriages Act, 1955;
- The Hindu Adoption and Maintenance Act, 1956;
- The Maternity Benefits Act, 1961;
- The Dowry Prohibition Act, 1961;
- The Medical Termination of Pregnancy Act, 1971;
- The Equal Remuneration Act, 1976;
- The Immoral Traffic (Prevention) Act, 1986;
- The Indecent Representation of Women (Prohibition) Act, 1986 and Rules 1987;

- The Commission of Sati (Prevention) Act, 1987 and Rules 1988.

In the field of social and criminal justice too, few changes have been brought about by way of amending the existing Acts or by way of fresh enactment to provide greater gender justice and to improve the social and legal status of women. Some of these measures are:

- Amendments to the Indian Evidence Act, 1872 in 1983 as part of the judicial reforms.
- Amendment to the Indian penal code (IPC) and additions of several new clauses during 1983 and 1986 as part of judicial reforms (which includes introduction of the concept of custodial rape, redefining of dowry death elaborating the term 'cruelty' etc.
- The family courts, Act 1984 to expedite disposal of select family dispute.
- The prenatal diagnostic techniques (Regulation and Prevention of Misuse) Act, 1994 to prevent the increasing incidence of female foeticides.

In India, during the last 50 years there have been some achievements, but quite a failure too. Female literacy has risen from 7.9 per cent to 39.43 per cent, expectation of life at birth increased from 41.7 to 60.4 years, average age at marriage increased from 15.4 to 19.5 for girls. Maternal mortality rate reduced from 27 to 04. As against this we also find 60 per cent of women still illiterate, over 80 per cent of women folk work in unorganized sector, and are still paid less for equal work. About 60 per cent of pregnant women are still anaemic. Sex specific mortality rates still show high death rate for female children. Violence and crime against women are on the increase. Convicts of rape are hardly punished. Dowry deaths show no decline. Media still represents women in an unfair manner, and immoral trafficking is on the increase.

Political Empowerment

Till the end of nineteenth century women in India were crushed under the weight of evil customs. They were socially weak, economically dependent and politically powerless and were influenced by the male members of the family. Hence in the political field the role of rural women was negligible. However, women with elite background and political families found it easy to have a smooth entry in politics.

The Constitution of India opened a new chapter in the matter of equality of women. Article 15(3) empowers the states to make any 'special provision for women and children' even in violation of the fundamental obligation of non-discrimination among citizens interalia of sex. Reservation of seats for women in local and educational institutions has been held to be valid according to the precisions. Ever since the first general elections in 1952, women voters, participation in various elections has been increasing. But their representation in national parliament has never crossed 10 per cent. In view of this, a modified strategy to increase the women participation in political decision-making by way of adopting a 'Quota System to Women' in the legislative bodies was adopted. The 73rd Constitutional Amendment providing for one-third of the seats to women members in all the rural local self-government institutions (Panchayat Raj Bodies), and 74th Constitutional amendment provides one-third of the seats to women (Municipal Bodies) are considered as an attainment towards political empowerment of women. A similar provision for one-third reservation to women in the Lok Sabha and in the Legislative Assemblies of the States by way of 81st Constitutional Amendment is under consideration of the Parliament. These provisions are basically to create more consciousness, among women and to 'strike a greater gender balance in the decision making. These Acts are expected to bring in silent revolution in the gender constitution of political structures in India. However, whether the presence of women will change the political culture in any symbolic ways is to be seen.

Though the political situation if women is changed in the constitutional document it will take time to make women politically equal in practice and enhance their status and development.

Need for Human Rights

As far as women rights in the context of India is concerned, it can be seen from independence period itself that human rights activists have been mostly from elite section of society specifically from upper castes because of which Scheduled Castes and Scheduled Tribes and other marginalized sections of the society did not get the importance they deserved. "Human rights, however, like democracy and all vibrant visions, are not static, nor are they the property of any group. While these concepts began in a particular historical movement, their dynamism and ongoing relevance stem from the fact that more people are claiming them and, in the process, expanding the meaning of 'rights' to incorporate their own hopes and needs. Much of the creativity of the human rights movement over the past sixty years has come from expanding the concept to address areas such as racial discrimination, disappearances, socio-economic rights, and the collective right to a sustainable environment. So, too, women are transforming the concept of human rights to address the degradations and violations that are fundamental threat to our human dignity and right to life, liberty and security of person".

"When women are denied democracy and human rights in private, their human rights in the public sphere also suffer, since what occurs in "private" shapes their ability to participate fully in the public arena".

Recent Global Trend in Women's Rights

This principle of non-discrimination on the basis of sex is clearly enshrined in the international law. Starting from the United Nations charter and the Universal Declaration of Human Rights, the principle found its way into the two main International Covenants on Economic, Social and Cultural Rights and the International Covenant on Civil and Political Rights.

In addition to these, other important provisions have also been included in these. The Universal Declaration of Human Rights calls for equal rights as to marriage, which it stipulates, "shall be entered into only with the free and full consent of the intending spouses. It also calls for equal pay for equal work, and for the protection of motherhood. The Covenant on Economic, Social and Cultural Rights states that all workers must be provided with "fair wages and equal remuneration for work of equal value without distinction of any kind in particular women being guaranteed conditions of work not inferior to those enjoyed by men with an equal pay for equal work". It too provides for the protection of motherhood, and calls for paid maternity leave or level with adequate social security benefits.

The Covenant on Civil and Political Rights Prohibits the use of the death sentence on pregnant women, provides equality between men and women during and at its dissolution. And for the right to participate in public life without discrimination while declaring, finally, that the principle of non-discrimination are enforceable rights.

A number of International Treaties are also devoted to the similar cause, mentioned below:

- The discrimination (employment and occupation) convention;
- The convention against discrimination in Education;
- The Equal Remuneration;
- The Slavery Convention;
- The Convention on the suppression of the Traffic in persons and of the exploitation of the Prostitutes and others;
- The Convention on the Nationality of Married Women;
- The Convention on the Political Rights of Women;
- The Declaration on the Protection of Women and Children in emergency Armed Conflict.

Various other Actions taken by U.N. for the Advancement of Women

- International Women's Year (1975);
- World Conference of the International Women's Year Mexico City, 1975 (first global conference ever held on women);
- The U.N. Decade for Women; Equality, Development and Peace (1976-85);
- Adoption of Convention on the Elimination of All forms of Discrimination Against Women by the United Nations General Assembly in 1979 (CEDAW);

- World Conference of the United Nations Decade for Women Programme of Action for the second half of the U.N. Decade for Women, Copenhagen, 1980;
- World Conference to review and appraise the achievements of the U.N. Decade for Women, Nairobi, 1985;
- The Nairobi forward looking strategies for the Advancement of Women;
- The fourth World Conference on Women; Action for Equality, Development and Peace, Beijing, 1995.

Nairobi Forward Looking Strategies for the Advancement of Women, Minimum Targets for the year 2000

- Enforcement of laws guaranteeing implementation of women's equality;
- Increase in the life expecting of women to at least 65 years in all countries;
- Reduction in maternal mortality;
- Elimination of Women's illiteracy;
- Expansion of Employment opportunities;

United Nations Decade for Women (1976-1985);

- The following are the concrete results;
- General equality firmly placed on global agenda;
- Critical role of women development process acknowledged;
- Adoption of the convention on the elimination of all forms of discrimination against women by the United Nations General Assembly in 1979;
- International Women's Movement expanded its net- work;
- Nairobi forward looking strategies adopted by 157 countries;
- Creation of two United Nations bodies devoted exclusively to women;

1. UNIFEM (The United Nations Fund for Women)
2. INSTRAW (International Research and Training Institute for the Advancement of Women).

United Nations Conference on Environment and Development, Rio De Janeiro, 1992;

"Women have a vital role in environmental management and development. Their full participation is therefore essential to achieve sustainable development".

The World Conference on Human Rights, Vienna, 1993. The Vienna Declaration and Programme of Action

- States that the human rights of women and girls are an inalienable, integral and indivisible part of Universal human rights, expresses concern for the various forms of discrimination and violence to which women continue to be exposed all over the world, urges the eradication of all forms of discrimination against women, both hidden and overt.

The Fourth World Conference on Women, Beijing, September 1995

Aims:

- To draw up a platform for action to perform to ensure the completion of the unfinished work in implementing the 1985 Nairobi Forward looking strategies;
- To address the question of how women can be empowered by effective participation in decision making on all issues which effect society.

ILO Declaration on Equality of Opportunity and Treatment for Women Workers (1975) "....all forms of discrimination on the grounds of sex which deny or restrict equality of opportunity and treatment are unacceptable and must be eliminated..."

ILO Resolution on Equal Opportunities and Equal Treatment for Men and Women in Employment

- The resolution outlines a comprehensive set of measures for national as well as ILO action to be undertaken in various areas which include;
- Equal access to employment and training;
- Promotion of full implementation of the principle of equal remuneration for work of equal value;
- Improvement of working conditions;

- Harmonization of family and job responsibilities;
- Equal treatment in social security coverage;
- Efforts to ensure the full participation of women in decision making process;
- Measures to establish and strengthen national machinery to promote equality of opportunities and treatment;
- Improvement of data base to reflect more fully the contribution of women.

ILO Plan of Action on Equality of Opportunity and Treatment of Men and Women in Employment (1987)

The main purpose of the plan of Action is;

- To ensure that issues relating to equality of opportunity and treatment are systematically included at each stage of policy formulation, planning and implementation in all ILO programmes and projects priority areas are as follows:

- International labour standards and human rights
- Training
- Industrial relations and labour administration
- Workers activities
- Employees activities
- Working conditions
- Sectoral activities
- Social Security
- Labour information and statistics

ILO Resolution concerning ILO Action for Women Workers (1991)

Stresses the need for a concerted effort between governments and employees 'and workers' organizations to implement the principle of equality.

These include:

- strategies to eliminate continuing barriers to the equal participation of women in employment.

- Inclusion of more women in delegations to the International Labour Conference and other major ILO meetings.
- Government measures to improve implementation of legislation on equality of opportunity and treatment in employment, including ratification of relevant conventions.
- New policies for the creation of full, productive a freely chosen employment and to help improve conditions in the informal sector.
- Promotion of equal opportunities and removal of discrimination in recruitment, promotion and training review of job evaluation schemes to prevent sex bias.
- Arrangements for the inclusion of part time workers in collective agreements.

India's Situation

India being a secular country and during post independence period it took various steps to bring gender equality and gender justice. Since human rights are fundamental rights and in Article 14 the Constitution guarantees justice, social, economic and political as well as equality before law and ensures non-discrimination on the basis of sex. Article 15(3) empowers the state to make special provisions for the promotion of the welfare and development of women.

India has committed herself to equal rights and inherent human dignity of women and men by ratifying the Convention on the Elimination of All Forms of Discrimination Against Women (CEDAW). India is firm in its resolve of full implementation of the human rights and fundamental freedoms.

It is well known that in various International Covenants, all states have been obliged to India, it has been seen that vast majority of population has been kept under utterly subhuman conditions.

National Perspective Plan for Women (1988) and the Shramshakti Report (1988)

These documents highlighted on the prevalence of discrimination against women and recommended various measures for the advancement of women.

A number of states have also come out with policies and Action Plans for women. The Central/State Social Welfare Boards, State Departments of Women's Development and Women's Development Corporations, National Commission for Women and Several State Commissions for Women have been setup to improve the status of women and to safeguard their legal rights. A number of schemes and programmes have been initiated, particularly with a view to promoting their economic advancement and social defence.

It is well known that in the period of globalization and scientific development though the clouds of darkness loom large over the horizon in regard to inequality and discrimination against women yet these are some silver lining.

Against this background, National Commission for Women was set up in 1993. Mrs. Mohini Giri, the chairperson of National Commission for Women has done tremendous work against the violation of women's human rights.

Evaluation and Future Strategies

Since Independence special measures have been taken to improve the status of women in almost all spheres of life-whether social, economic, political, cultural or religious. Consequently some improvements are visible during the last 60 years. Literacy rate has improved and women have registered their presence in all walks of life-administration, politics, economic activities, consumption, social setup etc. Credit goes to partly to the rise in female literacy and partly to equal opportunities provided under constitution, but reality is far from satisfaction.

Suggestions

The achievements under the shadow of empowerment become meaningless, if the following measures are not implemented strictly.

1. Quick disposal of cases of exploitation, torture, rape and atrocities against women.
2. Summary and in-camera trials of cases of rapes and other atrocities on women.

3. Drastic punishment for rapist.
4. Mandatory consent of wife in the sale of family property.
5. Compulsory and free education for girls up to 12th standard.
6. Better training facilities to enhance the skills.
7. Reserving one third of seats in legislature and in government employment.
8. Appointment of women administrators on key posts without any discrimination.

Conclusion

It has been concluded that in the last six decades since the Universal Declaration of Human Rights in 1948, remarkable efforts have been made to achieve human rights for women still there remains much to be achieved. For there are sustainable number of women in the society who have been living in semi-human conditions. Their human rights are violated for both at family and societal level. They are more deprived socially, economically, educationally, culturally and politically than their male counterparts. In order to achieve human rights for women considerable efforts have been made at National and Global level. As a result condition of women has noticeably improved. In addition, human rights awareness in them is also increasing.

REFERENCES

Dr. Shyam Sunder Singh, Chauhan and Gaurav Bansal "Various Dimensions of Women's Empowerment", *Social Welfare,* Vol. 49; No. 5 August 2002, New Delhi.

Dr. S. Mehartaj Begum "Trends in Women's Rights and Development" *Ibid,* p. 23.

Dr. B. Suguna "Strategies for Empowerment of Rural Women" *Ibid*, p. 3.

K.N. Gupta "Women's Empowerment and Protection of Their Rights' *Social Welfare,* Vol. 47; No. 12, March 2001, New Delhi.

B.K. Thapliyal and K.R. Sastry "Economic Development of Rural Women", January 1994, NIRD, Hyderabad.

Prof. D.P. Singh M "Issues and Initiatives in Women's Empowerment", *Social Welfare,* Vol. 48, No. 6, September 2001, New Delhi.

Sudha Kumari "Women workers in unorganised sector in India", *Yojana*, Vol. 33, No. 12, 1989, New Delhi.

Human Development Report, 1997.

Dr. Kulwant Singh "Women in Decision making" *Shelter*, Vol. 4, No. 4, October, 2000, A HUDCO/HSMI, New Delhi.

10

Political Empowerment of Women through Panchayat Raj Institutions

Women form almost half the population in our country. Though our Constitution guarantees equal rights and equal opportunities to both men and women, visible and invisible inequalities and inequities based on gender persist. The Report of the National Committee on the Status of Women in India, *Towards Equality* highlighted the process of the declining status of women and pointed out that this deterioration has accelerated since the last three to four decades. The Committee also mentioned several other disturbing trends about the status of women such as disparity in access to health care and medical services, increasing gap between men and women in literacy, education and training for employment, etc. There are several other unfortunate tendencies that have been conspicuous in India regarding women's status such as (a) decreasing sex ratio, increasing female infanticide and female foeticide; (b) malnourishment and undernourishment among girls and Women *due* to lower consumption of essential nutrients by girls and women, therefore, proneness to diseases; (c) higher maternal mortality rates in the lower age groups, because of inadequate health care and medical services.

When India was under the colonial rule it was only the few male members who could vote and contest elections while women were totally absent from the political scene. Even after independence the Indian Constitution did not mention or specifically provide reservation for women representation in parliament or state assemblies. It took nearly 40 years for women to find political representation in the formal political institutions.

As stated earlier, this was made possible through the 73rd Constitution Amendment Act, which had the landmark provision of reserving not less than one-third of the total number of seats in the local bodies for women. It provided the much-needed opportunity for women to actively participate in the decision-making processes of their locality through the political right that was conferred on them through the central Act. In this new era of panchayati raj, there are now more than one million women elected representatives elected to the three tiers of panchayats thereby giving greater meaning to democratic representation as women become spokespersons of the local community.

Women's political empowerment in the last nine years through the Constitution amendments has exploded several myths, like the belief that they are passive and disinterested in political institutions; that only the well-to-do, upper strata women will come through reservation; that only some powerful politicians will enter panchayats; and lastly and most importantly, that women are only proxy - 'namesake' - members and they do not participate in the panchayats. Without discounting the existence in panchayats of some women who do fit into this patriarchal oriented framework, one can say that these myths have now been exposed.

In many states there is a greater awareness about gender equality; women's organizations and especially where human rights initiatives exist, have taken it as a challenge to protect the interests of women in society. Initially, women were hesitant to enter this new political arena; political parties and vested interest groups took advantage of the situation and proxy rule prevailed. Thus the power remained in the hands of the traditionally powerful groups. A new class of 'sarpanch patis' also emerged where the husband of the woman sarpanch managed the affairs of the panchayat, while the woman acted only as a rubber stamp. A study in the state of Karnataka has shown that many women elected to the local bodies/panchayats are surrogates for husbands and fathers who could not contest because of reservation. Some were put in place by the wealthy and powerful, for their malleability - a kind of puppets, to serve the vested interests while appearing to be elected representatives.

Even after being given a space in the democratic process, women belonging to traditionally marginalized groups were at the receiving end of upper-caste atrocities. After more than a year of the election to the panchayats in Madhya Pradesh, there were reports from four districts—Raigarh, Chhatarpur, Raisen and East Nimar - of a lady sarpanch being stripped naked, another lady sarpanch being gang raped, an 'upa-sarpanch' (deputy president) being tortured and a dalit panchayat member being beaten up.

Meaning of Empowerment

Empowerment is the phenomenon of nineties and is defined as "giving power to" "creating power within" and "enabling". It is a multi-dimensional process, which enables individuals and groups to realize their full identity and powers in all spheres of life. Keller and Mbewe (1991) described empowerment as "a process whereby women become able to organize themselves to increase their own self-reliance, to assert their independent right to make choices and to control resource which will assist in challenging and eliminating their own sub-ordination". It thus envisages greater access to knowledge and resources, greater autonomy in decision making for self, greater ability to plan one's life, to have greater control over circumstances, and greater capacity to free one's self from traditions, customs beliefs and practices. The empowerment theme runs strongly through out the world, especially in the context of women. Most of the modern democracies and developing nations have a public agenda for the process of empowerment of women. It is a national commitment. A series of world women's conferences held in the last two decades with the United Nations support have strengthened this movement.

Political Empowerment

Till the end of the nineteenth century women in India were crushed under the weight of evil customs. They were socially weak, economically dependent and politically powerless and under total domination of the male members of the family. Hence in the political field the role of rural women was negligible. However, women with elite background and political families found it easy to have a smooth entry into politics.

The Constitution of India opened a new chapter in the matter of equality of women. Article 15(3) empowers the states to make any special provision for women and children even in 'violation of the fundamental obligation of non-discrimination among citizens. Reservation of seats for women in local and educational institutions has been held to be valid according to the provision. Ever since the first general elections in 1952, women voters' participation in various elections has been increasing. But their representation in Parliament has never crossed 10 per cent. In view of this, a modified strategy to increase women participation in political decision-making by way of adopting a "Quota system to women" in the legislative bodies was adopted. The 73rd constitutional amendment providing for one-third of the seats to women members in all the rural local self-government institutions - (Panchayati Raj bodies) is considered as a step towards political empowerment of women. A similar provision for one-third reservation to women in the Lok Sabha and in the legislative assemblies of the states by way of 81st Constitutional Amendment is under consideration of Parliament. These provisions are envisaged basically to create more consciousness, gender equality by politically empowering women. However, whether the presence of women will change the political culture in any significant way is to be seen.

Though the political situation of women is changed in the constitutional document, it will take time to make women politically equal in reality.

Practical Problems Attached to Women Empowerment

Without taking the environmental and social factors into consideration or any initiative for change of behavioural patterns of rural society towards women, mere statutory provision of reservation of seats for women in Panchayat Raj elections has proved to be a futile experience. There are innumerable problems and shortcomings attached to it. A few prominent ones may be enumerated below :

(i) The first and foremost shortcoming of empowerment of women in Panchayat Raj is that the electrol process may not reach the common rural poor women. Women from elite families, socially and economically affluent, may hijack power. This in turn will help to perpetuate elitism among rural women.

(ii) The most serious threat and challenges to women empowerment lie in the fact that participation by women representatives is masterminded by dominant male members of the family. Such acts diminish real empowerment of rural women. This trend gives rise to a mere structure without substance, a body without soul.

(iii) It is a common belief in rural areas, that politics is a dirty game. Hence women are told not to get involved in it. This belief also acts as a constraint on the empowering of women.

(iv) A more difficult problem for women in a rural society lies in trying to find time for political work. Running of a home and the raising of a family, both of which are full time jobs, in a patriarchal society leaves little time for other things. They have to work twice as hard and be twice as tough.

(v) A woman has to prove herself at every point. She may end up working much harder than her male colleagues and yet her bonafides are held suspect. Unless there is a change in the mindsets of the people, particularly in the male population, women will find it difficult to effectively participate in politics.

(vi) The problem of illiteracy, lack of political knowledge like understanding, the essence of Panchayat Raj, 'democratic decentralization work as hurdless in the smooth and proper functioning of rural political system.

(vii) Last but not the least politics in rural India has become increasingly prone to violence especially during election period; faction fighting and tense situation created by political parties lead to virtual stalemate which in turn helps in creating a vicious and insecure environment. There have been cases of trouble preventing women from taking part in election to the local bodies. This factor, unless given serious attention, will put the governmental initiative of empowering rural women in Panchayat Raj in jeopardy.

Reasons for Low Participation

Down the ages women have always been treated as subordinate to men in every aspect of life. Her identity was always attached to that of her father, husband or son. She had no independent identity of her own.

With the passage of time and reform movements and the growth of literacy, people came to realize that the development and empowerment of women are essential in modern times. Hence many economic and social changes were introduced for women's upliftment; however, the domain of politics was kept out of their reach. It is not that women in the past have not contributed substantially to politics, but because of their secondary status and low esteem, most of them were denied entry into political decision-making and at higher level of political parties.

After Independence, women along with men were given the right to vote. The objective behind this was to accord equal status to women *vis-a-vis* men and make them politically more aware and active. However, the status of women still remains low.

Although more women are entering politics, particularly in villages, the middle class urban women are still negatively inclined to join politics. Majority of women are not prepared to participate in politics beyond voting. Family responsibility, women's pre-occupation in the struggle to survive and the prevalence of violence and the role of money power in elections and women's lack of control or access over monetary resources are reported to be the main constraints.

In order to ensure their participation in politics, most women make use of their upper caste lineage and political connections, as widows, daughters, wives or daughters-in-law of well-known politicians. This has been possible because of the view that women are mostly silent and ineffective as participants. However, we see some exceptions to this rule among those who always uphold women's cause and / or take a stand according to their personal convictions. For women elected members to be constantly informed about women's needs it is essential for them to have frequent dialogue with women leaders.

Among the women who enter politics there are five distinct categories:

(i) Mainstream party women who also have connections with prominent politicians in their party or have strong political support at local/state levels.

(ii) Women who are members of the political parties but have no connections.

(iii) Women who have ambition to enter the electoral politics but have no choice but to stand as independent candidates.

(iv) Women who have moved up the party hierarchy on their own merit/performance/work.

(v) Women who already have family members in politics at local or state levels.

While the role of political parties in selecting women needs further research many women do not enter politics because of the following reasons :

(i) Widespread exploitation involved at local level.

(ii) Men are not willing to allow their women colleagues/ partners to enter active politics.

(iii) Most women do not have the necessary infrastructure facilities and enough resources to contest elections or consolidate their base at local level.

(iv) Communalization of politics.

(v) Criminalisation of politics.

(vi) Lack of party support and organizational structure at local level.

(vii) Discrimination in decision-making at party level.

(viii) Fear and insecurity.

(ix) Lack of confidence in public speaking and communication skills.

(x) Socio-economic background.

(xi) Family responsibilities.

Women need to enter the political decision making structures in order to change their subordinate social and economic status, change the political structures to a more human perspective promoting the interest and well-being of the poor, the children and women and eliminate the current trend of criminalisation and communalization of politics.

Conclusion

Since Independence special measures have been taken to improve the status of women in almost all spheres of life, social, economic political, cultural or religious. Consequently some improvements are visible during the last 60 years. Literacy rate has improved and women have registered their presence in all walks of life administration, politics, economic activities, consumption, social set up, etc. Credit goes partly to the rise in female literacy and partly to equal opportunities provided under the Constitution. But we still have to go a long way. It has been suggested that in the last five decades since the Universal Declaration of Human Rights in 1948, remarkable efforts have been made to secure human rights for women. Still there remain much to be achieved. There are still unacceptable number of women in our society who live in semi-human conditions. Their human rights are being violated at both family and social level. They are still deprived of their rights - socially, economically; educationally, culturally and politically. In order to achieve political rights for women considerable efforts have to be made at national and global level. It is only then that condition of women will be noticeably improved.

REFERENCES

Dr. Shyam Sunder Singh Chauhan and Gaurav Bansal, "Various Dimensions of Women's Empowerment", *Social Welfare*. Vol. 49, No. 5, August 2002, New Delhi.

Dr. S. Mehartaj Begum "Trends in Women's Rights and Development" *Ibid*, p. 23.

Professor D.P. Singh "Issues and Initiatives in Women's Empowerment", *Social Welfare*, Vol. 48, No. 6, September 2001, New Delhi.

Dr. Kulwant Singh "Women in Decision making" *Shelter*, Vol. 4, No. 4, October 2000, " A HUDCO / HSMI, New Delhi.

Dr. (Smt) Sneha Palnitkar,"Women in Local Government", *Ibid*, p. 43.

11

Empowerment of Agricultural Rural Women Labourers and Human Rights in the Context of Globalization

Women's right are human rights and should be treated as such. To quote former President K.R. Narayanan at the convention on Liberal values in New Delhi on January 6, 1996. "It would be seen that in the evolution of human Civilisation, Economic, Cultural, Social, Civil and Political aspects have come together to produce what are now called human rights. At the heart of the human rights lie rights and values associated with the individual human being, which in modern parlance or rather western parlance, are called liberal values, but which are inherent in every civilisation of the world."

It is the duty of the state to remove inequalities in the personal laws of various religions. Recently it has been made compulsory to include the mother's name along with that of the father in various forms required to be filled for an Indian child while seeking admission in a school and otherwise.

Women constitute atleast one-third of the country's economically active population, particularly in the unorganised sector. Low literacy levels, skill based and knowledge grounded technologies along with patriarchal social control restrain women's access to resource which might enable them to equip themselves to meet the challenges and take advantage of the opportunities provided by the new economic policy. A culturally steeped social and economic life is not conducive to a gender neutral wage policy.

Agricultural labourers, who constitute nearly 70 per cent of total rural labour households, suffer from seasonal unemployment, job insecurity, poverty, indebtedness, bondage, migration, inability to get statutory minimum wages, illiteracy, malnourishment, lack of access to assets like cultivated land, discrimination and incapability to form or join any organisation.

Since the agricultural rural women labourers do not have fixed employees relation as most of them work either as casual labourers or as contract labourers, they are not entitled for any protective social security benefits, which their counterparts get in industries the process of macro economic contraction (eg. lower public sector investment in farm and social sectors) and reduction in development role of the state, initiated during (1991) and thereafter, have actually worsened their economic condition. The qualitative restrictions lifted from agricultural products and attempt to dismantle PDS may have adverse impact on agricultural growth, which can result in reducing labour demand, leading to further deterioration in the condition of agricultural labour.

An important indicator of well being of agricultural labourers in the magnitude of real wages receive by them. As per the 55th round NSS, RWs of casual agricultural labourers in 1999-2000 was only Rs. 25.48 per day per male, which is much lower than the average of MWs of 14 states (average being Rs. 44.13 per day). This indicates that minimum wages Act has not been implemented effectively.

Although the average wage rate of both male and female have increased in real terms during the last five years, the growth is lowest among all rural activities. Thus, in spite of absolute rise in their wages, their position vis-a-vis their counterparts in other activities in both rural and urban areas have actually deteriorated.

Shrinking Opportunities

Gross Value Added per worker in agriculture has grown by 3.3 per cent per annum between 1993-94 and 1999-2000. The number of persons employed per 1000 population in rural areas declined from 444 to 417 and unemployment rate increased in case of rural male and females from 56 and 67 respectively in 1993-94 to 72 and 73 respectively in 1999-2000. It shows clearly that in spite of fairly high GDP growth rate during this period, there was sharp decline in rural employment. The average number of days the rural male workers worked dropped from 331 days per annum in 1993-94 to 327 days per annum in 1999-2000. However, is the average number of days the rural females workers worked increased from 241 to 246 during the same period. The increasing number of females work days reveals that the income earned by males were not adequate enough to support the family and females were compelled to work more to compensate for the meager income earned by their male counterparts.

Existing Provisions

Social security to agricultural labourers is the responsibility of both the Centre and State governments as it is enlisted in the concurrent list of the Indian Constitution. Although, Constitution of India has made provision to safeguard the interest of weaker sections, little has been done so far in this direction. Article 41 of the Constitution under Directive Principles of State Policy says, "The State shall, with in the limits of its economic capacity and development make effective provision for securing the right to work, to education and to public assistance in case of unemployment, oldage, sickness and disablement, and in other cases on under severed wants". However, even after 60 years planned development, state could not provide effective social safety net to poor workers.

During 1997, the then government prepared a comprehensive agricultural workers Bill to guarantee minimum wage and better working conditions. Sadly, several governments came in after that but the bill could not be passed in Parliament.

In Andhra Pradesh the situation of women in terms of literacy status is not very encouraging, as 66 per cent of them are still illiterate. Women worker are largely concentrated in the unorganised sector particularly in the agricultural sector, ecomprising of a formidable 88 per cent. The figure includes both cultivators and agricultural labourers in the unorganised sector. Women participate in all major agricultural operations which include preparation of land, sowing of seeds, transplanting, weeding, harvesting, winnowing, preparation of compost and manure pits, application of manure, spraying of pesticides and insecticides, storage of seeds and food grains. Majority of this work is not only time consuming but also strenuous. Hence, it leads to further depletion of the already scarce resources of the female worker. This in turn has an adverse impact on her health condition.

Due to globalisation the Indian agriculture has adopted new technology to tolerate its competitiveness in the production. This affects the Rural Agricultural Labourers workdays and violates the right to work. The rural labourers migrated to nearby urban areas like towns and cities for construction works and other jobs. As discussed above especially the agricultural rural women not in a position to live in their native villages.

12

Welfare Schemes, Policies and Programmes for Empowerment of Women in India : A Human Rights Perspective*

Empowerment may be defined as a function of economic, social, educational and cultural betterment of people. In Indian context not only various programmes and policies have been initiated for women betterment but their share has also been ensured as members and chairpersons in rural and urban local governments so that they can participate in decentralized decision making process for the development of their own and fellow citizens. It will not be out of context to say that women empowerment these days has become a buzz word. For women empowerment, the concept of women's component plan which was mooted as far back as in the Seventh Plan, put into practice in the Ninth Plan as one of the important strategies to earmark not less than 30 per cent of funds and benefits in all the women related sectors by the Centre and the State Governments. But if we see women empowerment from the perspectives of their social development we find that women are still at margin even after more than six decades of planning and development. The disparities between them and their counterparts is glaring, which is evident from the studies carried out by researchers and institutions from gender perspective. The main paper will discusses the impact of various welfare schemes for women empowerment in India and protection of their rights.

Human Rights and fundamental freedoms are the birth right of all human beings, their protection and promotion is the first responsibility of government. The world conference on human rights reaffirmed clearly that the human rights of women throughout the life cycle are an inalienable, integral and indivisible part of universal human rights.

Women and children are a grossly neglected section of society. This neglect of women and their oppression is seen in all fields, health, education, employment and politics etc. women's role is not restricted to home alone. They are responsible not only for the well being of family but also make a major contribution to the development of society. But they are deprived of every right.

The major landmark in promoting women's rights was setting up of United Nations Commission on the status of women in 1946 to monitor the situation of women and to promote women's rights. Thirty years of work culminated in the form of a Convention on the Elimination of all forms of Discrimination Against Women (CEDAW). CEDAW was adopted by the United Nations General Assembly on 18 December 1979 and it entered into force as an international treaty on 3rd September 1981 after the twentieth country had ratified it. By 1989, almost hundred nations agreed to abide by its provisions. These efforts for the advancement of women have resulted in several declarations and conventions of which CEDAW is the central and most comprehensive document. The rights of women in relation to life, liberty, equality and dignity of the individual are included in this document.

Measures for Women's Empowerment

The Constitution of India not only grants equality to women, but also empowers the state to adopt measures of positive discrimination in favour of women for removing the cumulative socio-economic, educational and political disadvantages faced by them.

International policies and India's Constitutional provisions, policies and programmes for women.

UN Human Rights Instruments

- Universal Declaration of Human Rights adopted in 1948.
- International Covenant on Economic, Social and Cultural Rights - adopted in 1966. Entered into force in 1976, monitored by the Committee on Economic, Social and Cultural Rights (CESCR).
- International Convention on the Elimination of All Forms of Racial Discrimination - adopted in 1965 - entered into force in 1969, monitored by the committee on the Elimination of Racial Discrimination (CERD).

- Convention on the Elimination of All Forms of Discrimination Against Women - adopted in 1979 and entered into force in 1981, monitored by the committee on CEDAW.
- Convention Against Torture and other Cruel Inhuman or Degrading Treatment or Punishment - adopted in 1984 - entered into force in 1987, monitored by Committee Against Torture (CAT).
- Convention on the Rights of the Child - adopted in 1989, entered into force in 1990, monitored by the Committee on the Rights of the Child (CRC).

Commitments at UN Conferences

- World Conference on Education for All (1990) Jomtien.
- UN Conference on Environment and Development (1992) Rio De Janiero.
- Second UN World Conference on Human Rights (1993) Vienna.
- International conference on Population and Development (1994) Cairo.
- World Summit on Social Development (1995) Copenhagen.
- Fourth World Conference on Women (1995) Beijing.
- Second UN Conference on Human Settlements (1996) Istanbul.
- World Food Summit (1997) Rome.
- Education for All Dakar Frame Work (2000) Dakar.

Constitution of India Guarantees

- Equality before law for women (Article 14).
- The State not to discriminate against any citizen on grounds only of religion, race, caste, sex, place of birth or any of them [Article 15(1)].
- The State to make any special provision in favour of women and children [Article 15(3)].
- Equality of opportunity for all citizens in matters relating to employment or appointment to any office under the State (Article 16).

- The State to direct its policy towards securing for men and women equally the right to an adequate means of livelihood [Article 39 (a)]; and equal pay for equal work for both men and women [Article 39 (d)].
- To promote justice, on a basis of equal opportunity and to provide free legal aid by suitable legislation or scheme or in any other way to ensure that opportunities for securing justice are not denied to any citizen by reason of economic, or other disabilities (Article 39A).
- The State to make provision for securing just and humane conditions of work and for maternity relief (Article 42).
- The State to promote with special case the educational and economic interests of the weaker sections of the people and to protect them from Social Injustice and all forms of exploitation (Article 46).
- The State to raise the level of nutrition and the standard of living of its people and the improvement of public health (Article 47).
- To promote harmony and the spirit of common brotherhood amongst all the people of India and to renounce practices derogatory to the dignity of women [Article 1(A)(e)].
- Not less than one third (including the number of seats reserved for women belonging to the Scheduled Castes and the Scheduled Tribes) of the total number of seats to be filled by direct election in every panchayat to be reserved for women and such seats to be allotted by rotation to different constituencies in a panchayat [Article 243 D(3)].
- Not less than one-third of the total number of offices of chairpersons in the panchayats at each level to be reserved for women [Article 243D (4)].
- Not less than one-third (including the number of seats reserved for women belonging to the Scheduled Castes and the Scheduled Tribes) of the total number of seats to be filled by direct election in every municipality to be reserved for women and such seats to be allotted by

rotation to different constituencies in a municipality [Article 243T (3)].

- Reservation of offices of chairpersons in municipalities for the Scheduled Castes, the Scheduled Tribes and women in such manner as the legislature of a State may by law provide [Article 243T(A)].

Various Welfare Schemes Implemented by Government of India for Development of Women

To increase employment among women, several initiatives have been taken by Government of India, and programmes have been launched for economic empowerment of women. Some of these are discussed here.

Swawlamban

The Swawlamban programme previously also called Women's Economic Programme and NORAD Scheme, was launched in 1982-83 with assistance from the Norwegian Agency for Development Co-operation (NORAD) to provide training and skills to women to facilitate them to obtain employment or self-employment. The target group under the scheme are poor and needy women and women from weaker sections of society, such as Scheduled Castes and Scheduled Tribes.

Under this programme, financial assistance is provided to Women's Development Corporation (WDCs), public sector corporations, autonomous bodies and voluntary organizations to train poor women, mostly in non-traditional trades and to ensure their employment in these areas. Some of the popular trades under the programme are computer programming, medical transcription, electronics, watch assembling, radio and television repairs, garment making, handloom weaving, secretarial practice, community health work, embroidery etc.

The number of projects sanctioned under Swawlamban programme as on 31-12-2004 are 868 and the number of beneficiaries benefited in India are 1,16,134.

Support to Training and Employment Programme for Women (STEP)

Support to Training and Employment Programme for Women (STEP) was launched in 1987 to provide skills and knowledge to poor and assetless women in traditional occupations such as agriculture, animal husbandry, dairying, fisheries, handloom, handicrafts, khadi and village industries, sericulture, social forestry and wasteland development for enhancing their productivity and income generation. This would enhance and broaden their employment opportunities, including self-employment and development of enterpreneurship skills. Women beneficiaries are organised into co-operatives. Services such as training, extension, infrastructure, market linkages etc. are provided, besides linkages with credit for transfer of assets.

Women in the dairy sector have been receiving the maximum support, keeping in view the nature of demands. This is followed by handlooms, handicrafts, sericulture and poultry. The number of women beneficiaries benefited under STEP are 1,41,131.

Hostels for Working Women

With the progressive change in the economic structure of the country, more and more women are living out of their homes in search of employment in big cities. These women are exposed to risks due to lack of suitable and safe accommodation. The Government of India acknowledged the difficulties faced by such women and decided to introduce a scheme for construction/ expansion of Hostels for Working Women.

The objective of the scheme is to provide cheap and safe hostel accommodation to working women living out of their homes. The target beneficiaries are single working women, widows, divorcees, separated women and working women whose husbands are out of town.

As on 31-3-2004 the number of working women's hostels with day care centres sanctioned are 914 and 329 respectively. The number of working women and children benefited hostels with day care centres are 56,214 and 8,681 respectively.

Support Services to Women

The Department of Women and Child Development, Government of India has undertaken several programmes and assists voluntary organisations providing services to various groups of women. Working women, widows, women in distress, and women from vulnerable backgrounds are in need of special services. To create an enabling environment to enhance the self confidence and autonomy of women so that they can take their rightful place in the mainstream of the nation's social, political and economic life, the government has started the following programmes for women's empowerment.

Short Stay Homes

The Central Social Welfare Board (CSWB) has implemented scheme of Short Stay Homes (SSH), which provide temporary shelter to women and girls who (i) are being forced into prostitution, (ii) are, as a result of family tension or discord, made to leave their homes and are without any means of subsistence and have no social protection from exploitation, or are facing litigation on account of marital disputes, (iii) have been sexually assaulted and are facing the problem of re-adjustment in the family or society, (iv) are victims of mental maladjustment, emotional disturbances and social ostracism, (v) have escaped from their homes due to family problems, mental or physical torture and need shelter, psychiatric treatment and counseling for their rehabilitation are re-adjustment in family and society.

The number of beneficiaries benefited as on 31-12-2004 are 16,900.

Integrated Child Development Services (ICDS)

ICDS is a centrally sponsored scheme, where in the Central Government is responsible for programme planning and operating costs and the state governments are responsible for programme implementation and supplementary nutrition.

The schemes aims at the holistic development of children (0-6 years) and pregnant and nursing mothers. It provides an integrated comprehensive package of services comprising (i) supplementary nutrition, (ii) immunization, (iii) health check-up, (iv) referral services, (v) pre-school non formal education and (vi) nutrition and health education. ICDS also involves adolescent girls in providing services at centres, and imparts training in life skills development.

The ICDS Scheme was introduced in 33 blocks in 1975 and expanded to 5,652 projects in 2003 of which 5,422 projects became fully operate and till March 2005. Currently, services under the scheme are being provided to about 40.3 million children and 8.1 million pregnant and missing mothers as on 31st March 2005.

Rashtriya Mahila Kosh (National Credit Fund for Women)

Several research studies had repeatedly highlighted the need of poor women to have access to credit facilities at reasonable interest rates. It was felt that the credit needs of poor women, particularly those in the un-organised sector, had not been addressed adequately by the formal financial institutions in the country. The government of India established Rashtriya Mahila Kosh (National Credit Fund for Women) on 30th March 1993. The main objective of Rashtriya Mahila Kosh is to facilitate credit support or micro-finance to poor women. It mainly channelises its support through Non-Governmental Organisations (NGO's) having experience of extending credit facilities to poor women, Women Development Corporations (WDCs), Women Co-operative Societies, Indira Mahila Block Samities (IMBS) under the Indira Mahila Yojana, and suitable state government agencies. 1066 NGOs assisted 4,35,535 beneficiaries upto 31-12-2002 during 2003-04; 32,765 and 2004-05; 8,729 are benefited through Rashtriya Mahila Kosh.

Swadhar

Swadhar was launched in 2001-2002 for the benefit of women in difficult circumstances, like destitute widows deserted by their families in religious places. Women prisoners released from Jail and without family support; women survivors of natural disasters who have been rendered homeless and are without any social and economic support, trafficked women/girls rescued and run away from brothels, victims of sexual crimes, who are disowned by the family or who do not want to go back to their respective family for various reasons; women victims of terrorist violence who are without any family support and without any economic means of survival; mentally disordered women who are without any support of family or relatives etc.

The package assistance for the scheme includes provisions for shelter, food, clothing, health care and counseling for such women, measures for social and economic rehabilitation through education, awareness, skill upgradation and personality development through behavioural training, help line for such women in distress etc.

The implementing agencies can be the social welfare, women and child welfare departments of state government women's development corporations, urban local bodies, reputed public/private trusts or voluntary organizations who are willing to take the responsibilities of rehabilitating such women.

Family Counselling Centres (FCC)

FCC were setup with the objective of providing preventive and rehabilitative services to women and families who are victims of atrocities and family maladjustment, through crisis intervention and systematic counselling. The number of beneficiaries benefited during 2004-05 are 64,250.

Swayamsidha

It is an integrated scheme for women's empowerment is based on the formation of women into Self-help Groups (SHGs) and aims at the holistic empowerment of women through awareness generation, economic empowerment and convergence of various schemes. It is to be implemented in 650 blocks benefiting 9.30 lakh women. Each block would have 100 SHGs, with 15-20 women in each group, nearly 59,940 SHGs have been formed.

Swa-Shakti Project

Is a World Bank and International Fund for Agricultural Development Supported Project, is being implemented in 57 districts of 9 States. With partnership of 218 NGOs, 17,647 women's Self Help Groups have been formed benefiting 2,43,962 women.

Support Measures for Women

- Creches/Day care centres for children of working and ailing mothers.
- National Creche Fund (NCF).
- Integrated Child Development Services (ICDS).
- Working Women's Hostels with Day care Centres.
- Swawlamban, erstwhile (NORAD).

- Support to Training and Employment Programme for Women (STEP).
- Mahila Samakhya (MS).
- Swayam sidha.
- Rashtriya Mahilakosh (RMK) (credit to women).
- Short Stay Homes for Women and Girls (SSH) (for women in distress).
- Condensed courses of Education and Vocational Training for Adult Women (CCE & VT).
- Family Counseling Centres (FCC).
- Rehabilitation of marginalised women of Vrindavan (widows and destitute women).
- Swa-Shakti Project (SSP).
- Women's Component Plan (WCP).
- Swadhar (Women in Difficult Circumstances).

The Government of India has a frame work for empowering women outlined in the policy document "National Policy for Employment of Women (NPEW), 2001".

The National Commission for Women has setup in 1990 to intervene in matters relating to human rights of women.

The various legislations enacted for the protection and promotion of women rights in India are:

1. The Family Courts Act, 1984.
2. The Dowry Prohibition Act, 1961 (Amended 1985).
3. The Hindu Marriage and Divorce Act, 1956.
4. The Hindu Widows Remarriage Act, 1956 (Amended 1985).
5. The Special Marriage Act, 1954 (Amended 1985).
6. The Christian Marriage Act, 1972.
7. The Muslim Personal Law (Shariat) Application Act, 1937.
8. The Foreign Marriage Act, 1969.
9. The Indian Divorce Act, 1969.
10. The Indecent Representation of Women (Prohibition) Act, 1986.

11. The Commission of Sati (Prevention) Act, 1987.
12. The National Commission for Women Act, 1990.
13. The Medical Termination of Pregnancy Act, 1971.
14. The Indian Succession Act, 1925.
15. The Married Women's Property Act, 1876 (Amended 1984).
16. The Hindu Adoptions and Maintenance Act, 1956.
17. The Hindu Minority and Guardianship Act, 1956.
18. The Hindu Succession Act, 1956.
19. The Pre-natal Diagnostic Technique (Regulation and Prevention of Misuse) Act,1994.
20. The Juvenile Justice Act, 1986.
21. The Infant Milk Substitutes, Feeding Bottles and Infant Foods (Regulation of Production, Supply and Distribution) Act, 1992.
22. The Equal Remuneration Act, 1976.
23. The Minimum Wages Act, 1948.
24. The Child Labour (Prohibition & Regulation) Act, 1986.
25. The Mines Act, 1952.
26. The Plantation Labour Act, 1951.
27. The Beedi & Cigar Workers (Conditions of Employment) Act, 1966.
28. The Factories Act, 1948 (Amended in 1949, 1950 and 1954).
29. The Contract Labour (Regulation and Abolition) Act, 1970.
30. The Employees State Insurance Act, 1948.
31. The Maternity Benefit Act, 1961 (Amended in 1995).
32. The Wormen's compensation Act, 1923.
33. Immoral Traffic (Prevention) Act, 1961.
34. The Code of Criminal Procedure, 1973.
35. Rape is an offence under Section 376 of IPC.
36. Supreme Court order regarding Sexual Harassment of Women at Work place and other Institution, 1999 (Section 509 IPC).

Recommendations

(A) Women and Poverty

(1) Review, adopt and maintain macroeconomic policies and development strategies that address the needs and efforts of women in poverty.

(2) Revise laws and administrative practices to ensure women's equal rights and access to economic, resources.

(3) Provide women with access to savings and credit mechanisms and institutions.

(B) Education and Training of Women

(1) Ensure equal access to education and eradicate illiteracy among women.

(2) Improve women's access to vocational training, science and technology and continuing education.

(3) Promote life long education and training for girls and women.

(C) Women and Health

(1) Increase women's access throughout the lifecycle to appropriate, affordable and quality health care, information and related services.

(2) Strengthen preventive programmes that promote women's health.

(3) Undertake gender-sensitive initiatives that address sexually transmitted diseases, HIV/AIDS and sexual and reproductive health issues.

(4) Increase resources and monitor follow-up for women's health.

(D) Women and Economy

(1) Promote Women's economic rights and independence including access to employment, appropriate working conditions and control over economic resources.

(2) Facilitate women's equal access to resources, employment, markets and trade.

(3) Strengthen women's economic capacity and commercial networks.

(4) Eliminate occupational segregation and all forms of employment discrimination.

(5) Promote harmonization of work and family responsibilities for women.

(E) Women in Power and Decision Making

(1) Take measures to ensure women's equal access to and full participation in power structures and decision making.

(2) Increase women's capacity to participate in decision making and leadership.

(F) Institutional Mechanisms for the Advancement of Women

(1) Create or strengthen national machineries and other government bodies.

(2) Integrate gender perspectives in legislation, public policies, programmes and projects.

(3) Generate and discriminate gender - disaggregated data and information for planning and evaluation.

(G) Human Rights of Women

(1) Promote and protects the human rights of women through the full implementation of all human rights instruments, especially the concentration on the Elimination of All forms of discrimination against women.

(2) Ensure equality and non-discrimination under the law in practice.

(3) Achieve legal literacy.

REFERENCES

Dr. K.C. Leelavathy & T. Padma Priya, "Human Rights of Women - Situational Analysis", *Social Welfare*, Vol. 50, No. 9, December, 2003, Central Social Welfare Board, New Delhi.

Sheetal Sharma, "Empowerment of Women and Property Rights to Rural Development", *Kurukshetra*, Vol. 54, No. 8, June, 2006, Publications Division, New Delhi.

"Factsheet on Women in India - 2005" Documentation Centre on Women and Children, National Institute of Public Co-operation and Child Development, 2005, New Delhi.

K. Usha, "Gender Equality and Development", *Yojana*, Vol. 47, No. 3, March 2003, Publications Division, New Delhi.

Dr. Mahipal, "Social Development of Rural Women in India", *Kurukshetra*, Vol. 52, No. 9, July 2004, Publications Division, New Delhi.

D. Sunder Raj, "SHGs and Women's Empowerment", *Social Welfare*, Vol. 50, No. 10, January 2004, Central Social Welfare Board, New Delhi.

13
Unorganised Sector and Violation of Rural Women Workers Rights

Introduction

The country's total labour force in unorganized sector consists of construction workers, fishermen, forest workers, agriculture labourers, handloom weavers, craft workers and child workers. Though their contribution to the economy is immense, they have been insulated from the nation mainstream. Take any unorganized labour, resignation to callous and in human exploitation has been the ordeal of the workers.

Every year a number of conferences, seminars and workshops are being held at national and international level for mainstreaming women of downtrodden, vulnerable sections of society. And every year the incidence of gambling, battering increasing. It has been inculcated in rural women that they have to sacrifice their lives for the betterment's of others in the household.

The economic reforms undertaken by Indian government lay stress on competition, minimizing cost, modern technology which is capital intensive, reduction in subsidies, declining role of the state in the economic sphere and economic stabilization. All these measures are likely to adversely affect, atleast in the short run, the interest of the weaker sections, particularly those working in the unorganized sector. Women in the unorganized sector will be the worst sufferers.

Plight of Rural Women

The National perspective plan for women had rightly observed, "There is continued inequality and vulnerability of women in all fields, socio-economic, political, education, healthcare, nutrition and legal. As women are oppressed in all spheres of life they need to be empowered in all walks of life".

Almost 50 per cent of female workers are classified as agricultural labourers and 37 per cent as cultivators. About 70 per cent of farm work is performed by women. However, the female work participation rate registered an increase from 14.2 per cent in 1971 to 22.3 per cent in 1991. There are about 30 per cent rural households headed by women who bear all the burden of earning and caring for the families.

Women's access to land ownership is extremely limited. Because of the seasonal nature of work, they get only 90 to 100 days regular employment in a year. The majority of rural women depend on agriculture which is the major unorganized sector in India. The lack of facilities to acquire skills and unavailability of opportunities to enter other fields have made them desperate and depressed.

The nature of work done by rural women as follows:

1. Domestic work
2. Agriculture work
3. Rearing small ruminants
4. Petty trades
5. Construction work
6. Kitchen gardening.

1. Domestic work

Almost everywhere in our country the picture of domestic work done by the rural women is similar in nature. Domestic activities like taking care of children, ailing household members, preparing food and rearing small ruminants are considered as basic responsibility of women in rural areas. Only variation is according to the region, caste, class and culture. It is a fact that everywhere women have their meals much later than the normal scheduled time as maintained for men. Generally women wake up in between 4.00-4.30 am and go to sleep in between 10.00-10.30 pm. Throughout the day women do a lot of work in the household. This includes sweeping and cleaning of corridors, verandah, cleaning of oven, utensils, cleaning cowshed, preparing breakfast, taking care of children and preparing them for school, preparing lunch, collection of fuel, washing clothes and serving lunch to household members etc. Again after having lunch they take care of small ruminants, do handicrafts for income generation, mend clothes, fetch drinking water, sweeping corridor, light incense-stick before the God/Goddess, preparing dinner, taking care of children, serving dinner to the household members, preparing beds for sleeping, washing floors and closing the doors before sleeping. There is no doubt that the extent of work done by the rural women has no boundary at all. There is no commensurate remuneration for their daylong services the household. It is considered a "service of love".

2. *Agricultural work*

This is the most important area that generates the highest employment of rural people in general and women in particular. The agricultural work done by rural women is an excellent task because they are doing it along with their daily routine of household work. However these women agricultural labourers are victimized with regsent to minimum wages paid to them in comparison to the wages paid to male. The men workers are doing the works like tilling and preparing land, sowing seeds, cutting crops, carrying crop to the home, selling in market, collection of money, decisive role etc, comprises of 31.5 per cent of total agricultural work. The women workers are doing the works like making seed-bed, plugging and transplanting saplings, lifting weeds, harvesting, threshing, boiling paddy, husking rice etc. comprises of 68.5 per cent of total agricultural work. But women are paid on an average ten to fifteen rupees less than the wages paid to male agricultural labourers. The discrimination varies from place to place.

3. *Rearing Small ruminants*

Women particularly play very vital role in the field of animal rearing which includes, cows, bullocks, goats, pigs, ducks, poultry, sheep etc. In most of the cases they are obliged to take care of all the domestic small ruminants and men are entitled to keep the cash returns from the same.

4. *Petty Trades*

In rural areas women run various kinds of petty trades. Such as rice and wheat shop, betel-leaf stall, tea stall, vending vegetables, sewing and knitting, selling of handicrafts etc. All these trades are run either at the dwelling unit or at the local market in the village concerned. Most of the women usually these trades along side their household work. But this kind of productivity is hardly recognized at the household as well as at the community level. Also these rural women do not bother for that. They move ahead with their daily routine. They earn but their husband enjoy. And they violates the rights of their wives in different forms.

5. *Construction work*

This is an important sector, which generates more employment for the women of weakers sections, broken families, and dis-advantaged section of the rural community. In this sector women have a sub-ordinate role. It includes, carrying soil, preparing bricks, carrying the bricks to the brick-bed for firing, supplying mixture materials and bricks to the mason etc. In all the work, women have to work more than the men workers do. Because of smoking and drinking tea, men workers usually enjoy breaks while women have to work without rest. Despite that these women are usually victimized for equal work or work of similar nature. The women cannot react for this unequal payment. Because, the women are in fear of not getting work the next day if they do like that. This kind of discrimination against the women continued till to day.

6. *Kitchen gardening*

In rural areas most of the rural women are engaged in kitchen gardening activities. They prepare the plot of land for kitchen garden around their dwelling units, how seeds and after a certain period they transplant the seedling to main plot of land. They regularly take care of the vegetable garden and sell the produce in the market. Sometimes the village middle men come and collect vegetables from these women at very low rates. Usually, no male household members take part in this kind of work to share the burden of women in the household. After selling the vegetables, most of the women cannot keep amount with them. They have to give the earnings to their husband or to their parents.

Besides all these activities, rural women complement their family income in different other ways. Such as by serving and knitting, weaving, bamboo-baskets, preparing mats, weaving cotton cloth and by doing different kinds of handicrafts. In all these activities women usually generate a good amount of earning. But the fact is the women inherit the obligations of labour while men inherit the ownership of properties.

Issues and problems

Though, development policies and performances have created a positive impact in women position in the society. They are facing many problems and difficulties violation of their rights at home and work place. Some major issues and problems indicate women status, which are as follows:

- Women are powerless (Treated as vulnerable in society).
- They have no choice regarding their job (Here the violation of right to work taken place).
- They don't have a principle occupation (especially rural unorganized women labourers).
- Women workers in rural areas perform dual role in society relating to production and reproduction (So that they are over burdened).
- Their contribution to the family economy and national economy remains largely invisible and valued (Especially in Domestic and Agricultural sector).
- Female worker do not have right to spend money themselves (Because the money is taken by their husband, it violates the right to property of women workers).
- Working for a longer time in unhygienic conditions affecting working women's health (This leads to violation of right to health) women have a low nutrition status.
- Women have a low level of participation in decision making (Due to illiteracy of unorganised rural women workers. At the same time the domination of the male in society).
- They have discrimination in regarding wages (violation of minimum wages and equal pay for equal work).
- The existing communication channels are not adequate and do not reach to the rural poor women.

- Lack of integrated approach in macro policies in tackling women issues.
- Unchecked exploitation of women in houses, at work places and public places.

Although there is no obvious discrimination on papers against women in plans and programmes but the poor women have been largely left outside the pole of development. They are getting lower income and lower status. Policies, programmes and seminars cannot change the women status. There is a greater need for attitudinal change in the society towards the working women of unorganised sector. It should recognize their creativity and enterpreneuership not as passive and defenseless poor women which is not looked for even 64 years of independence.

Suggestions

The problems of unorganised women workers in India are multifarious and multidimensional, these problems can be solved by changing the attitude of family, society and nation towards the women. Some suggestions as are discussed below:

- Women should be educated. When she is educated, she can manage here dual responsibility of home and work.
- Women should be given vocational training in their work so that their efficiency increases. They should be trained to develop their capabilities of decision making and individual thinking.
- Women should be made aware of their constitutional and legal rights both in their work and in the social sphere.
- The attitude of the husband and family members should be changed towards the women. Husband shou!d come forward to share her burden.
- She should be given adequate facilities.
- She should be given financial freedom.
- Baby care should be taken by other family members, when she is at work place.
- Maternity benefit schemes should be extended to the unorganised sector women.
- Wage gaps between men and women should be reduced.

- Better medical facilities and congenial atmosphere should be provided to them.
- Women should be change their attitude about themselves. They should be self confident in their approach.
- More seminars, conferences and workshops on women's rights should be organised at rural level to cover all the village women.
- They should be encouraged to participate in them and express their views.

Conclusion

There is a particular section of women who are really victimised only because of their lack of adequate knowledge and capacity building which is magnified because they are born and brought up in a "Culture of Silence". According to Greek philosopher "Plato", "naturally there is no difference between man and woman. Certain cultural beliefs, customs and norms of society make the difference between them" with reference to National Family Health Suivey - H (2000 AD), it is to be noted that 85 per cent women can decide over what to look and what to prepare for household while 41 per cent can themselves decide how to spend their own earnings. But 30 per cent can never decide how to spend their earnings. On the other hand 32 per cent of the studied women do not seek permission to go to market, 24 per cent of them do not require permission to go to relative's houses but the rest can never think of doing so by themselves.

It is a fact that rural women can work hard and can earn whatsoever amount it may be. But they face a problem in making decisions on how to spend it. In addition to government plans and programmes for the upliftment of women workers of unorganised sector, the Non Governmental Organisation also should participate for the women welfare. Then only the problems of unorganised women will be solved. The women will get equal rights with their male counterparts in all the sectors of the society.

REFERENCES

C. Hemalatha Prasad, "Unorganised Sector : Women in Beedi Making Industry - A Case Study", *Journal of Rural Development*, Vol. 18, No. l, January - March 1999, NIRD, Hyderabad.

Dr. Neeta Anand, "Working Women : Issues and Problems", Yojana, Vol. 47, No. 3, March 2003, Publications Division, New Delhi.

Dr. Gladis Abraham, "Female workforce participation : Need for empowerment, *Yojana*, Vol. 4, No. 5, May 2003, Publication Division, New Delhi.

Badal Chandra Das, "Women work, Men arc Paid", *Social Welfare*, Vol. 50, No. 2, May 2003, Central Social Welfare Board, New Delhi.

Dr. I. Satya Sundaram, "India's Economy and Rural Women Workers", Vol. 50, No. 5-6, August-September - 2003, Central Social Welfare Board, New Delhi.

14

Dr. B.R. Ambedkar's Perspectives on Caste and Human Rights

The caste system has denied four kinds of basic rights to the Dalits, the right to touch and the right to be touched, the right to share food with all human beings, the right to inter-marry across the caste bound social groups and the right to change occupations and acquire skills and knowledge in different fields. Ambedkar thought that all these restrictions should be removed in order to improve their mental and physical health. The individuals in a civilised society should feel that he/she has equal opportunities in all walks of life. The notion of human rights, therefore, entails that human dignity and self-respectable to be fully restored. But caste system has destroyed such a scope.

Introduction

Till Ambedkar came to the Indian scene, the question of human rights was not raised from the point of view of caste in modernist sense. Ambedkar was the first thinker to understand the role of caste in violating rights of the people. Though Buddha raised it, the Buddhist discourse of rights in terms of caste and untouchability got mythified in the process of history. The modern period, the Dalit bahujan discourse on human rights actually stands with Mahatma Jotirao Phule.

Mahatma Joti Rao Phule

Before we proceed to understand Ambedkar's perception of human rights it is important to understand the issues raised by Mahatma Joti Rao Phule, whom Ambedkar considered as his guru.

Phule emerged as a major social reformer in western India in the 19th century. He was the first OBC to revolt against the brahminical social order in the modern western India. He was born in 1827 and was a son of mali (Gardener). His mother and father used to make living out of selling flowers (phool) in Poona town. Their Surname Phule comes from their occupation. Phule got educated upto 7th class in a missionary school and got exposed to western values. He realized that in Western Societies, the rights of individuals and communities were respected by both the state and civil society. But in India one caste does not respect the other caste, there was a suppression of individuals and communities legitimate aspirations both through the institutional and ideological means.

Phule was influenced by the writings of Thomas Paine particularly the Rights of man The Age of Reason. He influenced the thinking of many of his friends that a society which believes in untouchability was no human society at all (in those days many sudra castes were also untouchable to Brahmin and Baniya castes). But Phule was the only person who went to the roots of Indian caste problem. He realized that the Brahmin Baniya castes of his contemporary society were mainly responsible for the suppression of human rights in India. He said that the Shetji Bhatji (Baniyas and Brahmins) were deceiving the sudras and Anti-sudras by means of trade and priest craft. Thus, he was the first persons to include untouchable in sudras and use the concept sudra not in a derogatory sense as Brahmin pandits did but in progressive and positive sense. He, coined the concept of Anti-sudra to denote Achuts or Chandalas. He decided to fight for the educational rights of sudras and Anti-sudras.

He wrote several plays and poetic verses in which he described as to how the rights of sudras and anti-sudras were suppressed by Shetji and Bhatji communities. He sees rights of sudra and anti-sudras in a historical perspective. He thinks that Rama killing Shambhuka and Vamana killing Balichakravarti as suppression of sudra rights by Kshatriya kings and Brahmin priests. The right to rule and the right to tapasya were made exclusive rights of Brahmins and Kshatriya. Such exclusivization of ritual rights destroyed the moral strength of Bahujan production masses.

By starting schools to educate the untouchable girls, boys and also by making his wife Savitri Bai Phule the first woman teacher, Phule made a revolutionary contribution to Indian social system. He also started an organization called Satyashodhak (discovering the truth). Many peasants and women were mobilized to fight for their rights under the banner of Satyashodhak. Thus, Satyashodhak became the main organization around which the sudra and Anti-sudras in different walks of life got mobilized.

Ambedkar's Arrival

Ambedkar drew inspiration from this historical struggle of Phule and Savitri Bai Phule and decided o fight for the rights of the untouchables and OBCs. We must, therefore, understand Ambedkar's perspective of human rights in the context of the anticaste discourse that was prevalent in western India.

The understanding of Ambedkar was rooted in his birth in an untouchable family. Ambedkar was born in a Mahar family of Maharashtra. As a child he experienced untouchability, as an officer he was humiliated and he experienced the same untouchability in the administration of Baroda Maharaja. This made him realize that the institution of caste and the practice of untouchability denied several forms of human rights to scheduled castes. In order to fight out atrocities against the SCs and to secure human rights for millions of Indians, Ambedkar worked out several socio-political strategies, of many strategies, reservations in legislative bodies, government services and educational institutions were some of the main, which had already shown some results in changing the attitudes of parasite (upper) caste people in India. By relating the practice of untouchability to human rights Ambedkar exposed the barbaric nature of Hindu caste system. He came to a conclusion that a society which does not believe in one human being touching another human being, eating together, living side by side can never make progress.

Ambedkar and Caste Question

The institution of caste was created after the Aryan invasion. The Aryan who waged a war on native agricultural and producers violently suppressed them and forced them to surrender all their rights. Ambedkar was the first thinker to realize that there was a close relationship between the Hindu religion and the suppression of human rights of SC's, OBCs and tribal (Dalit bahujans).

Ambedkar extended this arguments and said that violation of human rights in a casteist society takes place both at civil societal level and also at the institution of state. The institutional violence embedded in the system was, in fact, as an extension of Hindu religious violence. In his famous book Annihilation of Caste Ambedkar analyses how through various methods the caste system destroyed the very basis of human rights. He held, "caste system is not merely division of labour, it is also a division of labourers". These castes division created a social system of graded inequality and denied their human rights, which, in essence, stand for self-respect and dignity.

Sudras had no Rights only Duties

The Brahminical social forces had only rights but no duties except, the divine duties of worshiping Gods, advising the kings and vaisyas to serve them. The Kshatriya kings had only duties towards divine spirits and rishis but not towards people. The vaisyas business people were duty bound to serve the Gods, Brahmins and Kshatriya rulers. They could freely exploit the labour of sudra masses. Ambedkar through a process systematic study of Indian history established that the priests exploited the people through Dana and Dakshina economy and the vaisyas exploited through Gupthadhana economy.

Even with the Sudras there were various hierarchised castes like Reddy, Velama, Kamma, Kapu as a king of modern neokshatriya block. Down below them the Other Backward Classes and down below them are the Scheduled Castes. The SCs are forced to suffer untouchability and STs suffer other forms of social disabilities. According to Ambedkar the Hindu religion created graded unequal structures. In this graded inequality as we go down the ladder, more and more rights are taken away and more and more duties are imposed on them. In this process of "no duties but all rights" to non-producing parasitic classes and "no rights but all duties" to all producing castes created a complex social system in India. Ambedkar came to the conclusion that this kind of denial of rights to majority (Bahujans) and usurpation of all rights by minority was part of the Hindu social system. Ambedkar was one of the earliest thinkers who realized that while fighting against the Britishers, there must be a fight against caste system. He also argued for evolving a programme for abolition of a caste. But such an agenda of abolition of caste was met with opposition from Gandhi and the Congress leadership.

Ambedkar and Gandhi Debate

When Ambedkar argued that the human rights of SCs, STs and OBCs (depressed classes) need to be restored by abolishing caste. Gandhi opposed such a proportion. Since Gandhi was born in a Gujarati Baniya (Hindu family) which was part of the Hindu dwija community he felt that abolition of untouchability as acceptable but abolition of caste would destroy the Hindu social order. In order to silence Ambedkar he gave the title "Harijan" to the SCs which was opposed by Ambedkar, Gandhi felt the need for sustaining varna Dharma and agreed to work for abolition of untouchability because he wanted to build the Indian nation state as Hindu (Ramarajya) nation state. However, he also argued for equality of different religions. Later this came to be known as secularism but in such secularism there was no scope to address the caste question. The very existence of caste and untouchability go against the nation of secularism.

On the question of proportional representation to the depressed classes in assemblies and also Government services Ambedkar and Gandhi differed. Ambedkar felt that partial rights of the dalits could be achieved with growing "two votes and double membership constituencies" to them. Gandhi opposed such a system and went on "fast unto death hunger strike" in Errawada Jail of Poona. They finally signed an agreement called "Poona Pact" wherein both of them agreed on a compromised formula of reservation. The Poona Pact was a short term victory of Gandhi and long term victory of Ambedkar. It was this principle of reservation that led to the Mandal struggle. Gradually the theory of social justice came to occupy a space in Indian thought. The Mandal reservation and women's reservation are part of this social justice concept. Ambedkar gave his assessment of Gandhi's role and its historical limitation in his book "what Congress and Gandhi have done to Untouchables".

Applied creatively Ambedkar's thought to human rights questions it boils down to the fact that caste system has negated the very notion of human rights. What did caste do to human rights to SC, ST and OBC? Let us look at castes as an issue of human rights.

Caste and Human Rights

The caste system has denied four kinds of basic rights to the Dalits (a) the right to touch and the right to be touched, (b) the right to share food with all human beings, (c) the right to intermarry across the caste bound social groups and (d) the right to change occupations and acquire skills and knowledge in different fields.

Ambedkar thought that all these restrictions should be removed in order to improve their mental and physical health. The individuals in a civilsied society should feel that he/she has equal opportunities in all walks of life. The notion of human rights, therefore, entails that human dignity and self-respectable to be fully restored. But caste system has destroyed such a scope.

Ambedkar and the Concepts of Liberty, Equality and Fraternity

Ambedkar's understanding of human rights is quite clearly expressed in history of liberty, equality and fraternity. He felt that the western societies much before the French revolution took place, imbibed the spirit of liberty, equality and fraternity. In contrast, in India because of the Hindu Social order such spirit of liberty, equality and fraternity was never allowed to be a part of human consciousness. He was of the opinion that during the Buddhist period, as against the Hindu social order, an attempt was made to create a spirit of liberty, equality and fraternity. Irrespective of caste, creed and sex the right to become members of the sangha was granted. He, therefore, argued that revival of the Buddhist spirit was the only way in which an indigenous mode of restoration of rights can be made possible.

He was of the opinion that political and economic rights have their roots in social rights. The Hindu religion and caste system have cut at the roots of social rights of people. The Indian state is an extension of such Hindu civil society hence the state also has been denying rights to Dalits and other depressed classes. Ambedkar has shown that historically all those Kshatriya kings who believed in varna dharma did not grant any rights to Sudras and Chandalas. The right to read and write, the right to even enter into the temple, the right to learn from each other were denied. In other words their right to be human beings was denied.

In this situation the state has to consciously come to the rescue of the depressed classes. Reservation in education and employment, according to him, would only help them gain some rights but that is not going to solve the problem created historically. He, therefore, visualized a centralized state, which can play an interventionist role. In his "States and Minorities" document he argued for nationalization of industrial property and co-operativization of agricultural land. He was of the opinion that the SCs, STs and OBCs could get some say or get some hold on all forms of property only when it is in the hands of the state.

Human Rights and Violence

The suppression of human rights of depressed classes is also related to the nature of violence used in the Hindu caste system. Several sudra-chandala representatives were suppressed for asserting their rights to learn vidhya. Their right to practice tapasya and their right to administer the state were brutally attacked Ekalavya, Shambhuka, Bali and Vali were the examples, Dhronacharya, Vamana, Rama, violently killed the above mentioned sudras for assenting their rights.

Ambedkar was of the opinion that the Hindu religion "worshipped violence" as creed. This kind of worshipping of those who violently suppressed the rights of sudras and Anti-sudras created a sense of despair among the sudra-chandala masses.

He was opposed to Hinduism and communism, as he believed that both of them supported violence as a creed. He supported the socialistic ideas without violence. He came to the conclusion that the depressed classes cannot win back their rights in a struggle of violence. In a way he used the same argument against Hindus, which Gandhi used against the Britishers. Gandhi wanted to use non-violence method against violent Brithishers and Ambedkar wanted to use the Buddhist method of non-violence as against Hindu violence. He believed that the depressed classes would win over the rights they lost through democratic mobilization of masses. The basic difference between Ambedkarite and Gandhian mode of non-violence is that Gandhi used symbols like that of Rama and Krishna while taking about non-violence where as Ambedkar used a true symbol of non-violence like Buddha.

Conclusion

In conclusion it must be understood that the Dalit bahujan discourse standing with Buddha reached a definite stage with Ambedkar during the nationalist period. It looked Indian society quite differently from the Hindu thinkers like Kautilya, Manu, Rajaram Mohan Roy, Gandhi looked at the Dalitbahujan tradition believed in what Ambedkar called "Educate, Organize and Agitate" modes of action. While the Hindu tradition believed dividing the society into castes and sub-castes, even by using violence the Buddhist Ambedkarite tradition believed in resolving the contradictions through democratic means. It raised the level of human consciousness from "right of fewjan to rights of Bahujan" (right of minority to rights of majority). While drafting the Indian Constitution Ambedkar had this goal in mind. Though the Indian Constitution did not reflect all his scheme of human rights, as his original document on rights of states and minorities reflected, that every constitution began to play a transfor-matory role in post-colonial India.

In the post-Ambedkar period a major debate is on as to how to fight against both the civil societal and state suppression of human rights. Some Ambedkarites are of the view that the struggle for human rights should take place only through democratic mobilization and some are of the opinion that both Ambedkarism and Marxism must be combined in order to evolve a new theory of struggle for achieving human rights of SC, ST, OBCs and women. It must be remembered that Ambedkar resigned from his law ministry when the Hindu Code Bill, was not approved even by persons like Nehru. He was the first thinker to raise several substantial questions with regard to human rights of Dalitbahujans of India. He was also responsible for negating all forms of violence and creating a new understanding of human rights violence of all forms should be removed from the socio-political system.

REFERENCES

Dr. B.R. Ambedkar, *Annihilation of caste writings and Speeches*, Vol. 1.

Rosalind O'Hanlon, Caste, Conflict and Ideology.

Dr. B.R. Ambedkar, *Philosophy of Hinduism writings and Speeches*, Vol. III.

Gail Omvedt, *Dalits and the Democratic Reservation—Dr. Ambedkar and the Dalits Movements in Colonial India.*

Dr. Kancha Ilaiah, *Human Rights Discourse in Dalit Bhujan Tradition.*

Dr. B.R. Ambedkar, *Who are the Sudras?*

15
Dr. B.R. Ambedkar's Ideology and Human Dignity : A Human Rights Perspective*

Introduction

Babasaheb Ambedkar is the forerunner in the field of Human Rights and Human Dignity. Much before the United Nations adopted the Charter on Human Rights, Dr. Ambedkar propagated the necessity of struggles to be launched by the underprivileged, oppressed and suppressed, for establishing human rights. In fact, he led the first struggle in India for establishing human rights in early 1930's in the marathan movement started at Mahad, to establish the right to draw water from a public tank, by thousands and thousands of erstwhile untouchables. Dr. Ambedkar laid a road map for achieving human dignity, much earlier to the abolition of untouchability in the constitution of India and establishment of National Commission for Human Rights. Dr. Ambedkar visualised before anyone in this country, that by annihilating caste only, equality and human dignity can be bestowed and restored on Dalits, women and other vulnerable section of the society.

Dr. B.R. Ambedkar had liberal education in America and U.K. having seen the people there enjoying liberty, equality, dignity of person and education and denial to Afro-Americans (Negros); had developed humanism and ceaselessly worked for human dignity to his deprived social segments. Equally, Adivasis having

---

* Paper presented at U.G.G. sponsored National Conference on "Dr. B.R. Ambedkar's Ideologies : Revision & Vision" on 1st & 2nd March, 2007, organised by Centre for Ambedkar Studies, Sri Padmavati Mahila Visva Vidyalayam, Tirupati - 517 502, A.P.

lived away from the civilised society in forest areas, except their built in culture within their tribal groups, they too did not have access to formal education and cultural development in the modern sense. Having himself was the victim of social oppression, discrimination and of equal dignity, Dr. B.R. Ambedkar strived to secure civil, political, economic, educational and cultural rights for dignity of persons to the Dalits and Adivasis as a mission of life.

Ambedkar and Caste Question

The institution of caste was created after the Aryan invasion. The Aryan who waged a war on native agricultural and producers violently suppressed them and forced them to surrender all their rights. Ambedkar was the first thinker to realize that there was a close relationship between the Hindu religion and the suppression of human rights of SC's, OBCs and tribals (Dalit bahujans). In his famous book *Annihilation of Caste*, Ambedkar analyses how through various methods the caste system destroyed the very basis of human rights. He held, "caste system is not merely division of labour, it is also a division of labourers". These castes division created a social system of graded inequality and denied their human rights, which, is essence, stand for self-respect and dignity.

Sudras had no Rights only Duties

According to Ambedkar the Hindu religion created a graded unequal structures. In this graded inequality as we go down the ladder, more and more rights are taken away and more and more duties are imposed on them. In this process of "no duties but all rights" to non-producing parasitic classes and "no rights but all duties" to all producing castes created a complex social system in India. Ambedkar came to the conclusion that this kind of denial of rights to majority (Bahujans) and usurpation of all rights by minority was part of the Hindu social system. Ambedkar was one of the earliest thinkers who realized that while fighting against the Britishers, there must be a fight against caste system. He also argued for evolving a programme for abolition of a caste. But such an agenda of abolition of caste was met with opposition from Gandhi and the Congress leadership.

Caste and Human Rights

The caste system has denied four kinds of basic rights to the Dalits in India (a) the right to touch and the right to be touched, (b) the right to share food with all human beings, (c) the right to inter-marry across the caste bound social groups and (d) the right to change occupations and acquire skills and knowledge in different fields.

Ambedkar thought that all these restrictions should be removed in order to improve their mental and physical health. The individuals in a civilised society should feel that he/she has equal opportunities in all walks of life. The notion of human rights, therefore, entails that human dignity and self-respectable to be fully restored. But caste system has destroyed such a scope.

Human Rights and Violence

The suppression of human rights of depressed classes is also related to the nature of violence used in the Hindu caste system. Several sudra-chandala representatives were suppressed for asserting their rights to learn vidhya. Their right to practice tapasya and their right to administer the state were brutally attacked Ekalavya, Shambhuka, Bali and Vali were the examples, Dhronacharya, Vamana, Rama, violently killed the above mentioned sudras for assenting their rights.

Ambedkar was of the opinion that the Hindu religion "worshipped violence" as creed. This kind of worshipping of those who violently suppressed the rights of sudras and Anti-sudras created a sense of despair among the sudra-chandala masses.

He was opposed to Hinduism and communism, as he believed that both of them supported violence as a creed. He supported the socialistic ideas without violence. He came to the conclusion that the depressed classes cannot win back their rights in a struggle of violence. In a way he used the same argument against Hindus, which Gandhi used against the Britishers. Gandhi wanted to use non-violence method against violent Britishers and Ambedkar wanted to use the Buddhist method of non-violence as against Hindu violence. He believed that the depressed classes would win over the rights they lost through democratic mobilization of masses. The basic difference between Ambedkarite and Gandhian mode of non-violence is that Gandhi used symbols like that of

Rama and Krishna while taking about non-violence where as Ambedkar used a true symbol of non-violence like Buddha.

For the successful implementation of Dr. B.R. Ambedkar's ideology, the suggestions should be followed by the policy makers in India.

1. Compulsory education must be implemented in practice each and every corner of the Indian society.
2. Developmental programmes should be carried out at grassroot level with cent per cent commitment.
3. The reservation policy should be implemented in all sectors of developmental programmes to reach the grassroot level people effectively.

Conclusion

In conclusion it must be understood that the Dalitbahujan discourse standing with Buddha reached a definite stage with Ambedkar during the nationalist period. It looked Indian society quite differently from the Hindu thinkers like Kautilya, Manu, Rajaram Mohan Roy and Gandhi looked at, the Dalitbahujan tradition believed in what Ambedkar called "Educate, organize and agitate" modes of action. While the Hindu tradition believed dividing the society into castes and sub-castes, even by using violence the Buddhist Ambedkarite tradition believed in resolving the contradictions through democratic means. It raised the level of human consciousness from "right of fewjan to rights of Bahujan" (right of minority to rights of majority). While drafting the Indian Constitution Ambedkar had this goal in mind. Though the Indian Constitution did not reflect all his scheme of human rights, as his original document on rights of states and minorities reflected, that every constitution began to play a transforma-tory role in post-colonial India.

In the post-Ambedkar period a major debate is on as to how to fight against both the civil societal and state suppression of human rights. Some Ambedkarites are of the view that the struggle for human rights should take place only through democratic mobilization and some are of the opinion that both Ambedkarism and Marxism must be combined in order to evolve a new theory of struggle for achieving human rights of SC, ST,

OBCs and women. It must be remembered that Ambedkar resigned from his law ministry when the Hindu Code Bill, was not approved even by persons like Nehru. He was the first thinker to raise several substantial questions with regard to human rights of Dalitbahujans of India. He was also responsible for negating all forms of violence and creating a new understanding of human rights violence of all forms should be removed from the socio-political system.

REFERENCES

Dr. B.R. Ambedkar, "Annihilation of Caste Writings and Speeches", Vol. 1.

Dr. Justice K. Ramaswamy, "Dr. B.R. Ambedkar and Human Dignity", Dr. B.R. Ambedkar Memorial Trust, 2004, Hyderabad.

Dr. Joseph D'souza, "Who told us that Gandhi ended the caste system in India" An Agenda for Dalit Emancipation within the Twenty-first Century", Dalit Freedom Network, October 2006, New Delhi.

Dr. I. Subramanyam & Dr. B.V. Muralidhar, "Dr. B.R. Ambedkar's Perspectives on Caste and Human Rights", The PRP Journal of Human Rights, Vol. 10, No. 4, October-December 2006, New Delhi.

16

Dalit Rights and Constitutional Safeguards in India

The Indian caste system or the traditional socio-economic structure and system of India can be seen to be one of the gradation, degradation, deprivation and exploitation and in which there is a hierarchy of occupations also. Its design has been shaped in the self-interest of those in positions of privilege and prestige, to monopolize advantages and secure labour and services from those below:

The different problems faced by the dalits in Indian society are categorized as follows :

Social Problems

- Violation of rights such as the right to life with freedom, human dignity and self-respect.
- It is well known to any keen observer that throughout the whole of rural India, Scheduled Caste habitations are even today usually segregated, mostly on the outskirts of a village.
- The people belonging to Scheduled Castes and Scheduled Tribes are treated as untouchables and labour classes.
- Untouchability is undoubtedly the worst form of in human dignity.
- The Victims of Custodial Violence or illegal detention are mostly from the poor Scheduled Castes and Scheduled Tribes.
- They are denied a number of civil rights. They are subjected to various offences, indignities, humiliations and harassment.

- They have, in several brutal incidents, been deprived of their, life and property.
- Serious crimes are committed against SCs/STs for various historical, social and economic reasons.
- The dehumanizing practice of manual scavenging is yet another blot on the Indian society.
- Discrimination on caste basis at public places, wells, tanks, hotels and restaurants.
- Practice of Bonded Labour and slavery.

Economic Problems

- Discrimination in Educational Institutions based on caste.
- Village tea shops are a recent phenomenon in many villages. With this has arisen a variety of discriminatory practice such as no seating, separate seating, separate glasses, usually, old, dirty and cracked or chipped.
- Majority of the bonded labour belong to Scheduled Caste and Scheduled Tribe.
- The injustices suffered relate to property, wages and other resources on the one hand and the person on the other.
- The SCs/STs lose their land and even when title over the land has been conferred, they have been prevented from occupying the land and cultivating it.
- The SCs/STs families in many villages have been in permissive possession of house sites or homesteads which constant threats of eviction by the land owners or even the state.
- Practice of paying low wages to the agricultural labourers and unorganized labourers.
- Caste discrimination and practice of untouchability, severe discrimination against women, usury and indebtedness, wide spread illiteracy and terribly slow rate of spread of education among poor.
- The structure of surplus labour, unemployment and under employment, inequitable distribution of land and assets, low wages, distress migration and unjust social institutions

result in an environment which lead to the emergence and perpetuation of bonded labour.

- There are also large number of bonded labourers in brick kilns, stone quarries, limestone mines, match factories, carpet weaving, irrigation works and a variety of other occupations are mostly from SC/ST castes.
- Practice of bonded labour, migrant labour, contract labour, and child labour affects the economic rights of the SCs/STs.

Political Problems

The political rights like right to vote and right to contest in the elections are completely denied in the case of socially, economically disadvantaged people.

For Example: The votes of the SCs/STs are mainly denied and rigged by the upper caste people according to their favourite leaders. In this manner "The right to vote" has denied to SC/ST people.

The reserved seats in Panchayats are also not properly enjoyed by the disadvantaged groups. The upper caste people denied this right by threatening in different ways.

As described above the socially, economically disadvantaged people have still experiences the different problems in Social, Economic, Educational and Political aspects in their day-to-day life.

Constitutional Safeguards

The Indian constitution, as set out in its preamble, is a testament to secure to all its citizens Justice - Social, economic and political; liberty of thought and expression, belief, faith and worship; Equality of status and of opportunity and fraternity assuring the dignity of the individual and integrity of the nation. The founding fathers of the constitution, especially Babasaheb Dr. B.R. Ambedkar who was the Chairman of the Drafting Committee, were acutely aware of the iniquitous forces embedded in the social systems, economic institutions and political organizations in India in relation to the weaker sections and vulnerable sections of the society and therefore, considered it necessary to provide for specific corrective measures and mandates in the constitution in their favour.

The safeguards for the members of the scheduled castes relate to the removal of the disabilities as well as positive measures to enable them to acquire a dignified position in the national life. The major concern about the members of the scheduled tribes has been that of protecting and preserving their command over natural resources and the best in their tradition. The Indian constitution is a unique document which provides for a comprehensive framework for the socio-economic advancement of the scheduled castes and the scheduled tribes to achieve the objective of a just and humane society. The constitution incorporated a number of commands for the elimination of the inequities and inequalities prevalent in the Indian society and for promoting equality and social justice.

The constitutional perspective combines both the positive notion of rights guaranteed through the state and law as well as the notion of natural rights and includes horizontal rights applicable to all citizens and vertical rights to enhance the life chances of vulnerable groups such as scheduled castes, scheduled tribes and OBCs.

The following are the different fundamental rights provided in part III of the constitution of India.

Social Safeguards

The social safeguards provides protection against the social problems like abolition of untouchability, prohibition of discrimination on grounds of caste, race, sex, access to public places, wells, tanks, hotels, restaurants etc. Prohibition of forced labour and throwing open Hindu religious institutions etc.

Equality Before Law

The state shall not deny to any person equality before law or the equal protection of the laws within thte territory of India (Article 14)

Prohibition of discrimination on gounds of religion, race, caste, sex or place of birth.

Article 15

(i) The state shall not discriminate any citizen on grounds only of religion, race, caste, sex, place of birth or any of them.

(ii) No citizen shall, on grounds of religion, race, caste, sex, place of birth or any of them, be subjected to any disability, liability, restriction or condition with regard to—

(a) Access to shops, public restaurants, hotels and places of public entertainment; and

(b) The use of wells, tanks, bathing ghats, roads and places of public resort maintained wholly or partly out of state funds or dedicated to the use of the general public.

Abolition of Untouchability

Article 17 "Untouchability" is abolished and its practice in any form is forbidden. The enforcement of any disability arising out of "Untouchability" shall be an offence and punishable in accordance with law.

Rights Against Exploitation

Article 23 (1) Traffic in human beings and beggar and other similar forms of forced labour are prohibited and any contravention of this provision shall be an offence punishable in accordance with law.

Article 25(2) (b) Providing for social welfare and reform or the throwing open of Hindu religious institutions of a public character to all classes and sections of Hindus.

Educational and Economic Safeguards

These safeguards provides and promotes economic rights of the scheduled castes and scheduled tribes in the form of Reservations for admissions in educational institutions, reservation in public employment, claims in appointments to the services, promotion of educational and economic interests and protection from social injustice and all forms of exploitation.

Article 15(4)

"Nothing in this article or in clause (2) of Article 29 shall prevent the state from making any special provision for the advancement of any socially and educationally backward classes of citizens or for the scheduled castes and the scheduled tribes".

Article 16(4)

"Nothing in this Article shall prevent the state from making any provision for the reservation of appointments or posts in favour of any backward class of citizens which, in the opinion of the state, is not adequately represented in the services under the state".

Article 29(2)

No citizen shall be denied admission into any educational institution maintained by the state or receiving aid out of state funds on grounds only of religion, race, caste, language or any of them".

Article 24

Banned the employment of children below fourteen years in any factory or mine or hazardous occupations.

Directive Principles as Constitutional Safeguards

An important part of the constitution and of great significance to the poor is the Directive Principles of State Policy which are fundamental in the governance of the country.

Article 38

This article envisages a social order in which justice social, economic and political will inform all institutions of national life and the endeavour required on the part of the state to minimize inequalities in income, Status and opportunities.

Article 39

It visualises, among others, the right to adequate means of livelihood; the equitable control and ownership of the material resources of the community and that the operation of the economic system doesn't result in concentration of wealth and means of production to the common detriment. It also envisages equal pay for equal work for men and women as well as opportunities for children to develop in a healthy manner and without exploitation.

Article 41

Stipulates that the state shall within the limits of its economic capacity and development make effective provision for securing the right to work, the right to education and to public assistance in cases of unemployment, old age, sickness and disablement and in other cases of undeserved want.

Article 43

It calls upon the state to endeavour to secure a living wage to all the workers.

Article 45

Speaks of free and compulsory education for children until they complete the age of fourteen years.

Article 46

It mandates the state to promote with special case the educational and economic interests of the weaker sections of the people and in particular of scheduled castes and scheduled tribes and protect them from injustice and all forms of exploitation.

Suggestions

- The right to education must be implemented i.e. free and compulsory education for the children below 14 years at every nook and corner of the Indian society.
- The welfare schemes, programmes meant for dalits should be implemented effectively and efficiently.
- Practicing or encouraging untouchability should be eliminated in the Indian society.
- Effective implementation of the SCs & STs prevention of Atrocities Act 1989.
- Caste discrimination at public places must be eliminated.
- Practice of bonded labour, migrant labour, contract labour and child labour affects the rights of the dalit, so all the above should be avoided in the Indian society.
- Free and fair elections should be conducted for the political participation of dalits at all levels.
- In addition to the above suggestions the Indian government should take necessary steps to protect, prevent and promote the dalits rights in all spheres like education, health, employment and economic aspects.
- The government should amend the existing laws and legislations if necessary and should make new legislations for the benefit of the dalits in India.

Conclusion

The contradictions of socio-economic order in our society remain almost the same even after sixty years of independence. Half a century is a considerable period of time in the history of a society to correct it mistakes and imbalances but even at the closing end of the twentieth century neither the society nor the state in India has been able to resolve its contradictions. And despite the constitutional commitment of the state towards the goal of equality, liberty and justice, the age-old structure of inequality has not been dismantled. The ideas of social democracy and distributive justice remain elusive. On the contrary, the vast majority of the Indian population is subjected to multiple deprivations. The Dalits have yet to experience the so called fruits of development. Sixty years of our planning and money spend on development has brought several distortions like the rich becoming richer and the poor remaining poor. Moreover, the existing policies and programmes for eradicating poverty to generate employment has proved to be a failure. It is a great disappointment that we failed to eradicate poverty in our country. As a result of this, it has led to social tensions and a steep sense of insecurity among Dalits.

The constitution is thus an instrument heavily weighted in favour of the weaker sections of Indian society. Almost all the issues for which the poor struggle in their daily lives find a place in the Indian constitution whether it is equality, freedom, human dignity, discrimination, social and economic justice, right to livelihood, right to work, living wage or protection from exploitation.

REFERENCES

R.R. Prasad, "Journal of Rural Development", Vol. 19, 2000; NIRD, Hyderabad.

"Caste Action Programme", 2003, C.P.I. (ML), New Democracy, Hyderabad.

B. Myna Rao, "Dalits should they quit the Hindu Religion?", 2003, Hyderabd.

D.D. Basu, "Introduction to the Constitution of India", 1994, New Delhi.

R.R. Prasad, "Journal of Rural Development", Vol. 20, 2001, NIRD, Hyderabad.

P.S. Krishnan, "Theme Paper on Caste System and Dalits", Dalit and Minority Empowerment, Santosh Bhartiya, Raj Kamal Prakasham, 2008, New Delhi.

P.G. Jogdand, "Human Rights Violations of the Dalits: An inquiry into Indian Social Reality" *Indian Journal of Human Rights*, Special Volume (Human Rights: Dalits), Vol. 4, No. 1 & 2, Jan-Dec. 2000, University of Hyderabad, Hyderabad.

17

Violation of Dalit Rights in India in the Era of Globalization*

Globalization as a Concept

The term globalization is defined differently in different contexts. According to Robert McCorquodale "globalization is a contested term and there is no one accepted definition of it". In a broader sense it includes two things—integration of the world and interdependence of the sovereign nation-states. The term is all encompassing is defined and understood in both 'economic and non-economic contexts which broadly include socio-cultural, historical and political'.

Globalization refers to the process of the intensification of economic, political, social and cultural relations across international boundaries. It is principally aimed at the transcendental homogenization of political and socio-economic theory across the globe. It is equally aimed at 'making global being present worldwide at the world stage or global arena" [S.T. Kindle: 2002:12]

It deals with the 'increasing breakdown of trade barriers and the increasing integration of world market'.

Globalization is further seen in the context of ascendancy and dominance of capitalism; market forces and liberal democracy particularly in the aftermath of the collapse of the Eastern bloc in the late 80s and 90s. "Globalization" as quoted in S.T. Kindle means the "broadening and deepening linkages of national economies into a worldwide market for goods and services, especially capital". It aims at "removing all national barriers to

*Paper presented at National Seminar on "Human Rights in the Era of Globalization" on 3rd and 4th November 2006, organised by the Dept. of Political Science, University of Hyderabad, Hyderabad.

the free movement of international capital" reinforced by the "supersonic transformation in information technology. It is principally aimed at the universal homogenization of ideas, cultures, values, and even life styles as well as at the de-territorialization and villagization of the world".

The UNDP Human Development Report clearly spells out that the events of the 1980s and the 1990s that took place in the Eastern Europe and in the former Soviet Union spread the pace of globalization and deepened the interactions among the people. They have also defined the character of global integration, giving rise to new markets, new actors, new rules and new tools. And they have created an era of globalization that is intensifying contacts not just between countries but between people. Globalization, in sum, means connecting people, connecting places, connecting cultures and connecting values. As one commentator points out:

The last quarter of the twentieth century witnessed an upsurge in the process of globalization. The world has noted increasing integration of international markets for goods, services, technology and finance. Such an upsurge in international economic activity, which is now being referred to as globalization, has been interpreted by most social analysts, public officials and mass media alike as marking the dawn of a new era. The new era, with the breakdown of national boundaries, has been acclaimed as an era of "critical transformation" bringing about an "end of geography/ history", in a "new global village". The "new village" reflects the universal acceptance of the western arrangements and "management" of societal problems in a post communist world. It also increasingly shares a "world culture" dominated by the affluent West.

The current phase of globalization has three characteristic features. First, shrinking space, which means 'peoples lives—their jobs, incomes and health—are affected by events on the other side of the globe, often by events they do not know about'. Secondly, 'shrinking time, which is seen in the speed with which markets and technologies are changing. And more importantly, disappearing borders. National borders are breaking down, not only for trade, capital and information but also for ideas, norms, cultures and values. Peoples lives around the globe are linked more deeply, more intensely, more immediately than ever'. Globalization is also seen in terms of free movement of goods, services, capital and technology but not capital.

The concept of globalization has also been examined in terms of "universalization of particularism and particularization of universalism", that is, what is local is global and what is global is local. This two-fold process has many aspects. "Clearly it is a political, social, and cultural process, but it is foremost an economic process". Some scholars view globalization as the march and spread of American capitalism.

As John Harris puts it

Globalization is to great extent a euphemism for American imperialism. The power of capital is not only expressed through the financial flows that no one actually 'plans', but also in the very deliberately constructed policy networks linking government, corporate sector and *inter alia universities*, that operate behind barriers of official secrecy.

Globalization, Sovereignty and Nation-States

The phenomenon of globalization has seriously challenged the identity and sovereignty as well as the working of the nation-states. If globalization means emergence of borderless states then the very existence of the nation-state is questioned. Who controls the territory, population as well as the government in the globalized world? Not certainly the nation-states. Deterritorialization of the nation-states is taking place. Products and capital are moving with the least possible hindrance. As Human Development Report remarks 'national borders are also breaking down in economic policy—as multilateral agreements and the pressures of staying competitive in global markets constrain the options for national policy, and as multinational corporations and global crime syndicates integrate their operations globally'.

The states are in no capacity to take economic decisions such as what to produce, how to produce and, for whom and how much to produce. The process of liberalization and privatization has seriously weakened the control and functioning of the bureaucracy considered to be the backbone of the states. What we are witnessing, today, is the emergence of "contracted and atrophied states".

As more and more countries belonging particularly to the "Third World" are taking recourse to free trade, the national and international economic policies are being taken not by the national governments but by powerful international economic and financial institutions like the International Monetary Fund, the World Bank and, the World Trade Organization. These institutions are being ably supported by a new class of the people, called technocrats, who have taken over the role of the traditional bureaucrats. This process has gathered momentum in countries of Eastern Europe and the CIS where a dramatic transition from centrally planned economic system to market democracies has taken place. This is equally true in case of the so-called socialist countries like China, Mongolia and Vietnam.

While commenting on the nature of global governance, the HDR points out that (a) 'intergovernmental policy-making in today's global economy is in the hands of the major industrial powers and the international institutions they control—the World Bank, the International Monetary Fund, the Bank for International Settlement, (b) 'ad hoc and self selected policy' groups such as G-7 are making *defacto* global economic policy in which developing countries and G-15 have the least say, and (c) there is little participation of the poor countries in 'the formulation and implementation of the new rules that govern markets'. This was very much obvious during the Uruguay round of GATT negotiations and this is equally apparent in case of WTO negotiations where the poor countries have little capacity and skill to bargain with the rich countries. Their weakness in the negotiating capacity has further been compounded due to the breakup of the common "South" position on global trade issues.

This highly skewed system and arrangement of global governance has adversely affected the notion of sovereign equality as propounded by the UNO. As HDR remarks 'the rapidly increasing multilateral agreements—the new rules—are highly binding on the national governments and constrain domestic policy choices'. The 'unbalanced' Trade Related Aspects of Intellectual Property Rights (TRIPS) has further eroded the sovereign decision making power of the poor countries as almost all knowledge-based production is now subject to tight intellectual property protection. Moreover the TRIPS agreement *'provides an enabling environment for multinationals, tightening their dominant ownership of technology, impeding and increasing the cost of transfer to developing countries'*. In sum we can say that in the age of globalization the internal and the external behaviour of the nation-states is conditioned and governed by the multinational corporations as well as the multilateral institutions like the IMF, the World Bank and the WTO. Sovereignty belongs to those who are 'strong and powerful'.

The 'establishment of globalized economic institutions' like the IMF, the World Bank and the WTO has, on the one hand, been 'a symptom of and a stimulus for globalization' and, on the other, it 'indicates the trend away from the dominance of the state as the exclusive unit of analysis in international affairs'.

The World Bank report observes that the 'global events and international agreements are putting constraints on state's arbitrary action and are increasingly affecting it's choices' (World Bank Report: 1997:12, as cited in *ibid).* Besides, as McCorquodale puts it states no longer enjoy *'exclusive control over their economic, legal, political and sovereign affairs. Moreover, the current trend of globalization differs from past transnational influences on state sovereignty in the scale and speed of its operation'.*

The transnational flow of goods, capital, people, and ideas has equally affected the sovereign identity of the nation-states and so have the transnational corporations and inter-governmental institutions. The rise in popular participation at the grassroots level, emergence of civil-societies and the enhancement of non-governmental organizations have also influenced and limited the activities of the nation-states.

As one commentator points out

The globalization process has led to a corresponding decline in the role of the modern nation-state in regulating the nature of the growth of the political economy at the national level, as the multinational corporations driven by market forces have taken over. Economic reforms are being forced upon the nation-states so that national economies can be 'restructured' in accordance with the external changes taking place at the level of the global economy. Globalization has also forced the nation-states to "retreat" from their welfare activities and become the promoter of the interests of the global capital/capitalist class. The people are being left to the discipline and dictate of the market forces more and more brutally.

Dalits in the World of Globalization Indian Perspective

Globalization is repeatedly propagated to common people as a womb of 'progress'. People and nations who own resources and political power create conditions for others to follow this model of progress. Globalization is an economic system that does not talk of globalization of humanity, ethics or religion. Instead, it assures that benefits will flow to rich nations and the rich classes more than what they have now and wants others to believe that they too will receive some of the benefits in the process.

The rich nations and people in the world have welcomed the process of globalization. It is only those poor nations and poor people discriminated on the basis of caste, gender, minority status and colour, which resist globalization. They resist globalization because of their past experience and history, which has proved time and time again that no amount of progress, wealth or power in a nation has ever been equally distributed amongst all its citizens.

The Third World Social Forum continues to widen the debate on globalization. Since this forum is being held in India, naturally the debate is focused more around the Indian context. It is a well-known fact that India as a nation continues to be ruled more by caste than by its Constitution. Amongst the controversies and differences of opinion on whether or not globalization as a new world economic order is going to bring more progress, happiness or freedom for all, this folder specifically focuses discussion on how the globalization process is going to impact on Dalits.

How has India Responded to Globalization?

India has introduced its New Economic Policy in 1991 with several new measures such as liberalisation of its trade with other countries and structural adjustment of its own economy. This is an on-going process of 'reform'.

On the international trade front, India has provided market access and liberalised flow in the case of around 760 commodities.

Similar access is allowed in capital investment and flow. International companies are allowed in insurance and many other service areas.

A Structural Adjustment Programme (SAP) has been introduced into the domestic economy. It includes:

(a) Privatization of the public sector and services

(b) Removal of restrictions on private sector participation in the economy

(c) Withdrawal of the government from many development and basic welfare sectors

(d) Wage freeze and cuts in subsidies.

The government has also brought about major changes to the industrial sector. Whereas the Industrial Policy Resolution of 1948 reserved 18 sectors for government control, the 1991 Industrial Policy reserves only four sectors. Further services such as banking, insurance and education are now open for private sector investment. Similar changes are being brought about in the agricultural sector as well.

How Does Globalization Impact on Dalits?

How do Dalits experience globalization? What is the future for Dalits in the new economic world order that is based on privatization and the market economy? Dalits, 160 million Indian citizens known as 'scheduled castes', would be one fourth of the Indian population or 200 million if those converted from Hinduism to other religions are added to the category. Dalits are the most marginalised section of Indian society, sharing grinding poverty with other Indian poor. However, in addition and more importantly, Dalits suffer exclusion and intense discrimination in economic spheres - in the market and outside the market on the basis of caste, descent and occupation.

The policy so far had been

The central feature of government policies until the 1990s had been its active participation in the economic and social governance of the country. The framework of policies included government participation, market intervention and economic and social planning. This meant that the public sector played a more active role in providing anti-discriminatory measures such as reservations, and basic services like education, health, etc. Moreover, these measures were accompanied by policies and interventions in various markets such as agriculture, land, capital, labour, housing and others to improve the access of Dalits to sources of income.

The post-Independence *Indian Constitution* recognised the prevalence of caste discrimination and the need for an economic, political and social order that ensured equality and equal opportunity for all. This constitutional recognition was translated into special measures such as:

1. An affirmative action programme (reservations) that assured proportional representation of Dalits in governance, public sector jobs and higher education.
2. Anti-discriminatory and preventive laws such as the Untouchability Offences Act, the Protection of Civil Rights Act and the SC/ST (Prevention of Atrocities) Act.
3. Land reforms legislation.
4. Special welfare measures and programmes for economic, educational and social empowerment of the Dalits.

Through all these measures the focus has been to improve private ownership of fixed capital assets and human resource capabilities, and to ensure Dalits access to social and basic services like housing, health, drinking water, electricity, etc. While most of these measures still await adequate implementation, they were not exhaustive. The affirmative action policy applies only to government-run and government-supported sectors. It does not apply to the private sector where more than 90% of Dalit workers are engaged.

Now the policy has been changed

The New Economic Policy sets out to frame policies and programmes that imply a drastic reduction in the government's role in economic and social governance, framing of policies and programmes. Certain policies of the 1980s that were devised keeping in view the interests of Dalits and other poor and socially downtrodden classes have been revised. This can be seen from the following developments:

1. Land reform measures are now put on hold.
2. Ceilings on land holdings have been selectively relaxed.
3. Efforts are made to allow tenancies with no protection to mall lessees.
4. Private players have been granted entry into the field of education, particularly technical and vocational education, which makes such education costly, without provisions for affirmative action for discriminated groups such as Dalits.
5. Entry has been promoted for private insurance companies without making them pro-poor.
6. Industry, banking and insurance sectors are being privatised, which again means these private players are not bound by any affirmative action policy.
7. Expenditure reduction has been introduced for many anti-poverty schemes like the Integrated Rural Development Programme (IRDP), Employment Guarantee schemes, etc.
8. Labour reforms are being planned without taking into consideration adequate social security and other protective measures.

In so far as previous policies and programmes are now reversed, there is a departure from the past policies of the government towards facilitating a free market economy.

Privatization and the Market: Further Exclusion and Discrimination for Dalits

Apart from exclusion that Dalits face in the market due to lack of purchasing power, they also suffer particularly from lack of access to the market, which arises out of caste-based discrimination. In the context of privatization and the withdrawal of the government from economic governance, deregulation of various markets and changes to education, health, industry and financial sectors, Dalits are going to suffer more in the labour market and other markets such as capital, land, information, etc. They have already begun to lose their stakes in the employment market due to high levels of recruitment in the private sector through "informal channels", which is a hindrance for Dalits who lack adequate access to the network of opportunities and are relatively powerless.

Impact of Globalization on Dalit's Right to Land

(1) Landlessness among Dalits has increased: Landless and near landless households in 1991 accounted for around 70% of Scheduled Caste households, which has increased to around 75% by 1999-2000. Thus, since about three-quarters of Scheduled Caste households are either landless or near landless, their main occupation is primarily wage labour.

(2) Land reforms in favour of Dalits have come to an end: Post-Independence land reform measures of land ceilings and land assignments to Dalits had begun to provide bits of land of whatever quality to traditionally landless Dalits. Dalits had become producers, though marginal, in the agricultural sector. However, current policies of the government under globalization and structural adjustment induce a shift towards consolidation of agricultural landholdings for corporate farming, removal of ceilings for selective use in agriculture, policies of horticulture and aquaculture.

(3) Privatization has overtaken the process of land distribution : Over the past decade the government has put the brake on land assignments; existing land holdings are not being regularised and Dalits are not being given priority in the land market. Withdrawal of government intervention in the land market, in the form of land redistribution and other interventions, has a serious impact on Dalits' access to land. Selective efforts to remove land ceilings and encourage corporate farming are therefore destroying the livelihood of many poor Dalits.

National and International Safeguards

- To ensure that ownership and control of material resources are distributed so as to ensure the common good (Article 39(b) Indian Constitution: Directive Principles of State Policy).
- To ensure that no concentration of wealth and means of production takes place (Article 39(c) Indian Constitution: Directive Principles of State Policy).
- To guarantee the right of everyone to own property alone and in association with others, and not to be arbitrarily

deprived of her/his property (Article 17 Universal Declaration of Human Rights).

- To prosecute whoever, not being a member of a Scheduled Caste or Tribe, wrongfully dispossesses a Scheduled Caste or Scheduled Tribe from his/her land or premises or interferes with the enjoyment of his/her rights over any land, premises or water (section 3(1)(v) SC/ST (Prevention of Atrocities) Act).

Suggestions to Ponder Upon

- Appoint statutory committees with experts at national and states levels under the National Commission for Scheduled Castes and Scheduled Tribes to identify all lands illegally dispossessed from Dalits and restore the same to them with land title deeds within a specified time.
- Appoint special courts to initiate proceedings within a specified timeframe against all the illegal occupants of Dalit's lands and take punitive measures against the land encroachers.
- Fully implement land reforms and land ceiling laws through all possible measures, including the distribution of surplus land, government revenue lands and temple lands within a specific timeframe, so as to guarantee to every landless Dalit family a minimum of 3 acres of cultivable land to be registered in the name of the Dalit woman of the household.
- Issue strict guidelines to ensure that eligible poor Dalits and Adivasis can access development programmes like DPAP, DRDA and SJRY meant for these below the poverty line, and make key postings to these programmes open to officer from Dalit and Adivasi communities.
- Appoint a special agency to monitor the allocation and expenditure of funds under the Special Component Plan meant specifically for Dalit development.
- Where surplus land or common property resources are not available, focus upon the development of non-farm employment opportunities in rural areas to provide gainful and continuous employment to Dalits.

- Specifically include women, particularly single or landless women with preference given to Dalit and Adivasi women, in all development schemes to ensure they receive a fair share of the benefits.
- Work out short-term and long-term rehabilitation programmes for Dalit and Adivasi communities who have lost their lands and livelihoods due to government or World Bank funded development projects, or due to land appropriation by MNCs.
- Ensure that all future plans and schemes of investments involve local communities and make them priority stakeholders in all development projects.

Impact of Globalization on Right to Labour and Employment Opportunities for Dalits

(1) There are more Dalit wage labourers : Inadequate access to land (a fixed capital asset) has resulted in an exceptionally high dependence of Dalit households on manual wage labour. In 2000, Scheduled Caste wage labour dependent households accounted for 65% of rural and urban Scheduled Caste households.

(2) Dalits have moved from self-employment to wage labour: There has been deterioration in the quality of employment for Dalits in the 1990s, which coincides with the government's liberalisation policy. During the 1990s the percentage of households engaged in agriculture as self-employed cultivators has declined, accompanied by a corresponding increase in agricultural labour households and those in non-farm self-employment activities.

(3) Urban Dalits have moved from regular labour to casual labour : There has been a noticeable negative change in the employment pattern in urban areas as well in the 1990s, with an increased casualisation of Scheduled Caste labour. The percentage of Scheduled Caste regular wage earners has significantly declined, indicating their inability to participate in an equal measure in the salaried sector as in other sectors. There has been a greater shift towards self-employment and casual labour. This, in fact, reverses the trend of the 1980s, during which the proportion of both casual labourers and self-employed had declined by a substantial margin.

(4) Privatization has increased unemployment for urban Dalits : The trend in the unemployment rate in urban areas indicates that there has been a steady decline in the unemployment rate based on all status during the period 1977 to 1993. From the 1990s (1993-1999), however, there has been a complete reversal with an increase in the unemployment rate, especially in rural areas. There has been substantial reduction in regular salaried jobs in the public sector due to privatization.

(5) Privatization is leading to de-reservation by the backdoor : As part of the government's neo-liberal economic policy many public sector industries have been nationalised, and in many sectors in future the private sector will be the major player. While non-Dalits with their higher human resource development have gained more from new private sector jobs, Dalits have not likewise gained due to poorer human resources due to caste discrimination preventing access to education and skills, and employment discrimination.

(6) Credit market is also being liberalized : Privatization of banking and financial institutions as part of the liberalization policy has led to the gradual removal of priority lending and lending to Dalits and other poor. The banking sector was nationalised in 1969 precisely because it almost completely ignored the rural sector and the poor. Changes in the credit policy based on commercial considerations have reduced priority lending from 18% to 13% already, directly affecting the flow of funds to Dalits.

Persistence of Chronic Poverty

Poverty among Dalits continues to be high. In the year 2000 around 43% of Scheduled Caste persons were below the poverty line both in rural and urban areas, which is indeed higher as compared to 23% among other communities. Poverty is particularly high among Dalit wage labourers, i.e. 60%. Since 1983-84 there has been a decline in the poverty ratio for both Scheduled Castes and others in rural and urban areas. However, the decline in poverty for Scheduled Castes has been much lower in the 1990's by comparison, which means that the rate of poverty decline for Scheduled Castes has slowed down significantly in the 1900's.

National and International Safeguards

- To safeguard the right to work, which includes the right of everyone to an opportunity to gain her / his living by work which she/he freely chooses or accepts (Article 6 International Covenant on Economic, Social and Cultural Rights).
- To raise levels of nutrition and the standard of living (Article 47 Indian constitution : Directive Principles of State Policy).
- To ensure its citizens are free from hunger by taking measures, including specific progammes and agrarian reforms, which are needed to ensure food security for all (Article 11(2) International Covenant on Economic, Social and Cultural Rights).
- To protect the right of rural women to freedom from gender discrimination in their enjoyment of the right to adequate living conditions such as food security (Article 14 Convention on the Elimination of all forms of Discrimination Against Women).
- To protect the right of every child to a decent standard of living in order to ensure his / her development and well being (Article 27 Convention on the Rights of the Child).
- To make effective provision, within the limits of its economic capacity and development, for securing the right to work *(Article 41 Indian Constitution: Directive Principles of State Policy).*
- To secure for all workers a living wage, conditions of work ensuring a decent standard of life... and, in particular, promote cottage industries on an individual or cooperative basis in rural areas *(Article 43 Indian Constitution: Directive Principles of State Policy).*
- To make provision for reservations in matters of promotion of any classes of posts in government services in favour of Scheduled Castes and Scheduled Tribes to ensure their representation in these services *(Article I6A Indian Constitution Fundamental Rights).*

- To promote with special care the economic interests of the weaker sections of society, in particular the Scheduled Castes *(Article 46 Indian Constitution: Directive Principles of State Policy).*
- To safeguard the right to work, which includes the right of everyone to an opportunity to gain her/his living by work which s/he freely chooses or accepts *(Article 6 International Covenant on Economic, Social and Cultural Rights).*

Suggestion to ponder upon

- Provide subsidy measures to Dalit farmers so as to ensure their income and livelihood and prevent them from having to migrate to cities in search of work.
- Take every effort to restore wherever needed and to implement fully and effectively the PDS system in favour of Dalits and others belonging to the BPL category in a way that ensures the price of commodities are affordable and the PDS centres accessible.
- Bring in legislation to prevent all international and national institutions from making any inroad into the vital areas of human life such as food, water, labour, health and education.
- Eliminate child labour by ensuring allocation of sufficient funds to the National Child Labour Programme (NCLP), with a specially monitored commitment to eliminating this abhorrent form of labour within 5 years.
- Expand the value chain of agricultural production, providing assured markets for Dalit farmers that would enable them to diversify into higher value horticultural crops, as well as expanding employment by creating high quality non-agricultural.
- Fill up immediately all backlog vacancies under the reservation quota in both central and state government services and autonomous public bodies.
- Provide an enabling environment for the growth of small-scale industries and the informal sector where Dalits are concentrated by, for example, providing higher wages,

removing legal hurdles and putting in place social security measures.

- Give promotional support to small-scale industries such as technical assistance, market assistance and information to Dalit entrepreneurs.
- Review all laws and policies from the perspective of Dalit workers to ascertain any need to liberalize or change those laws and policies found to be anti-Dalit or anti-poor.
- Undertake a concerted and time-bound effort to promote improvement in the educational levels of Dalits, as well as the skill levels of working Dalits consistent with their level of education, and accordingly make radical changes to budget allocations for this effort.
- Make the reservation policy into law so as to ensure legally enforceable reservations for Dalits and Adivasis in both the public and private sectors.

Impact of Globalization on Right to Educational Opportunities and Access to Healthcare Facilities for Dalits

The impact of globalization on educational opportunities and access to healthcare for Dalits needs to be understood against the already existing exclusion in these sectors. Large gaps in literacy rates and levels of education between Dalits and others, high dropout levels for Dalit children from school, poor quality of education and caste-gender discrimination in schools are some of the problems faced by Dalits. There is also a wide gap between Scheduled Castes and others in health status and access to health services. High morbidly and child mortality among Scheduled Castes is closely linked with poverty and low educational status, and with discrimination in access to health services. The major impact of economic reforms in India under globalization is the reduction of government spending on public health and the withdrawal, therefore, of the government from fulfillment of the constitutional obligations.

(1) Privatization and commercialization of education : The government's withdrawal from the education sector, paving the way for privatization and commercialization of education, departs from its duty to promote and provide free education for Dalits.

Commercialization of education will reduce Dalits access due to inability to afford the higher cost of private schools.

(2) **Privatization will promote gender inequity among Dalits** : The present low literacy rate among Dalit girls will not improve due to the mere fact that Dalit boys will be preferred over the girls for increasingly costly education.

(3) **Consequences of globalization** : Manifested through high rates of illiteracy, poverty and discrimination will reduce the capacity of Dalits to demand, access and utilize public health services.

(4) Privatization does not guarantee access : Many Dalit villages are still unable to access public or private health facilities due to long distances from their villages, prevalence of untouchability practices in healthcare institutions, and/or negligence of health institutions in visiting their villages.

National and International Safeguards

- To provide, within a period of 10 years from the commencement of this Constitution, for free and compulsory education for all children until they complete the age of 14 years *(Article 45, Indian Constitution: Directive Principles of State Policy).*
- To promote with special care the educational interests of the weaker sections of the people, in particular the Dalits and Adivasis *(Article 47, Indian Constitution: Directive Principles of State Policy).*
- To recognize the right of children to education, to be achieved on the basis of equal opportunities.... to make educational and vocational information and guidance available and accessible to all *(Article 28 Convention on the Rights of the Child).*
- To recognize and achieve the right to education for all citizens, the government must do the following:
  (a) Make primary education compulsory and available free to all;
  (b) Make secondary education, including technical and vocational, generally available and accessible to all, in particular by the progressive introduction of free education;

(c) Make higher education equally accessible to all on the basis of capacity, in particular by the progressive introduction of free education. *(Article 13 International Covenant on Economic, Social and Cultural Rights)*

- ***"Though the right to education is not stated expressly as a fundamental right, it is implicit in and flows from the right to life guaranteed under Article 21 [Constitution]"*** (Supreme Court Judgment, 1993 in Unnikrishnan Vs. State of Andhra Pradesh & others).
- The National Plan of Action 1992 prescribes ***"reduction of disparities by emphasis on girl's education and special measures for children belonging to Scheduled Caste/Scheduled Tribe communities."***
- To raise levels of nutrition and the standards of living and to improve public health as one of the primary duties of governance (*Article 47 Indian Constitution: Directive Principles of State Policy*).
- ***To recognise:***

  (a) the right of everyone to just and favourable conditions of work that ensure safe and healthy working conditions;

  (b) the right to an adequate standard of living;

  (c) the right to the enjoyment of the highest attainable standard of physical and mental health;

The steps to be taken to achieve full realisation of this right shall include

(a) reduction of infant mortality and ensuring healthy child development;

(b) improvement of all aspects of environmental and industrial hygiene;

(c) prevention, treatment and control of epidemic, endemic, occupational and other diseases;

(d) creation of conditions which would assure medical services and medical attention to all. *(Articles 7, 11 and 12 International Covenant on Economic, Social and Cultural Rights)*

- To ensure the access of women to specific educational information in order to attain the health and well-being of families, including information and advice on family planning; and
- **To eliminate discrimination against women in healthcare so as to ensure:**
  - (a) on the basis of equality of men and women, access to healthcare services, including those related to family planning;
  - (b) appropriate services in connection with pregnancy. *(Articles 10 and 12 Convention on the Elimination of All Forms of Discrimination Against Women)*
- To eliminate racial discrimination and to guarantee the right of everyone, without distinction as to race, colour, or national or ethnic origin, to public health, medical care, social security and social services *(Article 5 Convention on the Elimination of All Forms of Racial Discrimination).*

Suggestions to ponder upon

- Chalk out a time-bound programme to provide compulsory, universal and free education for all Dalits.
- Allocate funds separately in the central and state government budgets for the education of Dalits proportionate to their numbers and levels of illiteracy.
- Ensure that SC/ST reserved panchayats have adequate power and authority to manage, control and regulate all the schools within their jurisdiction, and allocate adequate funds for this purpose.
- Set up "Dalit Women Education Committees" in each of the non-SC/ST reserved panchayats in order to monitor the overall functioning of the schools and teachers in the respective panchayats with regards to Dalit students, and allocate adequate funds for the functioning of these Committees.
- Conduct special trainings for Dalit students to secure admissions into public and private schools, colleges, professional and technical institutions.

- Provide enhanced scholarships to Dalit children as per their current needs.
- Ensure mandatory filling of reservation quotas for education and employment in all public institutions.
- Provide mandatory implementation of reservations in all private educational institutions at different levels, that is, from primary to technical and professional levels.
- Introduce a government-sponsored "Health Insurance Policy for All Dalits" in all the States and Union Territories.
- Abolish the policy of user-charges in public healthcare institutions.
- Establish a "Women Healthcare Statutory Commission" at Central and State Government levels with a view to monitoring the activities of public and private health institutions in the matter of protecting, defending and promoting the health rights of all women, especially Dalit women.
- Constitute "Dalit Women Health Monitoring Committees" in all the SC/ST reserved panchayats and provide them with adequate powers to supervise the functioning of the Primary Healthcare Centers and to take penal action against offenders as and when required.
- Allot funds to civil society bodies working with and for Dalits in order to impart health rights awareness and information to Dalits, especially children.
- Declare health rights violations against Dalits as "atrocities" and as such bring them under the ambit of the *SC/ST (Prevention of Atrocities) Act.*
- Ensure the regular release of funds for the health sector by the state governments' Social Welfare Departments under the Special Component Plan.
- Reduce infant and child mortality among the Dalit population to at least on par with the non-Dalit population within the next 5 years, and thereafter ensure steps to totally eliminate this problem.

- Provide all Dalit villages with proper transportation facilities to enable access to good and affordable healthcare facilities.
- Establish Primary Healthcare Centres and Sub-Centres in all the Dalit villages within the next 5 years.
- Set up special healthcare facilities and provisions for Dalits in primary, secondary and tertiary level hospitals.
- Regulate the private health sector by reserving a proportionate amount of services for marginalized groups, especially Dalits, at concessional fee rates.
- Provide all forms of important life-saving/costly drugs free of cost to Dalits.
- Ensure the eradication of untouchables in both public and private sector healthcare institutions through strict monitoring and enforcement of penalties for offenders.

Impact on Right to Water

Water serves both an economic as well as social function, especially in a highly agrarian set-up such as rural India, where the livelihood of millions of farmers depends upon adequate irrigation sources for crops from which millions obtain their staple foods. However, for the 160 million Dalits in India, access to water is a daily exercise of discrimination, humiliation and subjugation. It has provoked countless clashes, from heated verbal exchanges to more disturbing acts of violence and socio-economic boycotts. In India, Dalits, right to water is grossly violated with religious and social sanction.

Globalization and Water Accessibility, Availability and Quality

WTO/GATS, the World Bank, IMF, Asian Development Bank and other international money lending agencies are pushing for water privatization in India. Where water rights to major rivers and other irrigation sources supporting the livelihoods of small farmers and fishermen living by these sources are transferred to a private corporation without local community participation, the local community loses access to their source of livelihood. Private corporations divert water to large industrial belts and urban areas that can afford to pay for the increased costs.

The World Bank and IMF combine push water privatization as a pre-condition for loans. The result is a guaranteed profit margin to the investing corporation. They encourage cutting subsidies to those who cannot afford to pay, or increasing tariffs to take water supply out of the reach of India's poor. In 2000, 12 out of 40 IMF loans had requirements for partial or full privatization of water supply.

National and International Safeguards

- To raise levels of nutrition and the standard of living [includes right to water] *(Article 47 Indian Constitution: Directive Principles of State Policy).*
- To ensure the right to an adequate standard of living for the health and well-being of every person, [including the right to water] *(Article 11(1) International Covenant on Economic, Social and Cultural Rights).*
- To guarantee freedom from gender discrimination for rural women in their enjoyment of the right to adequate living conditions such as water supply *(Article 14(1) Convention on the Elimination of Discrimi-nation against Women).*
- To legally penalise any non-SC/ST who corrupts or fouls the water of any spring, reservoir or any other water source ordinarily used by Dalits or Adivasis *(Section 3(i) (xiii) SC/ST (Prevention of Atrocities) Act).*

Suggestions to ponder upon

- Elaborate and adopt plans, policies and programmes with sufficient funds and adequate monitoring, with regards to control and access to water sources, particularly for potable water supply. All such programmes and policies should contain clear guidelines in order to secure Dalits' right to water.
- Ensure that decisions about allocation and distribution of water resources are placed under democratic public control and Dalits have stakes in any such decisions.
- Declare water a permanent public utility and keep it out of the domain of WTO/GATS and private corporations, accordingly banning privatization of water supplies.

- Ensure that development or assistance projects that intergovernmental organisations, including inter-national financial institutions, and international donor agencies support take into account the economic and social situation of Dalits and work with this community in particular to ensure their right to water and other basic rights.

How Dalit Women are affected by Globalization

Dalit women, discriminated on the basis of caste, class and gender, are affected by globalization in a specific way due to the following factors:

(a) 71% of them work as agricultural labourers.

(b) Only 23% of them are literate.

(c) Their school dropout rate is an alarmingly high 64%.

(d) They have the highest work participation rate among women.

(e) They also suffer from reduced access to house amenities and poor health conditions.

(f) They are victims of sexual harassment and attacks by dominant caste men.

Globalization - induced reduction of government expenditure on social services has a direct impact on the health, education, security, development and livelihood of Dalit women. So too changing labour policies that affect this key labour force.

National and International Safeguards

- To ensure no discrimination on the grounds of caste and sex with regards to government or public employment (Article 16 Indian Constitution : Fundamental Rights).
- To ensure men and women have equally the right to an adequate means of livelihood (Article 39(a) Indian Constitution : Directive Principles of State Policy).
- To ensure equal pay for equal work for both men and women (Article 39(d) Indian Constitution : Directive Principles of State Policy).

- To renounce any practice which is derogatory to the dignity of women (Article 15 (a) Indian Constitution: Fundamental Rights).
- To ensure to women equal rights with men in the areas of education, economic and social life (Article 9 and 10 Convention on the Elimination of All Forms of Discrimination Against Women).
- To Prevent discrimination against women, which is fundamentally unjust and constitutes an offence against human dignity (Article 1 Convention on the Elimination of all Forms of Discrimination Against Women).

Suggestions to Ponder Upon

- Adopt and implement policies and measures to enable Dalit women to gain a minimum of 5 acres of cultivable land, registered in their name.
- Implement reservations in employment in both the public and private sectors for Dalit women, and specifically target Dalit women for capacitation and placement in reserved jobs.
- Take into account in all programmes and project planning free education at the formal schooling, technical and professional education levels for Dalit girls.
- Implement appropriate measures to prevent globalization exacerbating the situation of Dalit women's unemployment and poverty, including evolving national and state level perspective plans for mainstreaming Dalit women into developmental programmes and market enterprises.

Violence Against Dalits

Dalits continue to suffer from practices of untouchability and discrimination in public spheres. The following figures tell the story. During the 16-year period between 1981 and 2000 a total of 3,57,945 cases of crimes and atrocities were reported as committed against Scheduled Castes in the country. The number would be much more if unreported cases were also included. Most violence cases are centred on economic issues. In the context of shrinking space for economic growth for Dalits due to globalization, it is clear that in future this caste violence is going to increase to the disadvantage of Dalits.

Conclusion

Notwithstanding the gains, the disparities between Dalits and other sections of Indian society in many areas such as land ownership and literacy still continue and are growing. Coupled with evidence of discrimination in various market and non-market transactions, including access to social services like education, health and housing and in political participation, the cumulative impact of these disparities is reflected in high levels of poverty among Dalits as compared to other communities.

Dalits also suffer from continuing human rights violation and atrocities, which shows the magnitude of social and economic discrimination against Dalits in modern India. This also shows that there is a long way to go before Dalits can begin to imagine some degree of respectable and dignified life and livelihood. It is true, the Dalit situation today is somewhat better than what it was sixty years ago in terms of some Dalit households having acquired access to land and non-land capital assets from which they were previously prohibited. In urban areas 38% of Scheduled Castes have found employment due to the reservation policy. The literacy rate has slowly increased. As a cumulative impact of all these factors, the poverty rate for Dalits has slowly declined.

However, these little gains can also partly be attributed to factors such as anti-discrimination laws, government participation in economic and social governance and welfare measures. Another established truth is that all these small gains and the impact thereof are set to be wiped out with the New Economic Policy. Faced with this grim prospect, Dalits need to oppose the dominant processes of globalization.

REFERENCES

Gail Omvedt; *Dalit and Democratic Revolution, 1993,* Sage Publications India Pvt Ltd, New Delhi.

G.S. Bhargava and R.M. Pal *Human of Dalits Societal Violations,* 1999, Ganga Publishing House, New Delhi.

Om Prakash Sangwan, *Social System and the Dalit Identity*, Commonwealth Publishers, New Delhi.

Lal Prakash, *Globalization of Capital*, 1997, Rajwatpal Singh Publications, New Delhi.

S. Sivaram, *Globalization the Indian Scenario*, 1996.

Amrutha Sharma, *Caste in Social India*, 2001, Rajat Publications, New Delhi.

Dalits in the world of globalization, 1999, National Campaign on Dalit Human Rights-India, Secunderabad.

James Massey, *Dr. B. R. Ambedkar, A Study in just Society*, 2003. Lord son publishers, New Delhi.

Robert Deliege, Translated by David Phillips, *The World of the 'Untouchables' Pariars of Tamil Nadu*, 1997, Oxford University Press, New Delhi.

Baldevraj Nair, *Globalization and Nationalism*, 2001, Sage Publications, New Delhi.

Ram Sharan Sharma, *Sudras in Ancient India*, 1958, Motilal Banarasi Das Publishers, New Delhi.

Indian Journal of Human Rights, Vol. 6, No. 1 and 2, Jan - Dec 2002, University of Hyderabad, Hyderabad.

18

Status of Tribal Development in India : A Human Rights Perspective*

Introduction

The Scheduled Tribes were identified on the basis of certain well defined criteria including the traditional homeland of a definite geographical area, distinctive culture including shyness of contact, occupational traits such as pre-agricultural modes of cultivation and general lack of development. This list of scheduled tribes was notified by the President of India in accordance with the provisions of Article 342 of the Constitution of India. For the tribal population, there has always been a close traditional association with a territory or a tribal domain with the tribal community enjoying a collective command over the natural resources. There are certain states and union territories which are almost exclusively tribal such as Nagaland, Mizoram, Meghalaya and Lakshadweep. There are other areas or states where there is a substantial tribal population. The tribal areas are often hilly with large forest cover, undulating, with poor infrastructure and sparsely populated. The tribal economy revolves largely around land and land based resources, but land is more than a source of livelihood for the scheduled tribes. This paper discusses briefly about the Forest Rights Bill 2005 and concludes with some useful suggestions.

Many tribal groups practice shifting cultivation. A large number of tribal families dwell in the forests or live close to the forests and their economy is closely interlinked with the forest resources. The tribal tracts are often rich in minerals and natural resources.

---

*Paper presented at National Seminar on **"Tribal Development : A Myth or Pragmatic Reality?"**, during 26th and 27th February, 2007, organized by Department of Anthropology, S.V. University, Tirupati - 517 502, A.P.

The welfare and development of the members of the scheduled castes and scheduled tribes should be viewed at not merely in terms of material needs but equally or even more so in relation to non-material needs such as the right to live with freedom, human dignity and self respect. It is well known to any keen observer that throughout the whole of rural India, scheduled castes and scheduled tribes habitations are even today usually segregated, mostly on the outskirts of a village. The people belonging to scheduled castes and scheduled tribes, are indeed the labouring classes, on whose strength, sweat and toil the nation survives. But almost all of them suffered and continue to suffer from varying degrees of unfreedom and denial of human dignity. Untouchability is undoubtedly the worst form of inhuman indignity. The injustices suffered relate to property, wages and other resources on the one hand and person on the other. They lose their land and even when title over the land has been conferred, they have been prevented from occupying the land and cultivating it. There are severe problems in enjoying even the fruits of their own labour. The SCs, STs families in many villages have been in permissive possession of house sites or homesteads with constant threats of eviction by the landowners or even the state. In the urban areas, the problem is of living space itself, with just token space in unhygienic conditions and perpetual in security. The term slum clearance or encroachment removal is often an euphemism for uprooting the powerless migrates to low value sites, at the periphery leading to virtual economic extinction. The victims of custodial violence or illegal detention are mostly from the poor scheduled castes and scheduled tribes with little financial or political power to back them.

Despite various measures to improve the socio-economic conditions of the scheduled castes and the scheduled tribes, they remain vulnerable. They are denied a number of civil rights. They are subjected to various offences, indignities, humiliations and harassment. They have, in several brutal incidents, been deprived of their life and property. Serious crimes are committed against them for various historical, social and economic reasons. Because of the awareness created among the scheduled castes and the scheduled tribes through spread of education, they are trying to assert their rights and this is not being taken very kindly by others.

Occupation and the cultivation of even the government allotted land by the scheduled castes and the scheduled tribes is resented and more often these people become victims of attacks by the vested interests. Under the circumstances, the existing laws like the Protection of Civil Rights Act 1955, SC & STs (Prevention of Atrocities) Act 1989 and the normal provisions of Indian Penal Code have been found to be inadequate to check these crimes. A special legislation to check and deter crimes against them by non-scheduled castes and the scheduled tribes has therefore become necessary.

There are specific protective legislations and regulations for the scheduled tribes including laws and regulations under the Fifth Schedule of the Constitution prohibiting transfer of land to non-tribals, regulating and restricting money lending and trade and provision for monopoly rights in the collection and marketing of the tribal produce. The Sixth Schedule envisages a large measure of autonomy for the tribal areas in the form of Autonomous District Councils. The Panchayats (Extension to the Scheduled Areas) Act 1996, along with the conformity legislations of the states provides for a large degree of community management through the Gram Sabhas and empowers the tribal community to preserve and protect its interests and resources in the Fifth Schedule Areas. But these legislative measures are yet to be effectively translated into practice.

Since Independence, a variety of initiatives have been undertaken by the State for the socio-economic development of the scheduled castes and the scheduled tribes. They include an array of constitutional commitments and the enactment of a number of special legislations referred to earlier, reservations in public employment and in elected representative bodies, planned development programmes, budgetary allocations and in general, according to high priority in all the governmental activities. The series of land reform legislations, the land allotment rules and the myriad developmental programmes known as Poverty Alleviation Programmes, the scheme of reservations not only in public services but in various other fields including the allotment of land and housing, all these constitute positive measures intended to secure livelihood opportunities and enhance the well-being of these sections of the community.

Soon after Independence, the basic principles that should guide the approach to the development of the scheduled tribes were clearly set out by the former Prime Minister Jawaharlal Nehru in the form of five principles known as "Tribal Panchaseel" which was alter endorsed by the Renuka Ray team (1959), Dhebar Commision (1961) and the Shilu AO Committee (1969).

The Panchsheel laid down specifically:

- The tribal people should develop along the lines of their own genius and use should avoid imposing anything on them but rather try to encourage in every way their own traditional arts and culture.
- Tribal rights in lands and forests should be respected.
- We should try to train and build up a team of their own people to do administration and development.
- We should not over administer these areas or overwhelm them with multiplicity of schemes; we should rather work through and not in rivalry to their own social and cultural institutions.
- We should judge the results not by statistics or the amount of money spent but by the quality of human character that is evolved.

As the scheduled castes and scheduled tribes constitute a large segment of those below the poverty line, an overriding priority has been accorded to SC and ST families in all the Poverty Alleviation Programmes, particularly in the field of rural development. In the Integrated Rural Development Programme (IRDP), a minimum of 50 per cent of the total outlay was set aside for scheduled castes and scheduled tribes, they are also eligible for a higher subsidy of 50 per cent as against 25 per cent for others.

The Swarna Jayanthi Gram Swarozgar Yojana (SJSY) replaced the IRDP, TRYSEM, DWCRA, Million Wells scheme and Ganga Kalyan Yojana from April 1999. It has been stipulated that 50 per cent of Swarozgaris will be from scheduled castes and scheduled tribes. In sum, a policy of preference and exclusive allocation of funds under the various development and poverty alleviation programmes has been one of the significant features of the state efforts for the development of the scheduled castes and scheduled tribes in India.

Recently, the National Tribal Policy has also formulated some broad policy directions on the rehabilitation front incorporating the feedback from civil society. These principles acknowledge the tribal rights over forest resources and livelihood and are aimed at protecting the tribal interests in a holistic way.

Forest Rights Bill 2005

In keeping with the new policy framework and the pro-tribal policy priorities of the Common Minimum Programme (CMP), the UPA government has formulated the Scheduled Tribes (Recognition of Forest Rights) Bill, 2005 which aims to compensate the "historical injustice" done to forest dwelling tribes and provide the adivasis rights to forest resources. The bill for the first time recognises that tribals have rights over forests. The proposed forest rights include; the right to hold and live in the forest land, community rights over forest such as 'nistar', right of ownership access to use and dispose of minor forest produce, rights over disputed lands, rights for conversion of pattas or leases or grants on forest land into titles, rights of conversion of forest villages into revenue villages, right to manage any community forest resources, and any other traditional right enjoyed by the forest dwelling STs.

In concrete terms, the bill proposes pattas to forest lands occupied before 1980 but subject to a ceiling of 2.5 hectares per family. No tribal person is to be evicted from forest land until the process of determining rights is completed. The bill proposes wide-ranging powers for the gram sabha that include determining the nature and extent of forest rights, regulating access to forest resources and punishing those who violate the provisions.

Although the bill is a step in the right direction, it addresses tribal land issues in isolation from the related legislations on wildlife protection and forest conservation. Another weakness of the bill concerns the issue of displacement by development projects, the bill should clearly delineate the role of the gram sabha vis-a-vis development induced displacement. The rights proposed to be conferred with regard to the lands occupied before 1980 are essentially compensatory in nature. Because the bill tries to compensate the loss tribals suffered without looking at the processes that have resulted in land dispossession, nor does it refer to the failure of the state in restoring the alienated land and in providing adequate rehabilitation for the displaced. Because loss of land to non-tribals is among the major factors driving tribals to "encroach" on the forest land. The cut-off date of 1980 and the ceiling on the extent of land proposed to be regularised would drastically reduce the scope of the bill. It also excludes from its purview a large number of non-ST forest dwellers. Although the proposed legislation promises a great deal, the scepticism remains given the track record of the state in enforcing the earlier laws and the constitutional provisions.

Thus, very depressed, deprived and destitute tribals have already entered the process of development to some extent but they are still quite far away from the national levels of development and mainstream of economy and society.

Suggestions

- The tribal planning will be unreal, unless the cultural characteristics, environmental peculiarities and traditional skills etc. are not considered in the formulation of the developmental schemes.
- The basic question of tribal development is to stabilize the tribals in their area to discourage migration in search of work particularly in the rainy season. All the planning efforts of social development failed to deliver the goods due to their basic difficulty, hence tribal development has to concentrate on programmes.
- It is very essential to really emphasis on implemen-tation of the programmes when the actual outcome instead of target and quality along with quantitative change should be emphasized.
- A special planning will be required to develop agriculture for the tribals as per the geographical and ecological conditions to the tribal area impose limit on the degree to which tribal agriculture can be modernized.
- Traditionally tribals supplement their daily needs from forest produce and the forest department, therefore,

should evolve a scheme of forest management involving tribals assuring the minimum forest produce without damaging forests.

- There is a need to develop change in the mindset of tribals in a manner that they do not become victim of dependency syndrome but develop their confidence and capability.
- The participation of tribals in development plan has to be ensured by strategic efforts of promoting information system; delivery system, transparency and direct contacts of development agency.
- Finally, an intervention of few qualified NGOs, with appropriate administration of strong service motivation and professional competence, is absolutely essential to achieve expected tribal development objectives.

Conclusion

The welfare and development of scheduled castes and scheduled tribes since Independence has been rooted in the constitution which has been based on the values of equality, human dignity, social justice and the laws and policy prescription emanating from the constitutional mandates. However, in actual practice, there has been a disjunction between these values and the hierarchical and feudal values which continue to govern the society. On the one hand, the state has put in place laws, policies and programmes without which even the modest progress in the overall situation could not have been possible, on the other, these measures are as yet inadequate and have to be more effectively implemented to overcome the continued subordination of the scheduled castes and scheduled tribes. Commencing with the constitutional commitments and the special legislations to secure equality, human dignity and human rights, a large variety of measures have been taken up both as policy measures and developmental programmes in all the fields of development and welfare. The development of the members of the scheduled castes and scheduled tribes requires that there is not only a positive change in their socio-economic situation but that the rate of change is fast enough to ensure that the disparity in relation to the rest of the society is progressively minimised and ultimately eliminated altogether to facilitate the emergence of a just, human and equal society. Apart from the laws and state action, the society itself has to accept, imbibe and internalise the values of equality, non-discrimination, human rights, human dignity, justice and democratic practices. The development of scheduled castes and scheduled tribes is thus a part of a continued quest for equality and social justice, the objectives enshrined in the constitution and pursued since independence in free India.

REFERENCES

Government of India, Ministry of Social Justice and Empowerment, Annual Report, 1990-2000, New Delhi.

Government of India, Ministry of Tribal Affairs, Annual Report, 1999-2000, New Delhi.

Dr. Babasaheb Amedkar, Writings and Speechs, Government of Maharashtra Education Department, Bombay.

S.R. Sankaran, "Welfare of Scheduled Castes and Scheduled Tribes in Independent India—An Overview of State Policies and Programmes", *Journal of Rural Development*, A Quarterly of NIRD, Vol. 19, No. 4, October-December, 2000, Hyderabad.

S. Laxman Rao & Priya Deshingkar, "Tribal and Alienation in Andhra Pradesh Processes, Impacts and Policy Concerns", *Economic and Political Weekly*, Vol. XLI, No. 52, December 30, 2006, A Sameekhsa Trust Publication, Mumbai.

Dr. Dilip Shah, "Tribal Development: Planning and Performance", *Kurukshetra*, Vol. 51, No. 8, June 2003, Publication Division, Ministry of Rural Development, Govt. of India, New Delhi.

19

Right to Health with Special Reference to Vulnerable Groups*

"The enjoyment of the highest attainable standard of health is one of the fundamental rights of every human being without distinction of race, religion, political belief, economic or social condition," says the preamble to the constitution of the World Health Organisation (WHO) which was adopted two years earlier before the Universal Declaration of Human Rights was made.

The Right to Health in general, Article 25 of the Universal Declaration of Human Rights lays down that everyone has the right to a standard of living adequate for the health and well being of himself and his family, including food, clothing, housing and medical care and necessary social services, and the right to security in the event of unemployment, sickness, disability, widowhood, old age or other lack of livelihood in circumstances beyond his control. Article 12 of the International Covenant on Economic Social and Cultural Rights provides that right to enjoyment the highest attainable standard of physical and metnal health is recognized by every State party to the Government and they are under an obligation to take the following necessary steps for the full realisation of this right.

(a) To make provisions for the reduction of still-birth rate and of the infant mortality and for the healthy development of the child;

(b) To take steps for improvement of all aspects of environmental and industrial hygiene;

---

*Paper Presented at "First All India Conference of Social Sciences in Health", During November 14-15, 2003, Organised by Indian Society for Social Sciences in Health & Center for Women's Studies, Sri Padmavathi Mahila Viswa Vidyalayam, Tirupati.

(c) To take steps for prevention, treatment and control of epidemic, endemic, occupational and other diseases;

(d) The creation of condition which would assure to all medical service and medical attention in the event of sickness.

Linkages Between Health and Human Rights

The Scheduled Castes (SCs), Scheduled Tribes (STs) women and children are treated as vulnerable people in the society. The Scheduled Castes and Scheduled Tribes are most vulnerable when compared to the other people in the society. They live in unhygienic conditions, suffering with poverty, illiteracy, ill-health, malnutrition etc. This paper traces the different health problems faced by these people and the suggestions for the improvement of their conditions in the contemporary Indian society. And also analyses the health policies and programmes implemented by the government.

Impact of health policies, programmes and practices on human rights

The responsibilities of public health are carried in large measure through policies and programmes promulgated, implemented and enforced by or with support from the state. Therefore, this linkage may be best explored by considering the impact of public health policies, programmes and practices for the protection of health and human rights of SCs and STs. The three control functions of public health includes assessing health needs and problems; developing policies designed to address priority health issues; and assuring programmes to implement strategic health goals.

Health Impacts Resulting from Violations of Human Rights

Health impacts are obvious and inherent in the popular understanding of certain severe human rights violations of vulnerable groups, such as torture, imprisionment under inhuman conditions, summary execution, and "dis-appearances". For this reason, health experts concerned about human rights have increasingly made their expertise available to help document such abuses. Identification of health impacts associated with violations of rights and dignity will benefit both health and human rights fields. Using rights violations as an entry point for recognition of health problems may help uncover previously unrecognised burdens on physical, mental or social well-being. From a human rights perspective documentation of health impacts of rights violations may contribute to increased societal awareness of the importance of human rights promotion and protection.

World Health Organization (WHO) and "The Right to Health"

The "right to health" extends to all things, which promote health and well-being and prevent illness and diseases, not just access to medical care. This includes, among many others, the right to education, food and shelter, to freedom from discrimination and persecution to information and to the benefits of science.

Human Rights and Healthcare Professionals

As one of the most respected professions, health professionals hold a well-acknowledged commitment to the care of their patients. This provision of care, in the most basic and fundamental sense, includes a commitment to and advocacy for the patient's right to health.

The Relations between Health and Human Rights

1. Discrimination

Discrimination against ethnic religious and social communities, vulnerable groups as well as on account of gender, political opinion or immigration status, compromises or threatens the health and well-being and all too often, the very lives of millions. Discriminatory practices threaten physical and mental health and deny people access to care altogether, deny people appropriate therapies or relegate them to inferior care.

2. Health Policies that Violate Rights

Violations of human rights exist in the design and implementation of health policies. For example, population policies which fail to respect the conditions necessary for individual decision making are less effective. In the past few decades governments and international agencies have increasingly recognised that women must be able to make and effectuate free and informed choices about reproduction. Yet these choices are routinely infringed in the design and implementation of health policies, including clinical decisions.

3. Torture

Torture remains epidemic in most of the countries around the world. It brings both acute trauma and long-lasting physical or psychological suffering to victims, their loved ones, and society at large. Physicians themselves become complicit in torture when they certify individuals as able to withstand torture or falsify or fail to report evidence of torture in detention facilities.

4. Compromise of Medical Independence

People seeking health care are often denied the independent judgement of health professionals when the state imposes demands that the health professional show greater allegiance to the state ends than to the needs of the patient. Prisoners, detainees, undocumented immigrants, military personnnel and others are especially vulnerable to the effects of these conflicts of interest.

5. Lack of Access to Health Care

Throughout the world in countries rich and poor, people have no access to basic physical and mental health care and to immunization from infectious disease. Some people have no access because they lack the resources to buy it and the state does not provide it, others because there are no services available in their communities, and others because of discrimination or social stigma, such as their status as prisoners, detainees, refugees, immigrants or members of a lower class or caste such as SCs and STs.

6. Lack of Basic Sustenance

One fifth of the world's population lives in object poverty. They lack adequate food, clothing, housing, and social services and the opportunity to work. Extensive evidence, moreover, demonstrates that, in addition to absolute poverty, relative poverty within nations is associated with both diminished access to health care and to diminished health status.

7. Inhuman Labour Practices

Inhuman labour practices the world over significantly

compromise the health of millions. Vulnerable groups are under brutalizing, unsanitary and hazardous conditions for long hours or work without wages sufficient to support their families' basic needs.

8. Indiscriminate Harm from Weapons

Every human being's right to life is threatened by the existence and active deployment of the most destructive weapons ever devised nuclear, biological and chemical weapons. The lives and health of millions of people are jeoparadized daily by landmines, which kill and injure indiscriminately, and continue to do so for decades after the cessation of the conflict.

9. Denial of Dignity

Respect for human dignity is an essential element of health and well being for all people. In clinical settings, failure to respect dignity has stigmatized people with conditions such as HIV / AIDS and mental or physcial disabilities and resulted in denial of access to apropriate treatment and or being subjected to inappropriate clinical interventions or un-warranted longterm institutionalization.

10. Unethical Research Practices

Conventional practices in biomedical and behavioural research all too often violate human rights. Contemporary medical research studies often lack adequate informed consent procedures and have disproportionate risks in relation to benefits. Some members of the medical research community continue to use vulnerable populations for human experimentation at great detriment to their physical and mental health.

11. Lack of Education

Although education is one of the strongest predictors of health status and an intrinsic quality of well-being, more than 900 million adults are illiterate, two-thirds of whom are women and more than 300 million children are not in primary or secondary school. Most of these people belongs to vulnerable groups. Health professionals should promote adequate standards of education, which include human rights concerns, because these standards promote health and dignity of all members of the human family.

12. Exposure to Dangerous Environment

Prevention of environmental hazards, and mitigation of these hazards where they exist are critical factors in the promotion of health and the prevention of illness. Selective pollution areas like slums in urban areas without proper sanitation facilities, safe drinking water, unfit habitations in which poor or vulnerable people or others susceptible to discriminate life, often termed "environmental injustice", are an egregious form of denial of human rights.

Conclusion

From the perspective of human rights, health experts and expertise may contribute productively to societal recognition of the benefits and costs associated with realizing or failing to respect human rights and dignity. This can be accomplished without seeking to justify human rights and dignity on health grounds. In addition, the right to health can only be developed and made meaningful through dialogue between health and human rights discipliners. However, meaningful dialogue about interactions between health and human rights requires a common ground. The importance of health as a pre-condition for the capacity to realize and enjoy human rights and dignity must be appreciated.

The mutually enriching combination of research, education and field experience will advance understanding and catalyze further action around human rights and health. The health and human rights perspectives offers new avenues for understanding and advancing human well-being in the modern world.

20

Constitutional Provisions for the Protection of Human Rights of SC and STs

Introduction

The term Scheduled Caste has a long historical origin. Prior to the year 1935, when the Government of India Act was enacted, the communities suffering from the stigma of untouchability were being referred to as *'untouchables'* or *exterior castes* or *depressed classes* or by various caste names most of which were derogatory. As a part of the social and political changes sought to be introduced in the year 1935, the various castes which suffered social disabilities were listed in a schedule and from then, they came to be described as Scheduled Castes. After the Constitution of India was enacted, the list of Scheduled Castes was notified by the President of India in accordance with the provisions of Article 341 of the Constitution. The Scheduled Castes thus represent a constitutionally declared *collection of castes, communities* or *groups* their defining characteristic being the suffering from the traditional practice of untouchability. In terms of the provisions in Article 341, the Scheduled Castes have been specified separately in relation to each of the States and Union Territories. Seven Presidential orders have so far been issued specifying the lists of Scheduled Castes (SCs) in various States and Union Territories 471 communities.

The Scheduled Tribes (STs) were identified on the basis of certain well defined criteria including the *traditional homeland of a definite geographical area, distinctive culture* including *shyness of contact, occupational traits* such as *preagricultural modes of cultivation and general lack of development*. The list of Scheduled Tribes was notified by the President of India in accordance with the provisions of Article 342 of the Constitution. Nine Presidential orders have so far been issued specifying the list of Scheduled Tribes (STs) in various States and Union Territories were 540 tribes. This paper analyses the socio-economic and political problems faced by the SCs and STs, the various Constitutional safeguards and special protections provided by the Indian Constitution.

Problems of Disadvantage Groups

The different problems faced by the disadvantage people in Indian society are categorised as follows:

1. Social problems
2. Educational and economic problems
3. Political problems

Social Problems

(a) Violation of rights such as the right to life with freedom, human dignity and self-respect.

(b) It is well known to any keen observer that throughout the whole of rural India, Scheduled Caste habitations are even today usually segregated, mostly on the outskirts of a village.

(c) The people belonging to Scheduled Castes and Scheduled Tribes are treated as untouchables and labour classes.

(d) Untouchability is undoubtedly the worst form of inhuman dignity.

(e) The victims of custodial violence or illegal detention are mostly from the poor Scheduled Castes and Scheduled Tribes.

(f) They are denied a number of civil rights. They are subjected to various offences, indignities, humiliations and harassment.

(g) They have, in several brutal incidents, been deprived of their, life and property.

(h) Serious crimes are committed against SC/STs for various historical, social and economic reasons.

(i) The dehumanizing practice of manual scavenging is yet another blot on the Indian society.

(j) Discrimination on caste basis at public places, wells, tanks, hotels and restaurants.

(k) Practice of bonded labour and slavery.

Educational and Economic Problems

(a) Discrimination in Educational Institutions based on Caste.

(b) Village tea shops are recent phenomenon in many villages. With this has started a variety of discriminatory practice such as no seating, separate seating, separate glasses, usually, old, dirty and cracked or chipped ones.

(c) Majority of the bonded labour belong to Scheduled Caste and Scheduled Tribes.

(d) The injustices suffered relate to property, wages and other resources on the one hand and the person on the other.

(e) The SC/STs lose their land and even when title over the land has been conferred, they have been prevented from occupying the land and cultivating it.

(f) The SC/STs families in many villages have been in permissive possession of housesites or homesteads with constant threats of eviction by the landowners or even the State.

(g) Practice of paying low wages to the agricultural labourers and unorganized labourers.

(h) Caste discrimination and practice of untouchability, severe discrimination against women usury and indebtedness, widespread illiteracy and terribly low rate of education among poor.

(i) The structure of surplus labour, unemployment and under employment, inequitable distribution of land and assets, low wages, distress migration and unjust social institutions result in an environment which lead to the emergence and perpetuation of bonded labour.

(j) There are also large number of bonded labourers in brick kilns, stone quarries, lime stone mines, match factories, carpet weaving, irrigation works and a variety of other occupations are mostly from there two sections.

(k) Practice of bonded labour, migrant labour, contract labour, and child labour affects the economic rights of the SC/STs.

Political Problems

The political rights like right to vote and right to contest in the elections are completely denied in the case of socially, economically disadvantaged people. *For Example:* The votes of the SC/STs are mainly denied and rigged by the upper caste people according to their favourite leaders. In this manner "The right to Vote" is being denied to them.

The reserved seats in Panchayats are also not properly enjoyed by the disadvantaged groups. The upper caste people denied this right by threatening in different ways and not allowing them to contest from these seats.

As described above the socially, economically disadvantaged groups have still experiences the different problems in social, economic, educational and political fields in their day-to-day life.

Nature of violence of Dalit Human Rights violation are as follows: Murder, social boycott, rapes, naked parading, attacks, deaths in custody, seizure and destruction of property, practice of untouchability, caste discrimination in State.

Constitutional Safeguards

Fundamental Rights and Directive Principles under the Constitution

The Indian Constitution, as set out in its Preamble, is a testament to secure to all its citizens Justice - Social, Economic and Political; Liberty of thought and expression, belief, faith and worship. Equality of status and of opportunity and fraternity assuring the dignity of the individual and integrity of the nation. The founding fathers of the Constitution, especially Babasaheb Dr. Bhim Rao Ambedkar who was the Chairman of the Drafting Committee, was acutely aware of the iniquitous forces embedded in the social systems, economic institutions and political organisations in India in relation to the weaker sections and vulnerable sections of the society and therefore, considered it necessary to provide for specific corrective measures and mandates in the Constitution in their favour.

The safeguards for the members of the scheduled castes relate to the removal of the disabilities as well as positive measures to enable them to acquire a dignified position in the national life. The major concern about the members of the scheduled tribes has been that of protecting and preserving their command over natural resources and the best in their tradition. The Indian Constitution is a unique document which provides for a comprehensive framework for the socio-economic advancement of the scheduled castes and the scheduled tribes to achieve the objective of a just and humane society. The Constitution incorporated a number of commands for the elimination of the inequities and inequalities prevalent in the Indian society and for promoting equality and social justice. The Constitutional perspective combines both the positive notion of rights guaranteed through the State and law as well as the notion of natural rights and includes horizontal rights applicable to all citizens and vertical rights to enhance the life chances of vulnerable groups such as scheduled castes, scheduled tribes.

The following are the Fundamental Rights provided in Part III of the Constitution of India.

Social Safeguards

The social safeguards provides protection against the social problems like abolition of untouchability prohibition of discrimination on grounds of caste, race, sex, access to public places, wells, tanks, hotels, restaurants etc. Prohibition of forced labour and throwing open Hindu religious institutions etc.

Equality before Law

The state shall not deny to any person equality before law or the equal protection of the laws within the territory of India (Article-14).

Prohibition of discrimination on grounds of religion, race, caste, sex or place of birth.

Article-15

(i) The state shall not discriminate any citizen on grounds only of religion, race, caste, sex, place of birth or any of them,

(ii) No citizen shall, on grounds of religion, race, caste, sex, place of birth or any of them, be subjected to any disability, liability, restriction or conditions with regard to—

(a) access to shops, public restaurants, hotels and places of public entertainment; and

(b) the use of well, tanks, bathing ghats, roads and places of public resort maintained wholly or partly out of State funds or dedicated to the use of the general public.

Abolition of Untouchability

Article-17-"Untouchability" is abolished and its practice in any form is forbidden. The enforcement of any disability arising out of "Untouchability" shall be an offence and punishable in accordance with law.

Rights against Exploitation

Article-23 (1)-Traffic in human beings and beggar is and other similar forms of forced labour are prohibited and any contravention of this provision shall be an offence punishable in accordance with law.

Article-25 (2) (b)-Providing for social welfare and reform or the throwing open of Hindu religious institution of public character to all classes and sections of Hindus.

Educational and Economic Safeguards

These safeguards provides and promotes economic rights of the Scheduled Castes and Scheduled Tribes in the form of 'Reservations' for admissions in educational institutions, reservation in public employment, claims in appointments to the services, promotion of educational and economic interests and protection from social injustice and all forms of exploitation.

Article-15 (4)-"Nothing in this article or in clause (2) of Article 29 shall prevent the State from making any special provision for the advancement of any socially and educationally backward classes of citizens or for the Scheduled Castes and the Scheduled Tribes.

Article-16 (4)—"Nothing in this Article shall prevent the State from making any provision for the reservation of appointments or post in favour of any backward class of citizens which, in the opinion of the state, is not adequately represented in the services under the State".

Article-29 (2)—"No citizen shall be denied admission into any educational institution maintained by the state or receiving aid out of State funds on grounds. Only of religion, race, caste, language or any of them."

Artide-24-Banned the employment of children below fourteen years in any factory or mine or hazardous occupations.

Directive Principles as Constitutional Safeguards

An important part of the Constitution and of great significance to the poor is the Directive Principles of State Policy which are fundamental in the governance of the country.

Article-38-This article envisages a social order in which justice social, economic and political will inform all institutions of national life and the endeavour required on the part of the State to minimize inequalities in income, status and opportunities.

Article-39-It visualises, among others, the right to adequate means of livelihood; the equitable control and ownership of the material resources of the community and that the operation of the economic system doesn't result in concentration of wealth and means of production to the common detriment. It also envisages equal pay for equal work for men and women as well as opportunities for children to develop in a healthy manner and without exploitation.

Article-41-Stipulates that the State shall within the limits of its economic capacity and development make effective provision for securing the right to work, the right to education and to public assistance in cases of unemployment, old age, sickness and disablement and in other cases of undeserved want.

Artide-43-It calls upon the State to endeavour to secure a living wage to all the workers.

Article-45-Speaks of free and compulsory education for children until they complete the age of fourteen years.

Article-46-It mandates the state to promote with special case the educational and economic interests of the weaker sections of the people and in particular of Scheduled Castes and Scheduled Tribes and protect them from injustice and all forms of exploitation.

Legal Provisions

- Protection of Civil/Rights Act, 1955.
- The Scheduled Castes and Scheduled Tribes (Prevention of Atrocities) Act, 1989.
- Bonded Labour System (Abolition) Act 1986 (in respect of Scheduled Castes).
- The Child Labour (Prohibition and Regulation) Act 1986 (in respect of Scheduled Castes).
- State Acts and Regulations concerning alienation and restoration of land belonging to Scheduled Castes.
- Minimum Wages Act, 1948 (in respect of Scheduled Castes).
- The Employment of Manual Scavengers and Construction of dry latrines (Prohibition) Act, 1993.
- Laws to eliminate practice of Devadasi System.

Conclusion

The Constitutional safeguards for protection of Dalits remained only on paper and they were seldom translated into action. This is due to the apathy on the part of the State, and the law enforcing authorities. Caste has become Indian apartheid. The caste has survived not only the powerful impact of Buddhism, many centuries of Afghan, Moghal rule and inspite of Hindu, reformers who arised their voices against this caste discrimination. The caste system is alive today notwithstanding there is no law to enforce it. The status of Dalits and Tribes in Hindu Society is the lowest of the low.

The object of every religion is change of heart towards good. But inspite of its existence for thousands of years, the Hinduism failed to bring about a change of heart in the attitude of caste. Hindus towards their unfortunate untouchable brethren. The reason is that Hinduism carried caste system in its bosom althrough the ages. It is clear that caste is more of a divisive force than a cohesive force.

The depressed groups are the most disorganised people today. Education has only led to the emergence of an elite dalit class which had distanced from the Dalit movement. Inspite of religiously imposed caste, oppression on the dalits, some of the upper segment of the Dalits (who are advanced and developed by reservation system) are adopting Brahminical rites, rituals and all religious functions. Some of the Dalits, who are economically advanced may be under the mistaken impression that they are not affected by the caste disabilities such as untouchability, discrimination, inferior status by in virtue of their being rich. The question is whether one is leading dignified life of self-respect. In practice even the rich and highly educated dalits suffer from caste discrimination in one form or other. When millions of dalits suffer from discrimination, poverty, misery, the rich and advanced sections of dalits cannot be free from evils of caste system, in one way or other they have to suffer from the caste discrimination. It is like a person living with full comforts in a prison. The dalits are conditioned by the society consisting of iron bound caste, which is the peculiar set up of Indian Hindu society. The enjoyment of freedom by dalits is curtailed and conditioned by caste, even though the Constitution provides for sufficient provisions for ensuring civil liberties. In the Parliament and the Assemblies, the Dalit members belonging to different political parties are more loyal to the parties than to the millions of untouchables whom they represent. They remain silent even when worst carnages take place against

The Constitution is thus an instrument heavily weighed in favour of the weaker sections of the Indian society. Almost all the issues for which the poor struggle in their daily lives find a place in the Indian Constitution whether it is equality, freedom, human dignity, discrimination, social and economic justice, right to livelihood, right to work, living wage or protection from exploitation.

REFERENCES

R.R. Prasad (2000), *Journal of Rural Development,* Special issue on Welfare of Scheduled Castes and Scheduled Tribes in Independent India, part-l, Vol. 19, No. 4, October-December, NIRD, Hyderabad.

"Caste Action Programme", C.P.I. (M.L.), New Democracy, 2003, Hyderabad.

B. Myna Rao (2003), *Dalits should they Quit the Hindu Religion?*, Hyderabad.

D.D. Basu (1994), *Introduction to the Constitution of India,* New Delhi.

R.R. Prasad (2001), *Journal of Rural Development*, Special issue on Welfare of Scheduled Castes and Scheduled Tribes in Independent India, Part -II, Vol. 20, No. 1, January-March, NIRD, Hyderabad.

Prem. K. Shinde (2005), *Dalits and Human Rights*, Vol. 2, Dalits: Security and Rights Implications, Isha Books, New Delhi.

John. K. Thomas (2005), *Human Rights of Tribals*, Vol. 1, Status of Tribals in India, Isha Books, Delhi.

21

Federalism in India: Emerging Challenges

The Constitution of India provides for a federal system of government though the term "federation" has nowhere been used in the Constitution. On the other hand, Article 1 of the Constitution describes India as a "Union of States," an expression which has two implications. Firstly, unlike the USA, the Indian federation is not the result of agreement between the units. Secondly, the units have no right to secede from the federation.

It may be observed that the Indian Constitution does not possess all the features of a typical federation and makes numerous deviations. In view of these deviations the critics have challenged the federal character of the Constitution and described it as "quasi-federal". For example, Prof. K.C. Wheare says, "Indian Union is a unitary State with subsidiary federal features rather than a federal State with subsidiary unitary features." While Ivor Jennings characterises it as "a federation with a centralising tendency."

The federal features of the Indian Constitution are: written constitution, rigid constitution, division of powers, supremacy of the constitution, independent judiciary and bicameral legislature etc. It provides for a federal system for our country. "India, that is Bharat, shall be a union of States" is the expression used for our federation in the Constitution of India. India is federal in structure, but unitary in spirit as the distribution of powers between the centre and the states is in favour of the centre, which can be described under the heads centre-state legislative relations, centre-state administrative relations and centre-state financial relations.

Centre-State Legislative Relations

Legislative relations between the centre and the states have been spelt out in Articles 245-254 of the Constitution:

1. The Parliament can make laws for the whole or any part of the territory of India, while the state legislature can make laws for the whole or any part of the state.
2. The Constitution vests exclusive power in the parliament to make laws with respect to any matter enumerated in the union list, and in the state legislature to make laws for the state or any part thereof with respect to matters in the state list.
3. Both the centre and the states have been given power to make laws with respect to any of the matters enumerated in the concurrent list. In case of conflict between central and state law, the former prevails.
4. Power of parliament to provide for the establishment of certain additional courts.
5. Residuary power of legislation : The Constitution vests exclusive power to make laws with regard to residuary subjects (subjects not included in any of the three lists) in the parliament.
6. The Constitution also authorizes the parliament to legislate on any subject in the state list under the following conditions:
   (a) In the national interest, if Rajya Sabha passes a resolution.
   (b) Under a proclamation of National Emergency.
   (c) By agreements between states.
   (d) To implement treaty, agreement or conventions with any other country.
   (e) Under a proclamation of failure of the constitutional machinery in the states.
7. The centre exercise considerable control over legislative matters falling in the jurisdiction of the states, in the following cases:
   (a) Reservation of state bill by the governor for the consideration of the President.

(b) During the financial emergency, the President can direct the states to reserve money bill as well as other bills.

(c) The prior sanction of the President is necessary to introduce bills on certain matters of the State list.

Centre-state Administrative Relations

1. The executive power of every state shall be so exercised as to ensure compliance with the laws made by the parliament.
2. The executive power of every state shall be so exercised as not to impede the exercise of the executive power of the union. The central government is authorised to give such directions to a state as may appear to be necessary for that purpose.
3. The Constitution authorises the President to delegate with the consent of the government of the state, any function in relation to any matter to which the executive power of the union extends.
4. The states can also delegate certain functions to the centre with regard to matters to which the executive power of the states extends.
5. The Constitution says that full faith and credit shall be given throughout the territory of India to public acts, records and judicial proceedings of the Union and of every state.
6. Parliament may by law provide for the adjudication of any dispute or complaint with respect to the use, distribution or control of the waters of, or in, any inter-state river or river valley dispute and also provide for the exclusion of the jurisdiction of all courts, including the Supreme Court, to entertain such disputes.
7. The President can establish an inter-state council for enquiring into and advising upon inter-state disputes, if at any time it appears to him that the establishment of such council would be served by the public interest.

8. The President of India appoints the state governors. The state governors act as the agents of the union government. The governors submit periodical reports to the centre about the conditions in their states.
9. The central government dispatches the Central Reserve Police (CRP) to the states for tackling any situation of disturbance affecting law and order conditions in the states.
10. The President of India is empowered to constitute a joint public service commission to serve needs of two or more states.
11. The central government can exercise control over the state administration through its right to appoint enquiry commissions against the chief ministers for their acts of omissions and commissions.
12. The Comptroller and Auditor General of India supervises the auditing and maintenance of financial accounts of all the states through Accountant Generals under his control.
13. The zonal councils have been established by the State Reorganisation Act of 1956 with a view to securing co-operation and co-ordination between the states, the union territories and the union, particularly in respect of economic and social development.
14. The personnel of All India Services working in the states are appointed by the central government. They are governed by the rules, regulations and service conditions laid down by the central government.
15. The judges of the state high courts are appointed, transferred or removed by the union government.
16. The Constitution also provides for creation by the parliament common high courts for two or more states. For example, the states of Assam and Nagaland have a common high court.
17. The Constitution authorises the centre to impose the President rule in the state if there is a breakdown of constitutional machinery in the state.

18. There are other extra-constitutional and informal devices for securing consultations between the centre and the states and for bringing about co-operation and co-ordination between the States. Regular conferences are being held as a matter of practice like annual conferences of chief ministers, governors, chief secretaries etc.

Centre-state Financial Relations

1. The legislative power to make laws for imposing a tax is divided between the union and the states by means of specific entries in the union and state legislative lists in Schedule VII of the Constitution. There is no concurrent list in the matter of tax legislation.
2. Taxes belonging to the centre exclusively like custom duties and corporation tax etc.
3. Taxes belonging to the states exclusively like sales tax, motor vehicle tax, entertainment tax etc.
4. Duties levied by the union but collected and appropriated by the states like excise duties on medicinal preparations containing alcohol.
5. Duties levied as well as collected by the union, but assigned to the states within which they are leviable: duties on succession to property other than agricultural land.
6. Taxes levied and collected by the union and distributed between union and the states: taxes on income other than agriculture.
7. The principal sources of non-tax revenues of the union are the receipts from railways, posts and telegraphs, broadcasting and industrial and commercial undertaking.
8. The principal sources of non-tax revenues of the states are the receipts from forests, irrigation and commercial enterprises (like electricity, road transport) and industrial undertakings.
9. The union parliament may by law determine to provide grants-in-aid to states which are in need of grants (Art. 275).

10. Article 282 empowers the centre to make public purpose grants to the states and to any institution within the states.
11. The centre is empowered under Article 293 to grant loans to the states and also to give guarantee in respect of loans raised by them.
12. The President of India in consultation with the Comptroller and Auditor General of India prescribes the pattern in which the states have to maintain their accounts.
13. The union parliament may by law impose certain restrictions on the inter-state trade for any public purpose.
14. The President of India constitutes a Finance Commission for every five years to review the allocation of certain tax proceeds and the principles of grants-in-aid to the states.
15. The states of Assam, West Bengal and Orissa receive grants-in-aid in lieu of export duty on jute products on the recommendation of the Finance Commission.
16. During the Financial Emergency, all the money bills approved by the state legislature are reserved for the consent of the President. The President can also reduce the salaries and allowances of the judges.

The picture of dominance-dependency relationship between the centre and units of the federation is complete both in theory and practice. In the scheme of distribution of powers between the states and the centre, the balance tilts heavily towards the centre. Of the three lists specified in the Seventh Schedule of the Constitution, the union list consisting of 99 subjects is not only largest, it also contains most important subjects and the union government has exclusive authority to legislate on them. The 61 subjects of the state list are not only less important but also are subject to constant central encroachment. The concurrent list with 52 subjects being the smallest is common to both the centre and states. In respect to this list the centre has over-riding authority over the states. And finally, all the residuary powers belong to the centre. The centre thus not only gets lion's share of power but also dominates states.

It is widely known that our political system becomes a unitary government during an emergency (Art. 352 and 356), as the union government acquires all the powers to give direction to states. The parliament becomes all powerful to make laws. Therefore, Dr. Ambedkar, the founding father of Indian Constitution, described our political system as federal during normal times and unitary during an emergency.

But a closer analysis of our political system shows that Indian polity is not only unitary in the time of emergency but is also unitary even in the normal times. There are several legislative, administrative and financial provisions in the Constitution that necessitate central control and direction even in the normal times. In legislative field, Articles 248, 249, 251, 252 and 253 identify the numerous situations in which the legislative powers of the parliament have precedence over the state legislature. According to Article 249, the union legislature can legislate on the subject included in the state list if the Council of States by a two-third majority authorises to do so. Article 200 and 201 empowers the governors to reserve any bill passed by the state legislature for the consideration and assent of the President. And the President has power to refuse assent to a bill so reserved without giving any reason. Since there is no limit to the governor's power for reserving bill for President's consideration the power can be stretched to a point of bringing the entire state legislation under centre's review. Articles 3 and 4 of the Constitution empowers the union government to alter the boundaries of the existing states, create new states, abolish old ones and change their names without resorting to a cumbersome amendment process.

The administrative system, in addition, supports the supremacy of the centre. Article 257 categorically states that the executive powers of the state should be exercised in such a way as not to impede the executive power of the union. Failure to do so could result in operation of the union. Failure to do so could result in operation of Article 356. Again, the appointment of governors by the centre under whose pleasure they act, gives the centre additional leverage in dealing with the states in normal times. Armed with the power of dissolving or, suspending state legislatures and dismissing the democratically elected state ministries, reserving bills passed by state legislature for

President's assent, the governors serve as the agents of an omnipotent and centre.

In the administrative field also, the installation of All-India Service personel in key positions in the state puts the centre in commanding position. With the nerve of the state administration in the deft hands of these civil servants the centre ensures complete control over the states.

Apart from being politically weak, the states have been given a raw deal even in the economic sphere. The agencies that help concentration of economic power in the centre are the Finance Commission (Art. 280), Planning Commission, National Development Council (NDC) Zonal, Councils etc. With the introduction of planning and state-directed social and economic development, the prominent role of the centre has been strengthened further and the dependence of the states on centre for financial resources has been brought into sharper focus. In the division of financial powers, income tax, corporation tax, customs duty have been allocated to the centre. But on the other hand, the resource base of the states is very weak. Again through the Finance Commission, the central government distributes net proceeds of certain taxes and duties and grant-in-aid. This has given considerable flexibility to the central government to distribute favours to state governments and to use such patronage to create dependency and to enforce its own will on the content and pattern of development.

In addition to the above, over the years, in the name of national cohesion and integrated development, sectoral centralization has assumed significant proportions. Most initiatives in critical areas such as technology application, environment protection and education are based on central legislation. From water resources to wildlife, from forest to textiles, and from culture to entertainment are centrally established and controlled institutions.

From the above provisions, it follows that the division of power between central and state governments is both apparent and real. The unitary principles have over shadowed the federal one. The states have practically no existence of their own in this circumstance. The central hegemony over the states is absolute both in economic and political spheres. But this hegemonistic approach of the union government is unbearable for the survival and sustenance of healthy federal system in a pluralistic society like India. Centralization of power and the attempts to dominate the units of the union have been the cause of the rise of many regional forces in recent times.

Thus the need of the hour is to understand the new forces and to bring about practical changes in the federal system, and more particularly re-define the centre-state relations. The lists containing the provisions of distribution of power between the centre and states should be reconsidered, particularly the concurrent list. There is need to see how many subjects of the concurrent list can be transferred to the state list to make states genuine partners in a federal polity.

The centre has certain functions to perform and so have the states. There should not be any conflict. There is no denying the fact that the states are nearest to the people. They have to bear most of the burden. They are answerable to the people. Therefore, the states should be provided with all the administrative, financial and legislative powers so that they can achieve their objectives. In order to provide adequate powers there is an urgent need of decentralization of powers, from central to village levels, through panchayati raj institutions.

Apart from political sphere, there is also need for revamping the financial sphere. Under the Constitution, corporation taxes cannot be shared with the states. Suitable modification to this section will enable the states to have share of the corporate taxes.

Thus, the time has come to redefine certain aspects of federalism to accommodate the new forces. This will help to dilute the confrontal character of regionalism and will promote the chances of stable government at the centre and strengthen national unity.

Emerging Challenges to Indian Federalism

Demand for Separate Statehood

Regionalism in India has also made its appearance in other shapes. Demand for establishment of separate state is raised with a view to attain a distinct political entity for the people of a particular region. This type of regionalism gained momentum after the reorganization of the states on linguistic basis. The States

Reorganization Commission had made certain recommendations about the reorganization of states on linguistic basis but these recommendations created several serious problems and those regions which were not satisfied became violent in many parts of the country. All these demands for separate states, raised from time to time in different parts of the country are nothing but pure demonstration of regionalism.

Demand for Full-Fledged Statehood

These has also been a demand for a full-fledged statehood. After the passing of the States Reorganisation Act there were two categories of units in the country, viz. the states and union territories, Regionalism found its expression in the latter also when union territories became so vocal that with the passage of time the union territories of Himachal Pradesh, Manipur, Tripura, Mizoram and Arunachal Pradesh got full statehood. The union territory of Delhi also raised a demand that in view of its large population and financial viability, it should also be made a full-fledged State. But the union government turned down the demand, mainly on the ground that Delhi was the country's capital and separate statehood for it would not be in the national interest. But now Delhi has been conferred statehood. The demand for full-fledged statehood was also raised by the union territory of Goa, which took a violent turn in Goa, and this in turn led to the deployment of army there. Now even Goa has been conferred statehood. Currently, the demand for separate statehood is raised by the Telangana Rashtriya Samithi in Andhra Pradesh to form a separate Telangana State.

Inter-state Disputes

Finally, the regional tendencies in India have manifested themselves in the shape of inter-state disputes. There are some of the prominent inter-state disputes, which still remain, unsolved. For instance, dispute over Chandigarh between Punjab and Haryana, and the Maharashtra and Karnataka boundary dispute. Besides these, there are other disputes also like the dispute regarding the use of water resources of the three rivers namely, Narmada, Krishna and Cauvery.

The foregoing account, however, discloses that regionalism is at present a fairly widespread phenomenon in the Indian political system. Moreover, it is not likely to lose its sway over people's minds, at least in the foreseeable future. Further, Shriram Maheshwari aptly points out that as the various developmental programmes are carried out, regional disparities are becoming more marked and widespread engendering a sense of cumulative deprivations in the people of certain regions. This coupled with increasing politicization in the community is sure to impact sharper focus to regionalism, which would emerge more prominently as a factor of no small significance in Indian polity.

Pessimists argue that India faces the "dangerous" alternatives of either balkanisation or authoritarian rule as the movement for regional autonomy gains ground. There have indeed been such movements in the past and some exists even today. Once Prime Minister Mrs. Indira Gandhi also emphasised that for our political decision makers, regionalism is still an anathema, a very serious threat to the developmental progress and unity of the country. In fact, Amba Dutta Pant observes that regionalism or cultural pluralism do not necessarily impede the process of national integration. He further mentions that such pluralism at the regional level does not mean fragmentation. A real fragmentation is the result of the ruler's inability to effectively deal with the nation's problems or is the result of their using the method of exploiting one unit against the other. In an accommodative political system, demands of regional cultural units are properly met and there is no threat to national integration where all the constituents are equally valid and naturally interdependent while retaining the viability of the national system, that process is national integration. But Iqbal Narain remarks that, "politics does not create regionalism but it certainly accentuates and exploits regional royalties." Regionalism, he adds, is an important factor in party building and unless alternative secular loyalty bases are discovered or created, regionalism shall continue to flourish. The problem of regionalism could be tackled only with adopting a macro vision which takes within its sweep the macro-variations at regional levels within the nation. In this connection, he posed the problem of depoliticization of the planning process and allocation of resources and emphasised that politics can be secularised only if the political parties follow a policy of ideological polarisation in relation to problems to caste and tribe loyalties vis-a-vis the nation.

Regionalism is an essential co-ordinate of federalism. It is, therefore, a natural phenomenon in a society that is not only plural but also federal in its organization. It is, however, the operation of regional parties that provides strength to the various forces of regionalism.

REFERENCES

Durga Das Basu, "Introduction to the Constitution of India" Printice Hall of India, 1994, New Delhi.

Avasthi and Avasthi, "Indian Administration" 1974, New Delhi.

Shriram Maheshwari, "Indian Administration", 1989, New Delhi.

Himanshu Jha, "Policy Implication Institutions of Federal Financial Transfer in Australia and India", The Indian Journal of Public Administration, Vol. L. No. 3, IIPA, July-September 2004, New Delhi.

R.K. Barik, "The Centre-State Financial Relations: A Search for an Alternative Debate" Ibid.

Jayanta Pavida, "Redifining Federalism", Third Concept Vol. 12, No. 134-35, April-May 1998, New Delhi.

Dr. M.G. Khan, "Challenges to Indian Federalism", Third Concept, Vol. II, No. 126, August 1997, New Delhi.

Arshi Khan, "Withholding Federalism: A Case Study of President's Rule in Bihar", Third Concept, April-May 1999, New Delhi.

S.S. Tiwana, "Coalition Politics in India: Problems and Prospects", Third Concept, Vol. II, April-May, 1997, New Delhi.

22
Panchayati Raj Institutions and People's Empowerment*

Introduction

The concept of local government/Panchayati Raj was prevalent in ancient India, as mentioned in all historical accounts. Empires have been built and destroyed by invaders but the villages have remained intact. Village was an economic as well as administrative unit at the grassroot level.

After Independence several developments have taken place in the field of Local Self Government, particularly in rural local government. Now local government in India comprises two broad categories; rural and urban namely the Panchayati Raj and the Municipal Government. Recently both have been constitutionalized through 73rd and 74th Constitutional Amendments of 1992.

Panchayati Raj institutions were established in accordance with Article 40 of the Indian Constitution, of the Directive Principles of State Policy, which states, "that the state shall take steps to organize village panchayats and endow them with such powers as may be necessary to enable them to function as units of self-government".

Constitutional base for Panchayati Raj Institutions

The constitutional base for Panchayati Raj was required because State Governments were not enthusiastic about the creation of Panchayati Raj bodies and to share power with them in their states. In fact some states have taken back powers from

*Paper Presented at National Seminar on "Empowerment of Local Self-Government in India" on 8th and 9th January 2004 organised by Department of Public Administration, Osmania University, Hyderabad.

the Panchayati Raj bodies. Status and dignity to Panchayati Raj bodies to make them viable and responsive institutions was essential and this required constitutional support. In our Constitution local self-government and panchayati raj is a state subject and the Central government could not pass any legislation unless Constitution was amended. Hence, the 73rd Constitutional Amendment Act 1992.

The main characteristics of the (73rd) Constitutional Amendment Act are that the Act proposed to establish Gram Sabha consisting of all the voters in the panchayat area. It established a three tier system of Panchayat Raj, in an ascending order : (Except the states whose population is less than 20,00,000) the village panchayat at the village level, Samithi at the intermediate level and the Zilla Parishad at the district level. The members of all these panchayats are directly elected by the people. Members of the Lok Sabha/ Rajya Sabha (MPs) and the Legislative Assembly (MLAs) from the area would continue to be members of these bodies with the right to vote in the meetings of the Panchayats but they would have no right to vote in the election of Chairpersons of intermediate and district level Panchayats and they would also be debarred to be chairpersons of these Panchayats. The term of each Panchayat is five years and elections are held every five years under the supervision, direction and control of the State Election Commission/Commissioner and if superseded in mid-term, a mid-term election within six months will be held. The reconstituted panchayat will serve for the remaining period of five years only.

The Act also provided for reservation of seats, for the Scheduled Castes and Scheduled Tribes in proportion to their percentage to the total population of a panchayat. It has further reserved seats of Chairpersons for the SC and ST candidates in all the three tiers of the new Panchayati Raj system in direct proportion to their percentage to the total population of the State, out of these reserved seats one-third are reserved for SC and ST women. The 1992 Act also provides that one-third of the seats in the panchayats at all levels are reserved for women including SC and ST women. The Act directed the states that reservation be carried out by rotation in each and every panchayat at each level.

Another feature of the Act is that it has left to the states to decide the question of reserving seats for backward classes.

Financial paucity has been one of the main causes of Panchayati Raj bodies failure in the past. To remove this hurdle, the panchayats have been empowered to levy and collect appropriate taxes, duties, tolls and fees and they are entitled grants-in-aid from the Consolidated Fund of the State. Every five years the State Governor appoints Finance Commission to review and advise the State Government on the principles governing distribution of funds to the panchayats. The manner of audit of panchayat accounts as decided by the State governments. The state government would also devolve power to the panchayats to prepare plans for economic development and social justice. Significantly, a whole new schedule called the Eleventh Schedule has been drawn up to ensure a better utilization of central and state funds. The schedule contains entire agriculture and allied activities, minor irrigation schemes, land reforms and improvement, small scale industries including food processing, cottage industries, rural housing, drinking water, rural electrification, non-conventional energy programmes, poverty alleviation programmes, primary and secondary education, vocational education, health and family welfare schemes, public distribution system, welfare schemes for weaker and handicapped sections, etc.

Meaning of Empowerment

Empowerment is the phenomenon of nineties and is defined as "giving power to" "creating power within" and enabling. It is a multi dimensional process which enables individuals and groups to realize their full identity and powers in all spheres of life. Keller and Mbewe (1991) described Empowerment as "a process whereby women become able to organize themselves to increase their own self-reliance, to assert their independent right to make choices and to control resources which will assist in challenging and eliminating their own sub-ordination". If this envisages greater access to knowledge and resources greater autonomy in decision making for self, greater ability to plan one's life, to have greater control over circumstances and greater capacity to free one's self from traditions, customs beliefs and practices. The empowerment theme runs strongly through all the third-world countries specially in the context of women and weaker sections. Most of the modern democracies and developing nations have a public agenda for the process of empowerment of women. It is a national commitment.

Empowerment of Women and Weaker Sections Through the Panchayati Raj Institutions

Panchayati Raj Institutions-grassroot units, of self government have been proclaimed as a vehicle of socio-economic transformations in rural India. Effective and meaningful functioning of these bodies would depend on active involvement, contribution and participation of its citizens both male and female. The presence and participation of women and weaker sections in formal democratic process is usually indequate at all the levels Centre, State and local or grassroots. Consequently women oriented policies and programmes are neither formulated nor implemented with the desired women's perspective. Women in general and rural women in particular continue to constitute the single largest group of backward citizens in India who neither have access to power structure nor any other effective methods to overcome their age-old inequality and subordination.

India has hardly any record of deliberate discrimination worth mentioning against women in matters of female political participation. India is one of the few countries in the world that openly encouraged participation of women during the freedom struggle. Feminists believe that the early years of independence were years of promise, they seemed to herald a comprehensive social and economic revolution in the wake of political emancipation of the country. Nevertheless, women remained under represented in the decision-making bodies in the post-independence era despite the fact that they were active in the national movement as well as various social reform movements. Their presence in different democratic bodies has never been commensurate with their demographic strength.

The constitutional 73rd Amendment Act Proceeding for the establishment of a new Panchayati Raj system is a potent instrument for bringing about for reaching changes in our social, political, economic and administrative structure. The provision related to representation of women constitute the most revolutionary feature of the new system. The 73rd Amendment requires that one-third of the elected members of panchayats at all three levels would be women. But even more revolutionary is the provision that one-third of all panchayats at the village, intermediate and district levels would be headed by women.

It should be noted that empowering dalits and marginalised groups through ensuring their participation in the decentralised mechanism was one of the stated objectives of the central Act. However, the ground reality reflects some negative trends too. It was observed that high caste Hindu groups resorted to various measures to dilute or sabotage the attempts to empower marginalised groups especially dalits. These are instances where high caste groups challenge the reservation for scheduled caste/ scheduled tribes in the court of law, and when this attempt fails they announce a boycott of elections. There are also numerous cases of violence against dalits to prevent them from contesting elections or to influence them to favour other interest groups. If these efforts also fail and election do take place, they look for candidates who can be coaxed to carryout the whims and fancies of the dominant castes. On the other hand if somebody out of favour of the dominant caste manages to get elected, they do not cooperate with the person concerned.

Even after coming to positions of power, dalit elected representatives are restricted in effective exercise of their leadership. This is more in the case of women dalit members who have to face double oppression. Instances are not uncommon where the women dalit sarpanches sit on the floor during the course of the panchayat meetings while the male upper caste members sit on the chairs. Problems also arise when the gram sachiv (Panchayat Secretary) happens to be from the upper caste. On the positive side it was observed that the presence of a dalit sarpanch or dalit ward member has greatly contributed to the participation of greater numbers of the dalit community in gram sabha meetings. Disillusionment arises when the dalit sarpanches are forced to give priority to activities favouring the upper caste members.

The scheduled tribes include around 400 aboriginal communities, mainly inhabiting remote and forested areas of India. They constitute 7.8 per cent of India's population. The 73rd constitution Amendment's importance was that it aimed at achieving grass roots democracy guaranteeing adequate representation to the marginalised groups like the scheduled castes, the scheduled tribes and women. However, the 73rd amendment was not automatically applicable to the scheduled areas (geographical areas where the adivasis are concentrated) because of their unique characteristics and special needs. An Amendment act was subsequently enacted in December 1996 titled the provisions of the panchayat (Extension to the scheduled areas and the tribal areas are specified in accordance with the provision in article 244 and Vth and VIth schedules of the India Constitution. The Extension Act is one of the potent legislative measures of recent times, which recognises the tribal peoples mode of living aspirations, their culture and traditions.

Importance of the constitutional 73rd Amendment Act

As a result of 73rd and 74th Amendments of the constitution, India has moved towards what has been described as "multi-level federalism" and more significantly it has widened the democratic base of the Indian polity. Before the amendments, Indian democratic structure through elected representatives was restricted to the two houses of parliament, 28 state assemblies and two assemblies of union territories (Delhi and Pondicherry). And they had just 4,963 elected members.

Now there are nearly 600 (594) district panchayats, about 6,000 block panchayats at the intermediate level and 2,50,000 gram panchayats in rural India where 72.2 per cent of India's population lives. Urban India, with 27.8 per cent population, has 96 city corporations, 1700 town municipalities and 1,900 nagar panchayats. Today, every five years, about 3.4 million representatives are elected by the people through the democratic process, out of whom one million are women. Women headed about 175 district panchayats, more than 2,000 block panchayats and about 85,000 gram panchayats. Likewise, more than 30 city corporations and about 600 town municipalities have women chairpersons. A large number of exlcuded groups and communities are now included in these decision making bodies. As the Indian population has 14.3 per cent Scheduled Caste (SC) and 8 per cent Scheduled Tribes (ST), about 6,60,000 elected members i.e. 22.5 per cent of the total membership in the rural and urban local bodies will be from scheduled castes and tribes.

Suggested Measures

Indisputably, the 73rd Constitutional Amendment could be considered not only historic but also very radical in that for the first time in the history of the independent Inda, it has made mandatory provisions for the reservation of a minimum number of seats and offices of chairpersons to women as well as to the marginalized sections of the rural community. All States have incorporated these Constitutional imperatives in their respective Panchayat Acts. Elections were accordingly conducted, and in the process, a phenomenal number of about one-and-a-half million elected represen-tatives belonging to these disadvantaged sections have assumed office in the panchayats. However, in the context of the cultural conditioning of the Indian rural women, many of them entered the political arena for the first-time, due to persuasion of their family members, pressure from the local community, caste and political leaders. The male-dominated rural power structure is still not reconciled to their socialization in politics. This need not however them from actively involving and participating in decentralised democratic development process at the local level. Similarly, the marginalized communities are politically empowered and capacitated which they should take advantage of and strive to make their participation real and purposeful.

The male-dominated rural power structure should desist from applying social pressure on women-aspirants who possess the necessary enthusiasm and ability to assume political leadership. The menfolk in the villages should rather encourage and offer their unreserved cooperation and support to them. There is a great need for positive attitudinal changes and mental make-up of the menfolk in favour of women. The political empowerment of women and weaker sections demands that they must be able to think and act according to their conscience. Education and training being the sources from which they can access knowledge and understanding, the government may provide functional literacy to the illiterate elected women members of the panchayats after their election.

Training programmes exclusively for women Chairpersons of panchayats of different levels and for the women members of intermediate and district level panchayats must be organized. The State Institutes of Rural Development and the NGOs may be required not only to prepare appropriate curriculum for them, but also to organize the programmes. The training programmes for the chairpersons and members of the district panchayats, intermediate panchayats and village panchayats may be organized at the state, district and block levels respectively. The methods to be adopted at such training programmes may be made as simpler as possible. Group discussions, case studies and success stories should form part of the methods. Electronic media or visuals should also be extensively used in the training programmes. The content of the training should include not only the 'dos and don'ts of panchayat administration but also cover such aspects as may improve the knowledge base and exposure levels of the women relating to their rights, their role in the development process, rural development programmes, etc. Similar training programmes may also be organized for the elected representatives of the panchayats with specific focus on the issues that have a bearing on the welfare of the downtrodden. In order to compensate the income forgone by the elected chairpersons belonging to women and marginalized communities, the state government may provide for a reasonable monthly honorarium.

The state panchayat Acts may provide that any persons attending or presiding over the meetings of a panchayat on behalf of the legally-elected member or chairperson would attract severe punishment, and that the member or chairperson concerned would incur a disqualification from being a member of the panchayat concerned. The chief executive officers of the panchayats at various level should be required to report to the District Collector all cases of proxy participation by the kith and kin of the de jure members and chairpersons in the meetings of the panchayats. The District Collector may be required to initiate appropriate action against the person(s) as well as the member / chairperson concerned.

The state statutes governing the panchayats may be amended in such a way that all vacancies arising out of death, removal or resignation of the members or the chairpersons of the reserved seats or political offices should be filled only from among the other members belonging to the same reserved category. State governments may also introduce "incentive grants" for the panchayats headed by women or marginalized sections of the rural society for exhibiting good performance in terms of number of meetings held, attendance rate, civic and developmental activities taken up, internal revenue mobilization, organizing gram sabha meetings, etc. In the ultimate analysis, improvements in the literacy among women and weaker sections hold the key to their effective participation in decision making process and involvement with developmental activities in the rural areas. Political empowerment would be meaningful only if it is preceded or accompanied by 'capacity-building' among the women and the weaker sections of the Indian rural society. Therefore special attention on the improvement of literacy among these disadvantaged sections brooks no delay.

Conclusion

To conclude, awareness, willingness, and capacity building measures are the basic factors on which the overall development depends. Six decades of political democracy with the introduction of three tier Panchayat Raj Institute in the 90's have certainly raised the awareness among the rural people. Still, many improvements are possible with enhancement of capacity to participate and empowerment of all sections of the Panchayat Raj Institutes. Basic changes are needed in the socio-economic structures so as to enable the Panchayat Raj Institute to have its own effectiveness. We have already harnessed as Panchayat Raj Institute structure. Further progress and development depends upon the infrastructural facilities being created by the government on the one hand and adoptive response from the people on the other.

REFERENCES

Durga Das Basu "Introduction to the Constitution of India", Prentice Hall of India Limited, 1994, New Delhi.

Dr. Hoshiar Singh "Local Government in India After 73rd and 74th Constitutional Amendment : An Assessment", Local Government Quarterly, AIILSG, Vol. LXXI, No. 1-2, Feb-May 2001, Mumbai.

Dr. A.K. Paricha "Strategies for Empowerment of Women in Panchayati Raj Institutions", Local Government Quarterly, AIILSG, Vol. LXXII, No. 1-2, Feb-May 2002, Mumbai.

K.N. Gupta "Women's Empowerment and Protection of their rights", *Social Welfare*, Vol. 47, No. 12, March 2001, New Delhi.

"Georage Mathew, "Panchayati Raj Institutions and Human Rights in India" *Economic and and Political Weekly*, Vol. XXX VIII, No. 2, January 11, 2003, A sameeksha Trust Publication, Mumbai.

Dr. K. Siva Subramanyam "Empowerment of Women and Marginalized Groups in Panchayats", *Kurukshetra*, Publication Division, Ministry of I & B, Government of India, Vol. 50, No. 7, May 2002, New Delhi.

23

Political Violence in India: A Human Rights Perspective*

Political Violence–meaning and causes

Violence means the exercise of physical force so as to inflict injury or damage to persons or property. In the social context violence can be two types. It involves the use of physical or psychological force by the people against the state power or government to achieve group ends. This is violence by the people at large. On the other hand, there is also force used by the agencies of state power such as police, army etc. to maintain law and order. It is a legitimate use of force as is sanctioned by law. However, when force used by the agencies of the state exceeds its limits, it is known as state sponsored violence or official violence. Such incidences may lead to mass violence against the state repression itself. Some thinkers like Lewis Coser, Frantz Fanon argue that violence is a means of social communication, 'a danger signal' and a 'catalyst' in placing claims for scarce resources, power or status in society. When the government is not responsive to the needs of the people, the later tries to fulfil its demands through overt violent acts. Even where there is no real intention to use violence, the threat to use it many elicit desired concessions. Historically, many social movements have involved the use of violence at some point of time. Violence dramatises and helps in projecting the immediacy of a social issue which can then be used to justify the mass movement. **When violence takes place within a political community involving competing political groups against the political regime, its leaders or its policies, it can be**

*Paper presented at UGC sponsored National seminar on **"Factionalism and Human Rights"** during 30th -31st, March 2007 organized by Dept of Human Rights & Social Development, S.V. University, Tirupati - 517 502, A.P.

called as political violence. In other words, political violence seeks to directly or indirectly influence decision making and power relationships in a political system.

It is particularly manifest when political institutions fail to perform their roles or when political elites lose their authority and legitimacy. It can be motivated by a desire to maintain or change the existing social, political order.

Political violence inhibits the smooth functioning of democracy. In a democracy the representatives of the people are elected by popular vote. This election is uncoerced. Democracy also believes in equality which is practiced through the principle of one person one vote. All decisions are taken by a majority vote. Political violence militates against these principles of democracy and, therefore, political violence is considered undemocratic (Honderich, 1976).

Political Parties in India

In the words of Dr. B.R. Ambedkar, "The working of a Constitution does not depend wholly upon the nature of the Constitution ...... the factors on which the working of the organs (of government) depend are the people and the political parties. They will set up as their instruments to carry out their wishes and their politics, who can say how the people of India and their (political) parties behave?"

Our Constitution envisages not only a democracy of men, but also a democracy of institutions. Really there is no question that parties are important political institutions. People who want to bring about social, political change, along with those who prefer to maintain the social and political status have often seen parties as a means to promote or frustrate change. But very often the state of our political environment appears to drive one to the brink of despair. Reality of a democratic constitution worked by political parties which function none too democratically is barely followed, the conventions on which it is based is ignored. It is never to be forgotten that it is not the Constitution that has failed the people, it is our own chosen representatives that have failed the Constitution.

Until incorporation of 10th Schedule, our Constitution never mentioned political parties. Therefore, technically, there exists all sorts of problems to bind political parties to some form of constitutional morality. In the words of E.S. Venkataramaiah, "It is true that till recently the Constitution did not expressly refer to the existence of political parties. But their existence is implicit in the nature of democratic form of government which our country has adopted". The statement of the Apex Court of Pakistan, that political parties are now a necessary part of a democratic government" is a conclusion drawn liberally from ruling of our own Supreme Court. Injection of constitutional morality and a conscious cultivation of constitutional ethics alone can presence the democratic firmament.

The Problem

Political parties call for bandhs which lead to closure of commercial establishments, transportation unavailability, inability of employees to reach work places. There is the question of reconciling two rights here

- Right to associations to express dissent, or demonstrate dissent under Art 19, is a very strictly protected right in any political democracy.
- People keep away from the normal routine, falsely perceived as an expression of support to particular political party that calls for a bandh. But more often the common man sees thinly veiled threat to personal security when venturing out on a bandh day. Large scale government (State) inaction does nothing to protect his fundamental right of movement and work.
- Frequency of 'bandhs' as an expression of protest against specific government policies is, therefore, a problem of considerable magnitude.

If the States takes 'action' against demonstrators that will lead to criticism on the ground of refusing space for dissent/ protest in a political democracy.

Causes of Political Violence

The causes of political violence within any country are economic performance, ethnic dominance of a group, urbanization, type of political regime, and the role of military in that country. In India, the causes of political violence are caste, language, socioeconomic disparities, terrorism, communalism and criminalisation of politics. A brief discussion of each one of these follows.

Caste

There are conflicts in rural areas to get even with rival caste groups or suppress those belonging to lower castes. Bihar evidently tops the list in this kind of violence. Affluent upper caste people in Bihar began to have private armies (senas) to do away with rival castes for political reasons which have now become a common practice. During elections and political rallies there is an increase in the killings. Tamil Nadu, Uttar Pradesh, Madhya Pradesh and Rajasthan have also evidenced caste conflicts. The Parliament was informed 1994 that more than 52,534 cases of atrocities against the Scheduled Castes (SCs) were registered during 1991-93 (*Times of India*, 23 April, 1994). Violence by upper caste Hindus, sometimes with the tacit support of the police, includes the burning of dalit village, rape, torture, murder and deaths in custody. The policy of positive discrimination (the reservation of seats for Scheduled Castes and Tribes in public employment and higher education) and the Mandal Commission recommendations extending the reservations to Other Backward Classes (OBCs) has further exacerbated caste conflicts. During the anti-Mandal agitation in 1990-91, one witnessed widespread *bandhs*, riotings and self-immolations by the students. Sometimes the caste conflicts tend to overlap with conflicts for reorganization of economic system when landlords and peasants use caste factor to perpetuate violence.

Languages

In a multi-lingual and plural society like ours, it is difficult for any single group to occupy the centre stage of politics. Several groups of varied identities try to seek political power. Identities like language helps the aspirants of political mobility to appeal to a particular section of the people to create their vote banks. However, when two or more political opponents appeal to the same sectional identify (as language), it can inevitably lead to violence. Language as a basis of conflict has been the feature of independent India since 1950s. The demand for autonomy and protection of rights of a language group often merges with the demand for re-organization of states based on language. Despite states recognization in 1956 based on language, we have witnesses Haryana agitation for separate state in 1966, Telangana agitation in 1969, and also at present in Andhra Pradesh and language riots in different parts of the country.

Socio-economic Disparities

This was the major reason for violence by the ultra leftist groups. It began in West Bengal in 1960s and then spread to Andhra Pradesh and Bihar. Known as Naxalbari movement in West Bengal and Andhra Pradesh, the Leftist groups believe in radical socio-economic transformation in society which they seek to bring about through such extra-constitutional methods as using guns. They aim at establishing an egalitarian social system and redistribute the wealth proportionally among persons in society.

Terrorism

This form of violence in India is for territorial reorganization leading to the creation of their 'imagined homelands'. It first began in north-eastern parts of India followed by Punjab (since 1983), in Kashmir (since 1988) and in Assam. The problem has assumed serious proportions due to extra-territorial i.e., foreign support received by these terrorist groups in Punjab and Kashmir in the form of arms, ammunition, trained personnel and financial support. Indiscriminate killings, bomb blasts have made life unsafe for ordinary citizens in these states.

Grievance of Specific Groups

Various groups indulging in political violence to air their grievances include students, teachers, trade unions and the like. Growing indiscipline and unrest among the student community may take the form to bandhs, lathicharges, gheraos and even stabbing by the criminal elements on the campus. In fact, campus political organizations and trade unions have become a miniature version of national politics as various student political groups and trade unions are affiliated to or supported by the national/regional political parties. However, student power is a force that can also be used constructively for the betterment of society as Jaya Prakash Nayaran did in 1974 calling for socio-economic change and total revolution.

Group violence also includes tribal disturbances in regions like north-eastern part of India. Nagas, Kukis, Mizos, the Bodos and other tribes of the region are engaged in internecine violence in which several hundreds have lost their lives.

Criminalization of Politics

This is one of the causes for indiscriminate rioting and killing in India today. Riots are often engineered by the political parties to gain political mileage out of it in the elections or otherwise. Some officials in the state agencies like police and paramilitary forces also display evident complacency and connivance against the victims. Ranganath Mishra Committee Report accused the Delhi Police of inaction when rioters went berserk against the Sikhs in Delhi. Criminalization of politics can be seen during the elections when politicians take the help of criminals for 'booth capturing' and all the malpractice of impersonation, rigging and intimidation. This is so because the underworld dons have a heavy stake in the election of a candidate due to large contribution made by them towards election expenses.

In recent years, the role of criminals and politicians have converged to such an extent that several elected representatives in Assemblies and Parliament have long criminal record behind them. Thus, the nexus has been democratically institutionalized.

Mass Violence

In this we shall see three levels of violence depending on their intensity. *Bandhs* and *demonstrations* are forms of low intensity mass violence. These are usually a feature of protests by trade unions, bank and insurance employees in the service sector, and student protests in educational institutions. Though these protests begin on a peaceful note, they have the potential to turn violent when the leaders of the movement are unable to control the masses. Bandhs stop all work as a mark of protest where as a demonstration is a non-violent gathering or march by a group to invite attention of the concerned authorities towards their grievances.

Gherao, rasta/rail roko and lockouts are some of the means used by the political parties, interest and pressure groups to press their demands. Gherao involves surrounding or closing in on the top officials and decision makers by the aggrieved section of the people who are affected by the policies. Rasta/rail roko involves obstructing smooth movement of road and rail traffic. Rail roko agitation is particularly violent as sometimes the agitators cause immense damage to public property. In states like Assam, miles and miles of railway tracks are blown up by the United Liberation Front of Assam (ULFA) militants as part of their insurgency movement. Rail roko agitation assumes militant proportions and transforms into a high-intensity violence when tracks are blown up. Likewise, it is also common in our country to see students and angry mobs burning down public transport vehicles (buses) and police jeeps as a mark of protest.

Then there are more severe forms of political violence such as riots, arson, political assassination, insurgency movements and terrorism. They all come under high-intensity violence. Terrorism and internal war constitute the most severe forms of political violence. A riot is defined as a violent demonstration involving a large number of people acting spontaneously, impulsively and indiscriminately to loot or kill people. However, one may witness pre-planned, well-engineered riots in urban areas during political instability and turmoil. Political assassination implies eliminating prominent political leaders to express opposition to ideology, the leaders, policies or simply to seize political power. Mahatma Gandhi in 1948, Mrs. Indira Gandhi in 1984 and Rajiv Gandhi in 1991 were assassinated for ideological/political reasons. Political assassination also symbolizes an overt act of terrorism.

Impact of Political Violence on Human Rights

Human Rights and political violence have an inverse relationship. Greater the intensity of political violence, lesser are the prospects for human rights. Hence, steps taken to promote human rights can effectively check the possible outbreak of political violence. Conversely, violation of human rights sows the seeds of political violence. And, political violence in turn begets human rights violation. The impact of political violence of human violence on human rights can be at two levels - individuals and collective. At the individuals level it may include violation of civil and political rights and economic rights (i.e., the first generation and the second generation rights) such as loss of job, loss of life, sense of alienation etc. At the collective level, in a modernizing developing country like ours, two important rights (third generation rights) violated are right to peace and right to development. If one were to perceive society as an extension of individual's personality, then, the extent of human rights violation (or alternatively deprivation of its enjoyment) increases manifold.

Everything possible has to be done to curtail discontentment and promote conditions that are congenial to the enjoyment of human rights. The steps to be taken have to be both prohibitive and positive and by both the state as an agency of governance and civil society as the sphere of interaction between the state and the subjects. Three measures adopted by the state can be helpful: stable institutions of governance, sound legal regime of rights, and peaceful conditions in society (human rights are suspended in terrorist affected states). Above all, the basis of political mobilization itself has to be rationalized as it may contain roots of human rights abuse and political discontentment leading to violence. The more traditional cleavages like caste, religion or language are appealed to, the greater are the chances of retrogressive results. In a democratic society based on egalitarian-secular concept, traditional identities as a basis of authoritative allocation of values by the agencies of the state leads to disproportionate benefits accruing to a section of society at the cost of others. These have been some of the major causes of political violence in India as mentioned earlier.

At the people's level, civil society as an intervening sphere sustains and manages dissent and discontentment without allowing these to explode into difficult situations. It can be strengthened by encouraging representative institutions allowing wider participation of groups because; it represents human rights movement from below. Thus, democracy and devolution of power can be twin mantras to meaningfully stem the rot.

Political violence has had a subversive effect on Indian society and polity. It has made life of the citizen difficult and unsafe. It affects both our social life and our efficiency and productivity at work. Often life is paralysed for days at a stretch due to bandhs, riots and terrorist menace. It is a common knowledge that works in government offices and educational institutions comes to a stand still during bandhs as is the experience in the North Eastern

States in particular. This retards economic progress and implementation of developmental programmes by the government. Even when political violence does not actually break out, its imminence may induce the state to adopt such preemptive measures as imposition of curfew. This causes many hardships to the people. When terrorism was at its peak in Punjab and Kashmir, it was unsafe to move about after sunset. Outstation roadways buses were plying with the help of armed guards to protect lives of the civilian passengers.

Our state is spending huge sums of money and human resources to curtail political violence and maintain law and order. The scarce resources we are investing in maintaining various paramilitary forces such as BSF, CRPF, Rapid Action Force, Special Protection Group (SPG) for VVIP security can be usefully utilized for constructive and developmental activities. Political violence has undermined the functioning and effectiveness of our democratic political institutions. In fact, it has impeded healthy growth and strengthening of the roots of democratic institutions. This is a serious malady in that any danger to democratic institutions would mean a difficulty in governing our large and diverse country which can only be governed democratically. Therefore, any threat to democracy would imply a threat to our social and political unity and existence.

In view of the growing incidences of political violence in India, some steps have been taken to curtail violence at all levels. Most of the measures thus adopted are legislative in nature. A number of laws have been passed or amended to provide punitive measures against perpetrating violence. In some cases stringent administrative measures have also been introduced.

Lower castes and untouchables are the worst victims of caste-conflicts. Therefore, both negative laws providing punitive action for caste based discrimination and positive laws to ameliorate the socio-economic status of the backward classes have been adopted.

It is clearly evident that most of the measures adopted to check political violence are only in the law books and their implementation has not been very effective. Some more remedial measures should be adopted to make our society less violent.

Conclusion

Secular content of education and inter-faith dialogue should be encouraged to develop understanding and respect for other communities. The activities of all communal political parties and religious groups must be monitored and communally inflammatory speeches be curtailed as they are often responsible for fanning communal sentiments. Police and paramilitary forces should be broad based so as to be representative of all communities in India. This will go a long way in inculcating objectively, neutrality and discipline while performing their duties.

Root cause of terrorism today is the cultural alienation of some communities from the national mainstream. Linguistic and cultural suppression can be avoided by giving these communities more autonomy in their governance and allowing space for their cultural identities. Mass media can play a responsible and positive role through objective reports of the causes of violence without sensationalizing the issue. In today's information age, mass media has a significant role to play in educating the masses through both print and electronic media.

Above all, laws to oversee various aspects of political parties is the need of the hour. The least that can be done is to demand a mandatory disclosure of their sources of income. A responsibility rests on our polity and people to reduce the role of money in elections. A candidate seeking to contest elections be made to adhere to such requirements as clean police records, some formal educational background etc.

Besides the governmental efforts to check the menace of political violence, at the peoples level too we need to follow, to the extent possible, the Buddhist - Gandhian principles of non-violence.

REFERENCES

Ashok H. Desai, "Dangers to Indian Democracy", *Janata*, Vol. 61, No. 5, March 12, 2006, Mumbai.

Ibid, March 19, 2006, Mumbai.

B. Vivekanandan, "India should Build a Welfare State", *Janata*, Vol. 62, No. 1, January 28, 2007, Mumbai.

K. Savitri, "Political Violence in India: Implications for Human Rights", Perspectives on Human Rigths, Abdul Rahim, Kumar Suresh (editors), Manak Publications, 1999, New Delhi.

Dr. B. Meena Rao, "Human Rights: The challenge Ahead" *Third concept*, January 2000, New Delhi.

T.R. Sivaramjani and T. Ramakrishna, "Political Bandhs: whither Human Rights guaranteed by the constitution"? Occasional paper, centre for studies in Human Rights and social development, S.V. University, 1995, Tirupati.

24

Forms of Domestic Violence Against Women in India and Remedial Measures

Mahatma Gandhi had expressed *"The desire that women should be able to walk alone on the roads even at mid night, where as the situation today is no different and probably worse with women being subjected to violence in their homes"*.

Introduction

It is the establishment of control and fear in a relationship through violence and other forms of abuse. Violence against women is vide spread and involved as one of the cruelest social mechanism to suppress women. Unequal power relations have led to discrimination against women. Violence on women manifests even before birth and early life, married life as domestic violence, rape, murder, dowry death etc.

When the basic reason for violence against women is their inferior status educationally, economically, politically and socially in a male dominated society. Other factors responsible for increasing criminalization of society, media images, inadequate means to address the cause and consequences of violence, poor enforcement of legal provisions, unabashed consumerism and erosion of family values have all added to it. Over the past decade, there have been growing awareness of this phenomenon and its long term impact on women empowerment. The media reports extensively on dowry deaths, rape, molestation, incest, assault etc. and give out information that was virtually unavailable till a few years ago.

The Constitution of India grants equality to women and empowers the state to adopt measures of positive discrimination in favour of women for neutralizing the cumulative socio-economic, educational and political disadvantages. The state has enacted many women specific legislations to protect them against discrimination, violence and atrocities and prevent social evils like child marriages, dowry, rape, sati etc.

Abuses include mental, emotional, sexual and financial. Restricting her freedom of movement, for example, not allowing her to visit her parents or talk to the neighbours, denial of conjugal rights, sexual harassment, wife being dumped with an excessive work load and denied privacy. Driving her out of her matrimonial, deserting the wife and living with another women, forcing wife to leave her house, denying her food and necessities and the man abusing his wife's children.

Forms of Domestic Violence

Conjugal violence: This involves violence between husband and wife. In most situations the husband is more violent than the wife. Though in some cases the wife may also hit her husband, what ever be the method or type of violence, the effect of violence is often very serious both in terms of immediate and visible effects on the victims as well as long term effects that are often less visible. This is true not only for the victim and society at large. Over the years the myth has developed that wife battering is linked to dowry harassment. But research suggests that wife battering is a much wider cannot be entirely related to dowry.

Sex related violence: Spouses often hit each other in course of arguments and jealousy caused due to extra marital sexual relations.

Alcohol related violence: Association between alcohol intake and violence is well established. Alcohol is a solvent that boosts the super-ego and releases aggression and violence and almost invariably it is male violence.

Protective-reaction violence: This refers to situations where the wife starts a pre-emptive attack, which may be verbal provocation or otherwise, because she fears that her husband is getting ready to hit. The effort here is to hit the enemy before it strikes and cripple its capacity to fight.

Volcanic violence: This refers to violence that is caused due to the offender running out of patience due to externally caused stress, such as losing a job or persistently being nagged and provoked by the spouse with the spouse. Thus, the stress that is built up erupts into violence.

Dowry related violence: Most of the dowry deaths suicides, bride burning and harassment are apparently the result of dissatisfaction of in-laws over inadequate dowry brought by the daughter-in-law. Reviews of available studies on dowry victimization in India indicate that the victims of dowry related violence are in the age range of 18 to 30 years. They are not highly educated and are financially depended on their husband or in-laws. The problem of dowry surfaces largely during the early years of their marriage i.e., 2 - 5. In addition to the husband other family members, occasionally other members living in the family are involved. Dowry is seen as compensation for the cost of maintaining an economically un-productive humanbeing. But in the present scenario dowry harassment cases have been reported even where women are employed and are not an economic burden on the family. The explanation for this is situated in greed, desire for quick money and luxurious life style.

Child Abuse: Another form of family violence is the physical abuse of children. Many parents consider many violence as an effective tool for teaching and controlling children. Where parent child violence intersects with violence occurs. In such situations are parent uses force to discipline the child and the other disapproves which in turn results in secondary conflict between husband and wife. There are also situations where parents sell their children for labour and force them to work in hazardous employment for long hours or pledge them to bondage in lieu of the debt that they have to pay or indulge in child marriage. Incest and rape also takes place within the home and by persons having intimate relationships.

Infanticide and foeticide: These also become part of family violence because it is the parents who are involved in murdering the infant or getting the pregnancy terminated, especially if it happens to be a girl child. Most of the women reported that they killed their babies under pressure from their husbands. Many a time the husbands would beat up their wives and force them to kill the female child because she is an economic burden. Such situations occur more so among poverty stricken families.

Homicides in the family: In India apart from killing the born or unborn child and dowry deaths, the practice of sati burning of widows on the husband's funeral pyre, also amounts to homicide. The widows, usually against their wish, are brain washed and pushed into the burning pyre of their husband's by the family members and relatives.

Elder Abuse: Abuse of the elderly, like other forms of family violence, has increasingly become visible. It is part of the intra familial violence. The factors that make family life intimate may also make it prone to conflict and if the conflict is not resolved by negotiation and compromise then it may lead to violence. Getting information an extent of elder abuse often becomes difficult because family loyalty and dependency presents older persons from reporting abuse.

Whatever may be the type of violence, the effect of various forms of violence in the family are often very disastrous both in terms of immediate and visible effects on the victims as well as long term effects that are often less visible. This is true not only for the victim but also for the other members of the family, the family as a whole and society at large.

Causes for Increase in Domestic Violence

1. Geographical isolation and urbanization.
2. Household density leading to physical child abuse, bedroom sharing and sexual molestations.
3. Breakdown of ties leaving negative physiological and psychological impact of stress.
4. Unmanageable family composition in Joint family system.
5. Role disturbances in families leading to sibling quarrels and absence of an affectionate parent-child relationship.
6. Unequal distribution of power in the marital and strained father-mother relationship.
7. Poverty, materialism and greed for money and material comforts leading to dowry deaths, harassment of women by husband and in-laws.
8. Ineffective social control systems including religion and state authority.

9. Ineffective laws and their ineffective enforcement and collapse of criminal justice administration.
10. State of normlessness due to erosion of moral and spiritual values.
11. Growing sub-culture of violence in the society due to T.V. serials, Internet and cinema.
12. Lack of community awareness about the problem and their in difference to the problem.
13. Arguments over money, jealousy and suspicion, instigation by in-laws, housework, alcohol, women's desire to work or women's self-esteem and extra marital affairs of the husband.

Remedial Measures

The special enactments and legislations to safeguard women and their interests specifically are:

1. The Commission of Sati (Prevention)Act, 1987
2. The Medical Termination of Pregnancy Act, 1971
3. The Employees State Insurance Act, 1948
4. The Minimum Wages Act, 1948
5. The Factories (Amendment) Act, 1986
6. The Guardian and Wards Act, 1890
7. The Hindu Adoption and Maintenance Act, 1956
8. The Pre-natal Diagnostic Techniques (Regulation of Prevention of Misuse) Act, 1994
9. The Foreign Marriage Act, 1969
10. The Indian Succession Act, 1925
11. The Indecent Representation of Women (Prohibition) Act, 1986
12. The Hindu Succession Act 1956
13. The Christian Marriage Bill, 2000
14. The Immoral Traffic (Prevention) Act, 1956
15. The Child Marriage Restraint Act, 1929
16. The National Commission for Women Act, 1990 including the status of the chairperson and the members of the commission

17. Increase in the Maintenance Allowance under Section 125 of Cr.P.C.
18. Domestic Violence Against Women Act, 2005
19. Legal Awareness
20. Parivarik Mahila Lok Adalat (PMLA)
21. The Family Courts Act, 1954
22. Legal Feminist Jurisprudence
23. The Maternity Benefit Act, 1961 (Amended in 1995)
24. The Special Marriage Act, 1954
25. The Plantation Labour Act, 1951
26. The Dowry Prohibition Act, 1961
27. The Contract Labour (Regulation and Abolition) Act, 1976
28. The Equal Remuneration Act, 1976
29. The Criminal Law (Amendment) Act, 1983
30. Sexual Harassment of Women at Work Place Act, 1999.

Conclusion

As described, it appears that there is a persistent increase in all forms of violence against women. Government needs to make concerted efforts to curtail increasing incidence of crimes committed against women. There is a need for action plan to create awareness amongst women regarding their rights for better redressal. Otherwise any number of media campaign showing positive image of girl child and women's contribution to the society and family needs to be intensified to spread the message. Further there is a need for changing the mindset of men dominated society so as to give equal rights as enshrined in the Constitution of India, and also the special enactments and legislations to safeguard women and their interests.

REFERENCES

Dr. Snehalata Tandon, "Domestic violence and the role of the family counselling centers", Social Welfare, Vol. 50, No. 5-6, Aug-Sept-2003, Central Social Welfare Board, New Delhi,

Dr. Manjushree Pathak, "Domestic Violence and The Law", Social Welfare, Vol. 50, No. 9, December 2003, Central Social Welfare Board, New Delhi

Humane, "Violence Against Women," an occasional publication from forum for Human Rights, April 2003, No. 3 Guntur.

Dr. Snehalata Tandon "Domestic violence why and how? What to do?", *Social Welfare*, Vol. 50, No. 3, June 2003, Central Social Welfare Board, New Delhi.

Humane, "Combating Gender Violence," an occasional publication from forum for human rights, April 2004, No. 6, Guntur.

Dr. D.B. Krishna Kumari, "Intervention for combating gender violence," *Social Welfare*, Vol. 51, No. 9, December 2004, Central Social Welfare Board, New Delhi

A. Manohar, "Violence Against Women", *Yojana*, Vol. 50, October 2006, Ministry of Information and Broadcasting, GOI, New Delhi.

Facts sheet on women in India 2005, DCWC, National Institute of Public Co-operation and Child Development, New Delhi.

Annual report 2000-2001, National Commission for Women, GOI, New Delhi.

25

Rural Poverty in India and Remedial Measures*

In the simplest form poverty means the state of being poor. But the term poverty has multi-dimensions. Three perspectives have been used to define the concept of poverty, firstly, income perspective of poverty defined poor as people having income below the poverty line. Secondly, the basic needs perspective of poverty defines poor as the people who are unable to spend on minimum basic needs like food, shelter, clothing etc for their normal activities. Thirdly, the social perspective of poverty defines poverty as "Intolerable life conditions including social, economic, political, health, education and others. Development economists define poverty as the deprivation of opportunities and choices that denies social, political, economic, human rights claims and the decent standard of living.

As stated by Amartya Sen, one should not think poverty alleviation in terms of raising national income and per capita income but it should be in terms of enhancement of people's capability to lead minimally acceptable lives. Hence Sen advocated the social indicators like safe drinking water, health care, education, clothing and shelter as the measure of poverty.

Indian poverty estimates are based on household consumption expenditure. Any person consuming less than 2,400 calories per day in a rural area and less than 2,100 calories per day in an urban area is considered to be below the poverty line. Other aspects of poverty include access to medical care, schooling, indebtedness and insecurity but these do not figure in the official definition of

*Paper presented at U.G.C. Sponsored National Seminar on "Poverty Trends and Challenges with Special Reference to India" on 2-3 February, 2009, organized by the Department of Econometrics, Sri Venkateswara University, Tirupati- 517 502, A.P.

poverty. The percentage of poor population is higher in rural areas compared to urban areas.

Causes of poverty in India

1. The Indian caste system and the discrimination against low caste.
2. High level of dependence on primitive methods of agriculture.
3. Rural urban divide.
4. 75% of Indian population depends on agriculture where as the contribution of agriculture to the GDP was 22%.
5. While services and industry have grown at double digit figures, agriculture growth rate has dropped from 4.8% to 2%.
6. High population growth rate.
7. High illiteracy.
8. Unemployment and under employment.
9. Lack of employment opportunities in rural areas.
10. Low productivity of agriculture.
11. Uneconomical land holdings from the point of cultivation.
12. Dependence of agriculture on nature and lack of irrigation facilities.

Categories of Poor

Small and marginal farmers: It may also work as agriculture labourers. They are poor because they own uneconomic holdings.

Landless labours: For the landless labourers work is either available or not available seasonally. It includes tenant farmers, share croppers, rural artisans and unemployed people.

The Government has implemented a series of poverty alleviation programmes. The Planning Commission has the belief that employment is surest way to enable the rural poor to cross the poverty line. Land-Reforms were implemented to re-distribute the land holdings among the small farmers and landless labourers. But progress of these measures was less than satisfactory. Based on trickle down theory, agricultural development programmes were implemented during the plan period. The Green Revolution took place and agricultural production was increased much but they failed to solve rural poverty problem. The trickle down theory is challenged by a good number of economists. They argued that the agricultural growth might have had some link with income generation for the rural poor till the mid of nineteen sixties which increased the use of labour and thus benefited the rural poor. But according to Bardhan the new agricultural technology has stopped the trickle down effects i.e. machines and landlords have displaced the agricultural labourers, particularly women workers which reduced their income level.

In the seventies, for the first time Government used an ad-hocist approach i.e. rural development and rural employment programmes of eradication of rural poverty. The Fifth Plan proclaimed poverty alleviation as one of its principal objectives. Small Farmers Development Agency (SFDA), Marginal Farmers and Agriculture Labour Development Agency (MFALDA), Drought Prone Area Programme (DPAP), Crash Scheme for Rural Development (CSRE), Pilot Intensive Rural Employment Project (PIREP) and Food for Work Programme (FWP) were the various programmes implemented under an ad-hocist approach. But these programmes utterly failed to lift the rural poor above the poverty line.

In the latter phase of nineteen seventies, Government had implemented three major anti-poverty programmes namely Integrated Rural Development Programme (IRDP), National Rural Employment Programme (NREP) and Rural Landless Employment Guarantee Programme (RLEGP).

IRDP was introduced in 1978-79 with the initial coverage of 2300 development blocks. It consisted of both government subsidy and institutional credit at the ratio 1:2. The people below the poverty line were its beneficiaries and it aimed at supplementing the assets and income of the target group. During 1990-99, 20 million families were benefited under this programme. But there were lot of leakages, mismanagement of fund in its implementation. The IRDP was restructured into a single self-employment programme called "Swarna- Jayanti Gram Swarozgar Yojana (SGSY) and it came into implementation since April, 1999.

Food for Work Programme (FWP) was restructured and renamed as "National Rural Employment Programme" (NREP) in 1980. It generated 1500-2000 million man days' employment during 1985-89 by spending Rs. 2940 crores on development of rural infrastructure. The wage rate paid under this programme was lower than market wage rates. The selection of beneficiaries was also not proper. To supplement NREP Government launched 'Rural Landless Employment Guarantee Programme (RLEGP) in 1983. Since the objectives of both were same, Government merged them into a single programme called 'Jawahar Rozgar Yojana (JRY) in 1989. The programme solely targeted to help the rural poor below the poverty line but preference was to be given to Scheduled Castes, Scheduled Tribes and freed bonded labourers. The programme is being implemented under 80:20 Centre-State assistance. In 1993-94, the JRY programme was modified and implemented in three streams: Indira Awas Yojana and Million Wells Scheme is the first, additional allocation to identified 120 backward district is the second and the third stream is special innovative projects.

Watershed Development, Waste Land Development, Operation Black Board etc innovative and special employment projects were implemented to generate employment opportunities in rural areas. However the target of providing 90-100 days employment to every registered unemployed still remained as a distant goal.

The United Progressive Alliance (UPA) Central Government launched National Rural Employment Guarantee Programme (NREGP) in February 2006 under the provisions of National Rural Employment Guarantee Act, 2005. It is 80:20 Centre-State funding programme. The NREGP gives the guarantee of minimum 100 days employment in a year for at least one adult member in a family. The NREGP is different from the other employment generation programmes. It gives people work entitlement and makes the administration responsible for accountability.

All the anti-poverty programmes so far implemented by the Government have two objectives namely (i) creation of Self-employment and wage-employment and (ii) food security for rural poor. The former President of India APJ Abdul Kalam too suggested investments in dairy and animal husbandry, poultry, forestry, goatry, fisheries, cottage and small scale industries etc under his PURA (Providing Urban amenities in Rural Areas) programme.

A multi-dimensional approach to tackling poverty

The issue of tackling poverty requires a multi-dimensional approach. Sustained economic growth always remains a necessary condition. However, growth alone cannot ensure the eradication of poverty unless it is coupled with an enabling environment where the benefits of growth could be equitably distributed amongst the poor. A targeted and bottom-up approach involving the poor through their social mobilization, addressing the following remains critical for a successful poverty alleviation strategy.

- Defining the economic content of social mobilization processes at the micro level and indicating how these will be linked at the national level;
- Ensuring meeting the basic needs, including minimum food, shelter, clothing, healthcare and education entitlements, of all the poor;
- Providing income-generating opportunities through an enabling legal, financial and market environment;
- Given the success of micro credit in empowering the poor, up-scaling and replicating such best practices throughout the region;
- Ensuring adequate investment on children through programmes like food for education;
- Paying special attention to women in poverty with a view to freeing them from their perpetual entrapment;
- Mobilizing unemployed youth through various skill development and vocational training programmes;
- Taking special care of the disabled, aged and socially disadvantaged people through various social welfare benefit schemes;
- Emphasizing the need for rapid and sustainable economic development without degrading the environment and creating special safety nets for people living in ecologically vulnerable areas;

- Making affordable and sustainable technologies available for the poor so that they can reap the maximum benefits through better farming practices as well as from off farm activities;
- Attaching greater emphasis on rural poverty eradication programmes given the fact that majority of the poor still live in the rural areas;
- Resorting to Information and Communication Technology (ICT) for various poverty alleviation programmes;
- Encouraging more interaction amongst the government agencies and the NGOs, research institutions and civil society representatives at the regional level for better coordination and dissemination of ideas and information;
- Encouraging private sector to get directly involved in poverty alleviation efforts by offering tax rebates and other incentives;
- Emphasizing on decentralization and devolution of power at the grass roots level involving the poor in local level decision-making, which will also bring about more transparency, accountability and good governance at the local level;
- Ensuring, as far as feasible, a pro-poor element in national development planning in individual states with maximum provisions of investment of Human Resources Development.

Conclusion

The entire comprehensive poverty eradication programmes implemented by Government, however, have two different objectives viz. creation of self-employment and wage-employment in rural area and food security to the rural people.

But the major problem of these programmes is to organize public works to create durable assets by assigning them to contractors. The contractors recruit the labourers at low wage, complete the work in short-period and maximize their profits. But the solution to the rural poverty will require that the small farmers must be also given an access to land-augmenting innovation along with programme of well-conceived public works.

In addition, the rural industrialization with labour-intensive technique should also be taken seriously for alleviation of rural poverty.

As suggested by the former President Dr. APJ Abdul Kalam, "Providing Urban amenities in Rural Areas- (PURA) programme needs to be implemented to create new growth centers to take up investments in dairying and animal husbandry, poultry farming, fishing, forestry, goatry, small scale and cottage industries etc".

Encouragement of minor irrigation, creation of self-employment opportunities and development of education facilities in rural areas programmes will definitely help to eradicate the rural poverty.

REFERENCES

Prof. Arjun. Y. Pangannavar, "Self Help Groups and Rural Poverty", *Kurukshetra*, Vol. 57, No. 2, December 2008, A Journal on Rural Development, Publications Division, New Delhi.

Dr. K. Muthalagu, "Poverty Eradication in India under anti Poverty Programmes-Some Observations", *Kurukshetra*, Vol. 56, No. 2, December 2007, A Journal on Rural Development, Publications Division, New Delhi.

Dr. A. Ramachandran & N. Kavitha, " Eradicating poverty in Rural India", *Ibid.*

Dr. I. Subramanyam & K. Subramanyam, "Poverty and Human Rights: A Rights Based Approach to Development", Rights Based approach to Development, Dr. K. Sreenivasa Rao (Editor), 2007, S.V. University, Tirupati.

26

Slum-related Problems and Programmes in India

Introduction

The phenomenon of rapid urbanisation coupled with industrialisation has brought with it more rapid increase in the growth of urban slums. The existence of slums is essentially manifestation of poverty. Slums will continue to exist and grow further along with the economic growth and industrial development. The sprouting of slums in urban areas is a direct outcome of greater economic opportunities available in cities and towns. The demonstration effect of improved standard of living prevailing in urban areas has also attracted not only the population from smaller settlements but also the rural migrants to almost all the major urban centres resulting in proliferation of slums even in the heart of cities which occurred due to various factors, namely, the shortage of developed land for housing, the prices of land being beyond the reach of urban poor, large influx of population, migration to cities in search of jobs and inadequate provision of basic services and infrastructural facilities in urban areas.

The Census of 2001 revealed that urban population of India was 285.35 millions spread over 4000 urban agglomeration/ towns which is about 27.8% of the total population of the country. In 2001, there were 35 metropolitan cities with over a million people and their share in the total urban population was 37.8% i.e. about one-third of the total urban population where 375 Class I cities out of the total urban population. By 2010, around 450 million people will live in urban areas of this country. It is quite evident from the fact that there is a noticeable change in the urban population living in slums due to shortage of land and affordable housing. Unplanned urban growth has been accompanied by widespread poverty, marginalisation and neglect of children particularly those abandoned or forced into working. Besides this, there are other major forms of deprivation such as unhygienic environment, inadequate suitable housing stock, lack of access to safe drinking water, health, infrastructure, inadequate access to basic sanitation, education, etc.

The Concept of Slums

The concept of slums and its definition vary from country to country depending upon the socio-economic conditions of each society. Irrespective of location, whether in the heart of the city in the form of old dilapidate structures or on the outskirts in the form of squatting, slums have often been characterised in the following ways:

1. Physically, an area of the city with inadequate housing, deficient facilities, over crowding and congestion.
2. Socially, slum is a way of life, a special character which has its own set of norms and values reflected in poor sanitation, health values, health practices, deviant behaviours and social isolation.
3. Legally speaking, Section 3 of the Slum Areas (Improvement and Clearance) Act 1856 defines slums as areas where buildings:
   (i) are in any respect unfit for human habitation.
   (ii) are by reason of dilapidation, over-crowding, faulty arrangement of streets, lack of ventilation, light or sanitation facilities or any combination of these factors which are detrimental to safety, health and morals.

Chapter-II Section 3 of Slum Areas Act, 1956, defines slum areas by notification in the Gazette. The slum areas are declared which require (a) repair, (b) stability, (c) natural light and air, (d) system of dump, (e) water supply, (f) drainage and sanitary conveniences, (g) facilities for storage, preparation of cooking of food and disposal of waste water, the buildings deemed to be unfit if it is so for defective in one or more of the said matter and not found reasonably suitable for occupation in that condition.

Slum-Related Problems

- Generally slums are neglected parts of cities where housing and living conditions are appallingly lacking.
- Slums range from high density, squalid central city tenements to spontaneous squatter settlements without legal recognition or rights, sprawling at the edge of cities.
- Slums don't have basic municipal services like water, sanitation, waste collection, storm drainage, street lighting, paved foot paths or roads for emergency access.
- Slums do not have schools and clinics within reach, safe areas for children to play.
- The slum people don't have places for the community to meet and socialize.

Slums are Worsening

- As the average age of people in cities is increasing, the average age of slum dwellers is decreasing, so the youth suffer most from unhealthy conditions.
- Visible disparities between slums and better-off neighbourhoods increase the social tensions in poorer areas.
- Unplanned growth of settlements makes conventional service provision complicated.

Indian Scenario

The pattern of growth of cities and proliferation of slums bring out to the fore four aspects of concern.

Firstly, the movement of low income population into the city and its concentration and growth is an ever increasing phenomenon. Estimates indicate that about one-third of the population in large cities live in slums or slum like conditions and the proportion could be even higher in metros and mega cities. Further, whereas the population in urban settlements is growing at rates between 2 to 3 per cent per annum, the population in the slum and informal settlements in urban areas is estimated to be growing at the rate of 6 to 8 per cent per annum. Secondly, the proliferation of slums in cities is a result of the inefficiency and weakness of the urban system to respond adequately to meet the shelter requirements of the economically weaker sections, who migrate to the city primarily for economic reasons. In the absence of adequate access to shelter or land, the economically weak migrant population attempts to occupy the vacant lands. The abysmal environmental quality in the slum areas is compounded by the inability and awareness among the slum dwellers to take up self help initiatives for improvement.

Thirdly, there is a substantial ignorance and insensitiveness among the city population, in general, and civic administration, in particular, on the significant contribution of the slum dwellers for the overall growth of the urban economy and their self-help initiatives are treated 'insignificant' in the over all growth of the urban economy. Rather than citizens, the slum dwellers are considered as a "civic problem".

Fourthly, the marginalisation of the slum dwellers in the city fabric is total. A shelter in the "formal settlement" remaining unaffordable, geographic marginalisation of the "occupied" areas, which are often unsuited for human habitation, is absolute. The cumulative neglect and marginalisation of this crucial segment of population encompasses social, economic and political terms too.

Promotion of cities without slums offers a challenge that needs many initiatives of larger magnitude from the civic administration, the citizens and the slum dwellers. The imperatives cover wide ranging reforms like planning, administration and legal initiatives that would encourage assimilation of the slum population in the city fabric. The need is an effort to engineer an integration that encompasses social, economic, geographic and political aspects so that city develops as an inclusive entity, the slum dwellers feel part of the citizenry, and the general public perceive them as fellow citizens than as a civic problem.

The Issues in Scaling up

Moving from pilot slum upgrading projects to city wide and nation wide scales of action will require tackling the following critical development issues:

Good Governance

The capacity of local governments must be strengthened to carryout their responsibility for the equitable provision of infrastructure and services to all urban residents while planning for future growth. And the capacity of local, state and national authorities must be strengthened to ensure their critical normative roles, to establish facilitating policy environments, and to rid corruption from land markets and the provision of public services.

Legal System

Property rights and security of tenure are critical to sustainable approaches to upgrading. The vast majority of the residents of urban slums live without any form of secure tenure, often under constant threat of eviction, vitiating their ability to access credit and constraining their motivation to improve their homes and neighbourhoods.

Financial System

Coupled with security of tenure, access to credit is to unleashing the vast potential of the urban poor to improve their living and working environments and livelihoods. Micro-credit and other facilities to expand access to credit to the poor can provide critical elements of institutional support in creating financially self-supporting and sustainable urban upgrading programmes like Nehru Rozgar Yojana (NRY), Urban Basic Services Programme (UBSP), Prime Minister's Integrated Urban Poverty Eradication Programme (PMI UPEP), Shelter and Sanitation Facilities for Foot-path Dwellers (SASFFD), National Slum Development Programme (NSDP), Swarna Jayanti Shehari Rozgar Yojana (SJSRY), Urban Self-Employment Programme (USEP) and the Urban Wage Employment Programme (UWEP).

Social Framework

Community participation in the conception, development, financing and upgrading of infrastructure and services is a critical element of sustainable programmes.

Strategies for Slum Improvement in Urban Areas

1. Extension of Land Tenure

Extension of secure land tenure remains the single most appropriate method to ensure environmental improvement of poor income localities.

2. Realistic Land Policies for increased availability of land

The urban land policies need to forecast the realistic requirements for developed land, and formulate strategies and plans to ensure optimal availability of the land. Innovative initiatives such as land banking have been promoted in various states such as Tamil Nadu, Madhya Pradesh and others which need to be suitably adopted in all large cities.

3. *Slum dwellers to be recognised as partners in city development*

4. *City plans to be sensitive to the special shelter needs of slum dwellers*

In view of substantial quantum of home-based self-help economic activities undertaken by the weaker sections in general and slum dwellers in particular, the shelter designs advocated need to be on the pattern of workshed-cum-shelter.

5. Promotion of rental housing by Public and Private Sector

Large scale rental housing programmes need to be promoted which could be offered to the slum dwellers linked to their capacity to pay. The rental dues need to be so designed that with the increase in income levels, it would be preferable for the occupants to opt for a hire-purchase scheme rather than continue to pay the rental dues.

6. City planning to recognise slum dwellers as 'inhabitants' for infrastructure provision

The planning and development institutions continue to provide essential services to the various zones as per the original plan, which does not include the substantial quantum of population living in the slums in such zones of the city.

7. City plan to delineate integrated zones for planning

The civic bodies often identify the slum areas as independent zones, which results in apportionment of marginal developmental initiatives, in view of anticipated poor returns in relation to investments. The infrastructure availability in such zones occupied by the low income population continues to be poor, thereby underlining the spatial divide between the communities. In such cases, the authorities may delineate zones for infrastructure development which may have people of varied economic status. This would enable the availability of higher levels of infrastructure through cross subsidisation of the development costs for the weaker sections and low income groups.

8. *Initiation for economic emancipation and self-reliance of slum dwellers*

The ability to engage in multiple income-generating small scale enterprises is well recognised. It is in this context that there is a need to take up special promotional initiatives to extend financial and marketing support to the slum-dwellers in various self help activities that could enhance their income-earning capacity.

9. *Approaches to slum area development to be comprehensive rather than sectoral in emphasis*

To ensure an overall improvement in the quality of life, the development initiatives need to be comprehensive in their coverage, and address the economic, educational, health and shelter requirements of the slum dwellers. The programmes need to incorporate a substantial part of beneficiary involvement and contribution in order to ensure sustainability in the long run.

10. *Need for city wide strategies*

The strategies evolved for upgradation of slums, and also to control their formation and proliferation, need to be based on a whole town approach rather than through spatially sporadic efforts. The efforts in selected slum areas of the city, while resulting in improvement of the living conditions, may inadvertently fuel the proliferation of slums.

11. *Increasing the access to credit for self-help shelter initiatives*

The lending institutions need to evolve packages for this special category with appropriate repayment schedules and terms and security options. With substantial cohesion often seen among the residents particularly on issues relating to the shelter and environmental improvement, community-based securities/ mortgages being successfully experimented in a number of developing countries recently is another mechanism that has potential for adoption in slum areas.

12. *Need to involve slum dwellers in City Governance process*

In spite of the fact that about one-third of the population of the large cities live in slums and slum like conditions, their involvement in the urban governance process has been marginal.

A major initiative to promote awareness among the city population, in general, about the need for the involvement of the slum dwellers is an urgent necessity. They need to be enlightened on their potential contribution for ensuring sustainable city development in the long run. Neighbourhood groups in the slum settlements would be facilitated that may among other things identify collective actions for promoting a healthy environment.

13. Promotion of regional settlement system

There is a need to promote policies that would help to reduce the regional imbalances in income levels and the standard of quality of life as primarily reflected by the accessibility services.

Suggestions

- An effective approach towards community involvement right from the beginning for sustainable development in a slum situation.
- To provide proper facilities and real needs of the community to be correctly assessed and prioritised.
- To encourage the women's participation so that the needs and problems affecting their daily lives can be taken care by themselves.
- Community participation in the planning process gives due weightage to their perceptions in tackling the problems.
- Identification of problems and suggestions for possible solutions make the beneficiaries responsive.
- Transparency in the planning and close monitoring by the community helps in proper implementation.
- Gender-sensitisation takes place with the participation of women in large numbers.
- Base-level information on health, environment and socio-economic issues including literacy, income, etc. can be provided for the improvement of slums.
- Multi-disciplinary concept comprising engineering, health and community awareness.
- To approach slum development pragmatically, it is necessary to attack the root cause of such habitations, namely to search for economic opportunities.

- A well conceived economic development programme may be an effective intervention.
- Slum cannot be developed in isolation; effective networking between micro-interventions in slums and macro-infrastructure facilities in the metro-core is a must.
- Models of slum development will only succeed with parallel inroads into poverty alleviation schemes.

Conclusion

People's participation has to begin with an active interest by all city dwellers in civic affairs. In Japan there is a system of community management of civic services, such as street sweeping, garbage collection, maintenance of environmentally sensitive areas, gardens, parks, etc. Tasks in this connection are assigned to every family living in a locality and one sees the footpaths being looked after by one group of housewives, roadside plantations being attended by another group and garbage being properly collected and stacked by yet another. In India, we have yet to develop such a sense of community participation a very strong participatory programme in cities which is better managed by the citizens themselves.

Good local governance calls for a totally integrated approach in which government, the municipal body, the community and citizens, all play a coordinated role. To the extent the municipal body is able to empower its citizens, to the extent communities accept their responsibility to organise themselves to manage their local problems/ issues, to the extent that we are able to make all the citizens participate in the management of their own local problems, our cities will become better places to live. The 74th Amendment of the Constitution is only an enabling provision which starts the process of empowerment of people in urban slum areas.

REFERENCES

Government of India (1995) 'A Compendium of Central Schemes for Urban Employment, Poverty Alleviation and Housing', MOUA &E.

Gurumukhi, K.T. (2000), 'Slum Related Policies and Programmes', *Shelter* (Special Issue on Urban Poverty), 3 (2).

Jayapal, P. 'Cities without Slums-Imperatives towards achieving the dream', *Ibid.*

Palnitkar, Sneha (2000), "Promoting People's Participation for Local Governance in Urban Areas', *Shelter* (Special Issue on Urban Poverty), 3.

'Upgrading Urban Communities-A Resume Framework', (2001), *Shelter*, World Habitat Day, Special Issue on Cities without Slums, 4(3).

27

Threat to South Asian Security: Regionalism, Nuclearism and Terrorism—An Analysis

Introduction

In South Asian security discourse, regional, extra-regional linkages is an oft-researched area in which regional powers like India and Pakistan, on the one hand, and extra-regional powers like the USA, former Soviet Union, China, on the other have figured prominently. Perspectives of the countries outside India-Pakistan dyadic relations are often neglected. In the mean time, security scenario in the regions has undergone radical qualitative change in the wake of nuclear explosions by India and Pakistan. This has raised concerns among the non-nuclear countries in the region and beyond. While bulk of the one billion population are steeped in poverty. While rapidly deteriorating ecology in the region is taking its toll, nuclearisation of the region has added a new dimension of serious proportions so much so that powers that matter outside the region have expressed concerns, not to speak of the sanctions imposed by the western countries.

This Paper analyses the concepts of regionalism, nuclearism and terrorism and the impact on the South Asian security.

Regionalism in South Asia

The Foreign policies refer primarily to the countries which at present are the members of the South Asian Association for

---

Paper Presented at:

"Silver Jubilee Commemoration National Seminar on South Asia: Challenges to Security" held on 23rd and 24th January 2004 organised by Department of Defence and Strategic Studies, Guru Nanak College, Velachery, Chennai - 600 042, Tamil Nadu.

Regional Co-operation and which are Bangladesh, Bhutan, India, Nepal, Pakistan, Maldives and Sri Lanka. The foreign policies of these countries are usually shaped by their geopolitical situation *vis-a-vis* the regions and the outside world and their internal Politics. There is an over shadowing factor in the foreign policies of all these countries, which is the physical and political predominance of India in the region. This is not a question of political threats from India but its size and reach which makes it a major factor to reckon with. This aspect is heightened by Bangladesh were politically and physically a part of India, and Nepal and Bhutan were part dependent on it until post Independence times. Sri Lanka on the other hand enjoys sovereign Independence and Maldives was linked to it during colonial times with independence these countries have of course asserted their independence in their foreign policies but the tensions between India and Pakistan reflect the impact of India while the other states are watchful of their relations, with Sri Lanka enjoying a record of close friendship with India. There is no concerted policy on their part *vis-a-vis* India but that they are watchful of their relations with the big brother which is an acknowledgement of its impact. SAARC, which was established in 1980, is a conscious effort to harmonise relations between them and induce a collective approach apart from undertaking several collective activities for their common good.

It has a long way to go but no doubt a good start has been made which should enable them to reap the benefits like other regional bodies such EU and ASEAN membership of SAARC has not inhibited links with the wider world and several countries have excelled in it like Pakistan's links with the Islamic World, Sri Lanka's open economic policy and non-alignment and bonds between SAARC countries and ASEAN. In international relations the strategic significance of South Asia was a factor in the cold-war, which made it an object of interest of the superpowers.

South Asian countries have shown their awareness of these internal and external challenges and Sri Lanka has set an example with this steadfast record of friendship with India and non-alignment in international affairs.

Apart from the external and security factors, foreign policy is decided upon by the government of a country and it is necessary to consider the character of governments of South Asia. Basically these are of two kinds, which are parliamentary democracies, where power is vested in a particular party and authoritarian regions. In parliamentary democracies foreign policy is the decision of the government in office, which in turn represents the philosophy and outlook of the parties which installed it. To that extent foreign policy becomes a party issue and this can result in a lack of continuity, which can cause a sense of uncertainty in international relations. However, the multiplicity of states and creeds in the world our time have given it a truly multilateral character which can absorb political vicissitudes in states. Foreign policy is a key issue in party politics.

Regionalism has been considered as something that is antifederal and hostile to the basic interests of a well integrated polity. Regionalism is often regarded as "a very serious threat to the development, progress and unity of the country". The term "regionalism" is of comparatively recent origin. Haqqi, S.A.H., says, "whatever the context of parameter, region may be said to connote an area, at least sufficiently large in size, which is differentiated and distinguishable from others by a variety of factors, such as language, culture, caste/creed, socio-economic life, political background, historical background, geographical continuity and certainly, group consciousness and of being neglected, deprived or discriminated by the majority or those in authority". Regionalism was inspired, not merely by the factors like caste, linguistic groups and attitudinal anti-cultures, but also by prevailing economic conditions of different regional communities.

It is clear that regionalism is rooted in South Asia's cultural, ethnic and linguistic diversity. It is posing threat to national unity and territorial integrity. Regionalism, always, should not be viewed as a threat to our federal system, but as a reaction against our centralisation and a reflection of people's desire to maintain their cultural identities and demand for more balanced development. It is only be adopting a healthy and constructive approach towards the problem of regionalism based on a careful study of the diverse milieu where in its roots lie, that the efficiency of the political system and the process of national and international integration can be better assured and the twin goals of development and democracy assured. The Indian political system has to evolve an accommodative structure for a co-operative union. The goals of unity, development and democracy can be achieved only through participative and accommodative models of politics. The aspirations of various regions are in reality unfulfilled. But as the Punjab and Kashmir problems have shown, the worst of situations can be dealt with by a mixture of effective retalisation and accommodation, strengthening the body of the nation state in the ultimate analysis.

Nuclearism in South Asia

Since India detonated its first nuclear explosive device in 1974, the spector of a nuclear arms race has loomed large over the Indian Sub-Continent. Today both India and Pakistan have acquired the source of the fissile material for nuclear weapons as well as substantial command of the technology for manufacturing weapons. They also aircraft that are capable of delivering nuclear weapons to targets inside each others territory and missile technology advances in both nations are strengthening rival delivery capability. China whose actions strongly influence the South Asian proliferation landscape, has also launched as ambitious programme to expand its nuclear armoury and has made important strides in recent years. Significantly, however, neither India nor Pakistan has chosen to develop a declared nuclear weapons arsenal. This restraint, which is due to both international pressure and subcontinental strategic considerations, provides some hope that some arms controls and confidence building measures can be constructed to stop the further spread of nuclear weapons in the region.

According to American strategic specialists, Levis A. Dunn and Herman Kahan have listed as many as fourteen reasons or pressures encouraging a country to go nuclear. They have classified these reasons under several heads such as security, status or influence, bureaucratic and domestic factors. They have also identified eight types of events as 'Trigger' activating consideration on the pressure or reasons for a country going nuclear.

These are Involvement in foreign crisis, reduction in alliance credibility, nuclearisation of other countries; weakening or break down of international constraints; domestic crisis, changed perception and utility of nuclear weapons.

According to another analyst Mayer, notes three basic types of incentives, first incentives of international political prestige and image building. These can affect the country's appearance and posture. Second incentives to advance national military and security objectives, to minimize external threats to the country and to strengthen its relative power position and strength. Third, incentives to support and promote domestic policies and to prevail in domestic political struggles. Fourth, sets of arguments are frequently advanced by threshold states aiming to retain the nuclear options - military security, political prestige and influence, economic gains and domestic pressures and compulsions.

So far as South Asia is concerned, national security concern has been the principal factor in the process of nuclearisation. South Asia proliferators border hostile countries or nuclear weapon potential countries. Indo-Pakistan hostility has been there since partition in 1947, and there have been two wars on this front. There has been another war between India and China. The key territorial issue of Kashmir has its roots in the colonial history of the sub-continent and involves Pakistan, India and China. India and Pakistan continue to claim the entire state of Kashmir for themselves. Since 1984, India and Pakistan have engaged in sporadic battle over the control of the Siachen glacier in Kashmir. In December 1987, poor communications and mutual misperceptions almost led to war, and by the spring of 1990, many expected a sub-continental nuclear war between the two.

From a strategic view point, Islamabad's nuclear programme is driven mainly by its threat perception and security concern with respect to India. In contrast, India's nuclear calculations are centered on China a which has an expanding nuclear arsenal. Pakistan sees its potential nuclear forces as a deterrent to India's conventional military advantages and strategic ambitions. India, whose military build up was spurred by its humiliating defeat in the 1962 war with China, views its nuclear programme as the vital component of a strategic plan to deter against a more powerful China.

John J. Schulz has rightly observed that, "The rationale presented by leading government officials in New Delhi and

Islamabad to justify the current state of their weapons programme is analogous to the ocean food chain-big fish eats small fish which has just eaten the small fish. China created its nuclear deterrent with fears of Moscow and Washington in mind. China is feared by India and India is feared by Pakistan. All three countries justify their present nuclear policies as a solution to security problems. A fully declared arsenal in China, a nuclear weapons 'option' in India and now in Pakistan. "An ability to assemble", as the equalizing deterrent".

Terrorism in South Asia

Terrorism has indeed become a global phenomenon with increasing and rather well identifiable links between terrorist groups or organizations. They use each others areas or organizations for recruitment and training, exchange illegal weapons, engage in joint planning and ventures and also provide administrative and other logistic support.

Many different definitions of terrorism have been proposed, the commonest elements mentioned in these are use of force, political purpose, terror or fear, threat and anticipated psychological effects or reactions by third parties or practice of using violent and intimidating methods especially to secure political ends. No single definition is authoritatively accepted in the academic world because various commonly used definition have many defects. Earlier the statistics suggests that international terrorism is not a serious threat, but recently it is taken as one because of its opposition to democracy and the violation of human rights.

Terrorism perpetrated by both left and right using extremists, continues to threaten peace and democracy. Such a terrorism does not have a precise definition as employed in the west, especially, bourgeoisie pluralism and eclecticism refuse to relate terrorism to class specific struggle.

Recently, South Asia has emerged as a hub for international terrorism with Pakistan and Afghanistan providing support to international terrorist groups. The US State Department in its reposition terrorism, which was released recent, says that both Pakistan and Afghanistan are providing support to international terrorism and specially to Pakistan, has sent mixed messages on terrorism by harbouring and aiding terrorism including many who are fighting in Jammu and Kashmir like Harkat-Ul-Mujahhideen, Harakat-a-Taiba, Lashkar-a-Taiba etc.

The US apparently has tough words for Afghanistan primarily related to Osama Bin Laden (Who is responsible for terrorist activities in the world). But it restrained Afghanistan or Pakistan to the list of nations sponsoring terrorism. Adding a country to the list entails some sweeping penalties, primarily on the economic front. The report on terrorism is one of the many report cards, the US issues every year on and about the world. The US has also said these are credible reports that Pakistan continues to support groups such as the Harkat-ul-Mujahideen, one of whose leader Maulana Masood Azhar was freed from Indian prison in exchange for hostages abroad on Indian Airlines plane in December, 1999.

Suicide terrorism is the new phenomenon in the sphere of international relations, mainly in south and South East Asia. The concept of suicide terrorism was acquired by emulation or by the transfer of technology through group to group contact. The groups currently engaged in suicide terrorism have Political, Military and Financial links with several other groups. The number of groups engaged in suicide terrorism has increased between the 1980's and the 1990's. Islamic group of Egypt in Pakistan and Croatia and LTTE in Sri Lanka and India. Among the contemporary terrorist groups engaged in suicide attacks, the LTTE has conducted the largest number of attacks. The Black Tigers are constitued exclusively of cadres who have volunteered to conduct suicide operations.

The suicide terrorism syndrome which has become acute in South Asia and West Asia in the past two decades, has not driven states most affected by the menace to study and uproot it. By acquiring and comparatively analyzing a wide range of datas, a deeper understanding of the distinction between suicide and non-suicide terrorism must be gained. This is essential to evolve solutions to suicide terrorism.

Coming in closer to LTTE suicide terrorism in Sri Lanka, the two terrorist outfits in Kashmir, such as the Laskar - Toiba and

Hizbal Mujahideen have made it chillingly evident that cross-border terrorism has become a deadly menace in the Kashmir Valley.

Nuclear terrorism is another important and latest development in international relations. Nuclear Terrorism is discussed within the over all context of world wide violence and terrorist, particularly the growing problem of state supported terrorism initiated as a means of advancing revolutionary foreign policy. The ever increasing proliferation of nuclear weapons and materials makes the threat of their being stolen by or supplied to terrorists. Besides nuclear weapons, terrorists are now seeking biological and chemical weapons of mass destruction as also practicing cyber terrorism. There is a geographic shift too with terrorism moving East to South Asia, especially Afghanistan. The political ramifications of such an incidents are very serious.

Terrorism by its nature seeks to destroy a nations political will as well as violates individuals rights. Some of the characteristics of terrorism include:

1. Political assassination,
2. Mass intimidation by murders, physical or mental harm,
3. Continuing crime,
4. Generic genocide,
5. A co-operative crime functionally and technically,
6. Plurivalent activity,
7. Propaganda by action,
8. Kidnapping and plane hijacking and
9. Narco - terrorism

In order to establish international equilibrium and protect human rights, the following efforts were to be made:

(a) The genocide convention,

(b) Charter and resolution law on aggression,

(c) Treaty law on the protection of air communications,

(d) Protection of diplomats,

(e) Primacy of the international qualification of international offences, and

(f) The strict adaptation of international law to control acts of terrorism. Although terrorism is usually associated only with extremist groups, governments can also be responsible for acts of terrorism. Before international law can be formulated to reduce and punish terrorist acts, elimination of a double standard must be guaranteed, acts of terror by small groups and by national governments must be prosecuted with equal vigor. Only when no individual or groups is considered to be above the law, will the world be free from terrorism. In spite of the attempts made to curb genocide, little has been done to combat terrorism. The need for an anti-terrorist law at international level is just as important as law concerning the prevention of terrorism.

Conclusion

Having aware of the danger posed by the spread of regionalism, nuclearism and terrorism and harmful effect on peace, co-operation, friendship and good neighbourly relations and which could also jeopardise the sovereignty and territorial integrity of states, the member states of SAARC, at Bangalore summit of November 1986, adopted a regional convention on suppression of Terrorism. The heads of state or Government of SAARC expressed serious concern on the spread of terrorism in the region affecting the security and stability of all member states and unequivocally condemned all acts, methods and practice of terrorism, as criminal. They deplored all such acts for their impact on life, property, socio-economic development and political stability as well as on regional and international peace and co-operation.

Terrorism, nuclearism of any kind, whether it is national or international is obviously results in the destruction of wealth and life of the innocents is nothing but a violation of human rights. International terrorism, nuclearism specially sponsored by fundamentalist states failed to protect the basic rights and immunities of the diplomats. Therefore, it is necessary to plan with conviction the best and workable methods to face the challenges thrown by international terrorism to humanity in the twenty-first century.

REFERENCES

Dr. S.A. Palekar "Regionalism : A Threat to International Security", *Third concept*, Vol. 12, No. 134-35, April - May, 1998, New Delhi.

Dr. Aftab Alam "Nuclerisation in South Asia, Incentives and Motivations", *Third concept*, Vol. 11, No. 127, September 97, New Delhi.

Dr. Chandrakant Yatanoor "International terrorism. Violation of Human rights", *Third concept*, Vol. 4, No. 164, October 2000, New Delhi.

Abdur Rob Khan "South Asian Security in the New Millenium: Bangladesh Perspectives", *Liberal Times*, A forum for liberal policy in South Asia, Volume IX, Number 4, 2001, New Delhi.

Dr. Vernon LB Mendis, "Foreign Policies in South Asia", *Liberal Times*, Volume XI, Number 2, 2003, New Delhi.

28

Poverty Alleviation Programmes Indira Gandhi's 20-point Programme

The package of economic measures announced by the Prime Minister, Smt. Indira Gandhi, on July 1, 1975 is indeed the need of the hour. The main contents of the 20-point programme are:

1. Measures to check the price rise

According to the 20-point programme, continued steps shall be taken to bring down the prices of essential commodities. Production plans have been streamlined and procurement and distribution of essential commodities has been taken up by the government on a quite large scale. Strict economy in government expenditure is also to be observed.

2. Implementation of Agricultural land ceilings

Under this economic programme implementation of agricultural land ceilings and speedier distribution of surplus land and compilation of land rewards occupy a special place.

3. Provision of house sites for landless and weaker sections

The 20-point economic programme aims at stepping up provision for house sites for landless and weaker sections of the society. Small Farmers Development Agencies (SFDA) and Marginal Farmers and Agricultural Labourers Development Agency Programmes were also undertaken for the development of weaker sections.

---

*Paper presented at UGC sponsored National Seminar on Smt. Indira Gandhi's Garibi Hatao (Relevance, Revival & Restructure) during 16th & 17th March 2007, Organized by centre for Indira Gandhi studies, Sri Padmavathi Mahila Visvavidyalayam, Tirupati 517 502.

4. Abolition of Bonded Labour

The practice of bonded labour is barbarous, inhuman, unjust, degrades human dignity, illegal and will be abolished.

5. Plan for liquidation of Rural Indebtedness

This includes imposition of moratorium on the recovery of debt from small agriculturists. After complete liquidation of rural indebtedness, government is also making a provision of alternative sources of credit for small agriculturists.

6. Review and Improvement of Minimum Agricultural wages

It aims at providing higher minimum wages to the farm workers. In order to achieve this objective, serious efforts have been made. New laws prescribing enhanced minimum agricultural wages and revision of existing low wages has been taken up.

7. Programme of increasing the area under irrigation

Twenty point economic programme basically aims at improving the performance of agriculture the programme also aims at integrated rural development.

8. Accelerated power Development programme

In this economic programme for economic progress, there are measures to increase infrastructure resources through the expansion of major, medium and minor irrigation projects and accelerated power development programmes. Efforts have also been made to tackle the problem of unemployment to a certain extent by introducing apprenticeship schemes.

9. Development of the Handloom Sector

The Programme also contains a new development plan for the development of the handloom sector.

10. Improvement of the controlled cloth Scheme

Prime Minister said, "In the mill sector the controlled cloth scheme is being improved, so that dhothis, sarees and cloth will be of better quality and are sold through a larger number of outlets in rural and urban areas.

11. Socialization of Urban and Urbanisable land

Speculation in land and the concentration of urban property have led to glaring in equalities and to great deal of haphazard urban growth. Legislation is being initiated to impose ceiling on the ownership and possession of vacant land, to acquire excess land, to restrict the plinth area of new dwelling units and socialize urban and urbanisable land.

12. Appointment of Special squads for valuation to Conspicuous construction and prevention of Tax-evasion

Another very important provision of the 20-point economic programme is the appointment of special squads for valuation of conspicuous construction and prevention of tax-evasion. There is a provision of summary offenders shall be given.

13. Confiscation of smugglers properties

The 20-point economic programme wants to end the smuggling completely. Under the new economic programme, special legislation for confiscation of smugglers properties shall be enacted.

14. Liberalization of investment procedures and check on the misuse of import licences

Liberalization of investments below which no licence is at all required and simplication of licensing procedures shall also augment production. Introduction of schemes like worker's participation in management will succeed in getting more co-operation from the labourers and thus maintaining industrial peace and harmony on the one hand and increasing national productivity on the other hand.

15. Schemes for workers participation in industries

Schemes for workers participation in industries particularly at the shop floor level and production programmes were introduced.

16. National permit Scheme for Road Transport

Prime Minister said, "The movement of food grains, coal, steel and cement by railways has improved in the last few months.

Constraints on the movement of goods by trucks will also be removed. For this purpose, we are introducing a system of national permits".

17. Income Tax Relief to the middle class

Under this programme Income Tax relief has provided middle class and to encourage small savings.

18. Provision of essential commodities at controlled prices to students residing in hostels

Provision of essential commodities at controlled prices for the students in hostels and, similarly, provision of books and stationery. Controlled prices will be provide a great financial relief to the parents and students.

19. Provision of Books and Stationery at controlled prices

Under this programme Books and Stationery shall be provided to students at controlled prices.

20. Introduction of new apprenticeship scheme for enlarging employment and training opportunities, especially for the weaker sections. At present the following schemes are look after by the SHG wing of Rural Development

1. Swarnajayanti Gram Swarozgar Yojana (SGSY)
2. Self Help Groups (a) State Revolving Fund, (b) SHG Bank linkage & Interest subsidy, (c) Deepam, (d) Gruhini
3. Special projects
4. TRYSEM
5. DRDA Administration
6. (NSAP) National Social Assistance Programme

Swarnajayanti Gram Swarozgar Yojana (SGSY)

This is a centrally sponsored scheme funded by the government of India and the State Government in the ratio 75:25. All the existing schemes upto 1998-1999 IRDP, TRYSEM, TOOLKITS, DWCRA, GKY and MWS have been merged in the new Scheme called Swarnajayanti Gram Swarozgar Yojana (SGSY). This programme has come into existence w.e.f. 1.4.1999. The objective of the SGSY is to bring poor families above the poverty line by providing them income generating assets through a mix of bank credit and government subsidy. The key elements in this programme are the choice of activity based on local resources and aptitude as well as the skills of Swarozgaries.

S.G.S.Y. focuses on group approach. This would involve organization of the poor into Self Help Groups (SHGs) and their capacity building. Efforts are being made to involve women members in each SHG. Besides, exclusive women groups will continue to be formed. At the level of the Mandal, almost all the groups are exclusively women groups. Group activity will be given preference and progressively, majority of the funding will be for Self Help Groups. The scheme consists of 5 major components:

1. Infrastructure, 2. Training, 3. Revolving Fund, 4. Group Loan and 5. Individual Loan.

Relevance of the 20-point programme as on today

After 1991 the new economic Policy stresses the need for the increasing the productivity in the economy. At the same time, it does not provide for enough safety for large section of the rural poor. The new economic policy suggests that the benefits of economic reform would reach the poor. This can be in the form of price stabilization and new jobs, resulting from the increased dynamism in the economy. However, in a country like India where the increase in the rural poor to wait for the benefits of the new economic policy which would flow much later.

Due to liberalization, globalization and privatization the Indira Gandhi's 20-point programme's objectives are undermined. The Nationalization Policy reversed to privatization and the allocations for poverty alleviation programmes in real terms have been going down. If we adjust the allocations made under these programmes to the general increase in prices, it is clear that the state's support for poverty alleviation is coming down.

As a result of the economic reform the share of indirect tax in the overall revenue collections has been increasing. This would further led to the erosion of purchasing power of the rural poor. Hopes on the agricultural export potential are not materialising. International agricultural market is infact very small. When a country like India offers to export the basic food products like rice, sugar, the international prices come down. Similarly, when India has to import the rice, the prices would go up. This clearly establishes the disadvantageous position of India in its negotiating capability.

Poverty Alleviation Programmes and Women

A woman is an economic producer, a home manager, a scarcity manager, a child bearer, a food provider, a caretaker of children and the elderly. Women work longer hours with fewer resources and for lower rewards. Their work is largely unremunerative and therefore, when valued against market standards, their contribution is invariably undervalued. House-hold work is a classic example. Therefore, any debate on the impact of economic liberalization on women is necessarily a part of much wider debate on how women's concerns and women's participation can be brought from the margins of development to more central position, as economic policies play an increasingly major role in society. In other words, women's concerns and women's perspective have been generally peripheral to the process of development planning, the world over, it is extremely difficult to try and isolate any impact due to a particular economic policy measure, say economic liberalization on women. It is the combination of relatively slow process of economic liberalization of women that have contributed to unfounded and impressionistic accounts of any impact of these policies on women.

Generally, the literature regarding the impact of liberalization process on women relate such impact to three broad causative factors.

1. The first of these relate to the nature of these processes which many affect women via inflation, leading to greater household demands on fewer resources, which given the skewed and discriminations intra-household distribution patterns, can further marginalize women and girls in poor families. Through reduced public expenditure and high user costs, these measures are also expected to result in a partial transfer of costs of various social services to the household, which once again affects women more, given intra-household gender discrimination.
2. The second stream of factors are related to labour market changes resulting from such factors as increasing expert orientation which are likely to squeeze out the handicraft and subsistence agricultural sectors both of which are large employers of women.
3. The third stream of factors relate to increased industrial competitiveness and the technology intensive nature of development, which given women's low skill level and low literacy, are likely to further undervalue women's contribution and marginalise them in the job market.

The crux of the problem is to prepare women to face a society which is increasingly becoming not just labour intensive or capital intensive, but knowledge intensive.

Women must be prepared to device the maximum benefits from the liberalization process. Enabling women to overcome their traditional impediments to face the employment market an equal terms with men is a major task. Education, skill development, literacy, organization, support services to meet gender needs, training and retaining pertaining to new areas are some of the critical inputs that are necessary.

Conclusion

The government has always been conscious of the efforts that are required to mitigate the possible negative short-term impact of the liberalization policy on women. However, such efforts cannot just be limited to expanding safety nets. Women's needs, concerns and perspectives have to be voiced and articulated so that adjustment programmes assist their empowerment and advancement. The multiple facets of women's roles have to be taken into account and efforts have to be made to identify potential growth areas, women should be provided with the necessary skills, contacts and bargaining power to take full advantage of new openings, a rising out of the impact of new economic policies. But one has to understand the relevance of 20-point programme and its pragmatic approach in alleviating poverty especially among rural poor. But unfortunately new economic policies affecting the empowerment of women instead of help them in all corners of life.

REFERENCES

All India Congress Committee Meeting, May 29-30, 1976, New Delhi.

Prime Minister's broadcasting on July 1, 1975 on 20-point Economic Programme.

B. Sudhakar Rao, "Social Welfare and poverty alleviation in the context of new economic policy" NIRD, Nov 1998, Hyderabad.

Annual Report 2005, Dept of Rural Development, GOAP, Hyderabad.

29

Role of Urban Local Bodies in Poverty Alleviation in India

Introduction

The local government is the tier of the government which is closest to the people. In India, Urban Local Bodies came into existence several decades ago. However, they have had limited exposure to various policies and programmes which have been formulated to address urban poverty issues directly. All these programmes were mainly formulated at the national level without any involvement of local government. However, of late, things have been changing for a greater involvement of in the formulation and implementation of Urban Poverty Alleviation programmes.

Role of Urban Local Bodies

Though Urban Local Bodies came into existence several decades ago in India, they could undertake ever increasing demand for the municipal services in an effective manner due to a variety of reasons like scarcity of funds, lack of power and technical expertise, restriction of certain functions and frequent dissolutions and supersessions. During 70s and 80s, some of the primary civic functions were withdrawn from the Urban Local Bodies and were given to several non-representative statutory authorities. Urban Local Bodies were left only with functions like street lighting and registration of birth and deaths, etc. They were not really involved in any of the poverty alleviation policies and programmes in an effective manner. They were not consulted

---

*Paper presented at National Seminar on "Urban Poverty Alleviation" During 25-26th July, 2005. Organised by Regional Centre for Urban and Environmental Studies, Osmania University, Hyderabad - 500 007, A.P.

by the national and state governments while formulating Urban Poverty Alleviation programmes. It was only when these programmes failed to live up to the expectations, the realisation of true decentralisation planning came in the beginning of 90s.

Nagar Palika Act (74th Constitutional Amendment Act)

The Government of India enacted the famous 74th Constitutional Amendment Act in 1992 to provide constitutional base for the Urban Local Bodies and gave them the status of a third-tier of government. This Act, better known as "Nagar Palika Act" aims at systematic constitution of Urban Local Bodies, proper representation of all sections of people in the council, regularity in the election, well-differentiated financial allocations and all devolution of planning down to grass-root level. It added the 12th schedule municipalities where urban poverty alleviation has been treated as a legitimate municipal function. The Act facilitated the fruitful partnership between ULB-higher levels of government and also decentralisation in the implementation of programmes.

However, it is not hard to find that after more than 19 years of enactment of Nagarpalika Act, not much progress has been made as yet. Many states have yet to incorporate the all important 12th schedule in their legislation. Moreover, things not changed for strengthening institutional arrangements at town/local level for effective implementation of the Urban Poverty Alleviation programmes. There is, thus, a felt need for a system at local body level to secure and ensure the people's participation in anti-poverty programmes. The best systems is one that is created by the participate target families in planning, implementation and monitoring of the programmes.

Urban Poverty Alleviation Programmes in the 90s

Quite a few developments for urban poverty alleviation got underway as a fall out of the 74th Constitutional Amendment Act. The Urban Poverty Alleviation programmes which were in operation like NRY, UBSP were modified to enable the participation of Urban Local Bodies and communities in the implementation. The Eighth Five Year Plan which started in 1992 gave further momentum to the urban poverty alleviation drive with a couple of new programmes viz; (i) Prime Minister's Integrated Urban Poverty Eradication Programme (PMIUPEP);

and (ii) National Slum Development Programme (NSDP). In 1997, the beginning year of IX plan, NRY, and PMIUPEP programmes were withdrawn and merged to form a new scheme "Swarna Jayanti Sahari Rojgar Yojana" (SJSRY). The role of Urban Local Bodies in some of the programmes implemented in 90s is described in the following paragraphs:

(i) Nehru Rozgar Yojana (NRY)

The Nehru Rozgar Yojana was launched in 1989 to cater to the economic needs of the urban poor by providing them employment opportunities through skill upgradation and assistance in setting up their micro-enterprises. The components of the scheme were: (i) Scheme for Urban Micro Enterprises (SUME); (ii) Scheme of Urban Employment (SUWE); and (iii) Scheme of Housing and Shelter Upgradation (SHASU).

One of the most important objectives of the NRY was involvement of Urban Local Bodies in various aspects of the programmes so as to enable them to play a major role in the analysis and selection of employment-oriented activities in the municipal areas, identification of beneficiaries, provision of land and space for employment activities and organising Nehru Rozgar Centres as effective platforms of co-ordination between specialised agencies, financial institutions, public authorities, municipal institutions and beneficiaries. However, due to some inherent weaknesses, Urban Local Bodies could not show genuine commitment to reach the target group through the NRY programme.

(ii) Urban Basic Services Programme (UBSP)

Urban Basic Services Programme (UBSP), a modified version of the earlier UBS programme was launched in 1992. It was a multi-dimensional and community-oriented scheme involving centre, state, Urban Local Bodies and the community. The programme was based on the seven guiding principles, namely, child and women focus, community involvement, cost-effectiveness, convergence, full coverage, continuity commitment of actors. It was a need-based strategy centred on consultation partnership between urban poor and the Urban Local Bodies for meeting the common needs, education, healthcare, water supply, sanitation, income generation, etc.

Urban Local Bodies were given the overall responsibility of implementing the programme in towns. A Urban Poverty Alleviation cell was to be created under the ULB to generate local municipal contributions, promoting linkage and convergence with all the sectional departments. Initially the Urban Basic Services Programme was successful but later due to various reasons including lack of clarity about the specific roles to be played by the agencies involved, the programme could not produce desired results and finally was scrapped in 1997.

(iii) Prime Minister's Integrated Urban Poverty Eradication Programme (PMIUPEP)

Consequent upon the 74th Constitutional Amendment Act, the Prime Minister's Integrated Urban Poverty Eradication Programme was launched in 1995 for improving the quality of life of urban poor by creating a facilitating environment for them through community based planning and implementation. Prime Minister's Integrated Urban Poverty Eradication Programme envisaged to involve Urban Local Bodies actively in the planning, implementation, monitoring and evaluation of this programme with this objective in view, a separate 'Urban Poverty Eradication Cell' (UPEC) was created in each town being covered under the programme, which functioned under the Urban Local Body. It also emphasised the establishment of a separate 'Town Urban poverty Eradication Fund' under the Urban Local Body in each town by pooling resources from central government, state government and Urban Local Body. As a following up of the 74th Constitutional Amendment Act, states are required to devolve funds to Urban Local Bodies by earmarking special grants for urban poverty reduction. Also Prime Minister's Integrated Urban Poverty Eradication Programme envisaged to bring about attitudinal changes among officials of the Urban Local Bodies as well as communities through suitable training, seminars, workshops and filed-based orientations. The responsibility of the Urban Local Bodies lied in identification; preparation of town action plan; project formulation and execution maintaining Town Urban Poverty Eradication Fund; co-ordination with NGOs/CBOs and other stakeholders; monitoring and reviewing of the programme.

(iv) Shelter and Sanitation Facilities for Footpath Dwellers

This is a central sector plan scheme formulated in 1988 and being implemented through HUDCO. The aim of the scheme is to ameliorate the living conditions and the shelter problems of the absolutely shelterless people in urban areas till such time they can secure affordable housing. This aim is sought to be achieved by construction of community night shelters, community pay and use toilets, improved sanitation facilities and upgradation of civic infrastructure. The role of Urban Local Bodies is very significant as the projects are formulated, constructed and operated and maintained by the Urban Local Bodies themselves. HUDCO is responsible for appraisal, financing and monitoring of scheme. The Urban Local Bodies are given prescribed subsidy through HUDCO along with the loan component from HUDCO. Urban Local Bodies are also required to conduct systematic survey identification, etc.

(v) National Slum Development Programme (NSDP)

"National Slum Development Programme" (NSDP) was introduced by the Government of India in 1996 as a special central assistance to states for upgradation of the urban slums by making provisions for physical and social amenities, community infrastructure, shelter etc. The scheme is designed to be implemented at the grass-root level by Neighbourhood Committees (NHCs) and Community Development Societies (CDSs) under the overall responsibility of Urban Local Bodies. Every Urban Local Body is required to create a separate sub-head in the budget for slum development and urban poverty reduction. Urban Local Bodies are also expected to set up a Slum Development Committee with co-opt representatives of NGOs/ CBOs, etc., to oversee all slum development programmes. The monitoring is also the responsibility of the Urban Local Bodies.

(vi) Swarna Jayanti Sahari Rozgar Yojana (SJSRY)

The Swarna Jayanti Sahari Rozgar Yojana (SJSRY), the latest urban poverty alleviation programme of the government of India which became operational in December 1998, seeks to provide gainful employment to the urban unemployed poor through encouraging the setting up of self-employment ventures or provision of wage employment. It is based on creation of suitable community structures on the Urban Basic Services Programme pattern. It consists of two special programmes, namely, (i) The Urban Self-employment Programme (USEP); and (ii) The Urban Wage Employment Programme (UWEP).

SJSRY recognises that the Urban Local Bodies are strategically placed to undertake local long-planning of the Urban Poverty Alleviation through the participation of Government, NGOs and CBOs. The involvement of Urban Local Bodies in various sectoral areas of operation with institutional co-ordination and monitoring and facilitating community participation is very much emphasised in this new programme.

However, the programme though implemented very recently, has many limitations. It only touched upon the employment generation aspect of the urban poverty reduction rather than an integrated approach considering the multi-dimensional nature of urban poverty.

Future Role of Urban Local Bodies

The present role being played by the Urban Local Bodies are very limited. In order to reduce urban poverty in an effective and sustainable manner, the Urban Local Bodies need to play much more proactive roles which could include: initiating planning process (Community Action Planning); formulating, evaluating and reviewing urban poverty reduction plans; coordinating and networking with other Urban Local Bodies and stakeholders; etc.

Conclusion

The strategies for poverty alleviation need to be integrally linked to the process of economic growth rather than treated as a supplement. The objective should be to integrate the poor with the process of economic growth rather than offer some poverty alleviatives. It is not necessary for the Government to directly provide employment to the poor or loans for setting up enterprises. Policies, which promote employment, may be far more effective. Thus unbundling of infrastructure services and their privatisation can open up avenues for increased employment for the poor.

The civil society will have to play a much greater role in alleviation of poverty. A large number of NGOs are involved in these programmes. There is need to multiply their efforts. It needs to be seriously considered whether the strategy should be multiplication of NGOs or scaling up of activities of NGOs. In our view the former is a superior option since community participation which is a necessary component of Poverty Alleviation strategy, tends to lose out in the latter case.

References

Akshaya Kumar Sen - *"Role of Urban Local Bodies in Poverty Alleviation Programmes"*, Shelter, Special issue on Urban Poverty, Vol. 3, No. 2, April, 2000, A HUDCO HSMI, New Delhi.

Govt. of India (1994) - *"73rd and 74th Constitutional Amendment Act"*, MOUA&E, New Delhi.

Govt. of India (1996) - *"India National Report"* for Habitat II, MOUA&E, New Delhi.

Govt. of India (1982-83) - *"Report on the Study Group on Constitution, Power and Laws of Urban Local Bodies"* New Delhi.

Govt. of India (1995) - *"A Compendium of Central Schemes for Urban Employment, Poverty Alleviation and Housing"*, MOUA&E, New Delhi, December.

Govt. of India (1997) - *"Swarna Jayanti Sahari Rozgar Yojana"*, New Delhi.

30
Drought Impact in Rayalaseema: Remedial Measures

Introduction

"The theme of the year 2004 was observance of World Water Day is "Water and Disasters: Be informed and be prepared". Water-related disasters - including floods, droughts, hurricanes, typhoons and tropical cyclones - inflict a terrible toll on human life and property, affecting millions of people and provoking crippling economic losses. As ever, it is the poor and vulnerable who are most adversely affected, but as we saw in Central Europe in 2002, even industrialized nations can suffer immensely. However much we would wish to think of these as strictly natural disasters, human activities play a significant role in increasing risk and vulnerability. And of course, there are also strictly man-made disasters, such as oil-spills and toxic run-off that do great damage to our precious water resources.

Modern society has distinct advantages over those civilizations of the past that suffered or even collapsed for reasons linked to water. We have great knowledge, and the capacity to disperse that knowledge to the remotest places on earth. We are also the beneficiaries of scientific leaps that have improved weather forecasting, agricultural practices, natural resources management, and disaster prevention, preparedness and management. New technologies will continue to provide the backbone of our efforts. But only a rational and informed political, social and cultural response -and public participation in all stages of the disaster

---

Paper presented at UGC sponsored National seminar on "The Political Economy of Drought and Deterioration of Tank Irrigation in Rayalaseema" on October 27-28, 2005, organized by Dept. of Economics, P.V.K.N. Govt. College, Chittoor 517 002, A.P.

management cycle - can reduce disaster vulnerability, and ensure that hazards do not turn into unmanageable disasters.

Drought conditions in Rayalaseema—causes and remedies

Agriculture is the backbone of the country's economy and also in Rayalaseema region of Andhra Pradesh. It contributes nearly 24 per cent of Gross Domestic Product (GDP); while about 65-70 per cent of the population is dependent on agriculture for their livelihood. Being a state subject, the primary responsibility for increasing production rests with the State governments whereas the Central government supplements and coordinates the entire mechanism so that the farming community benefits.

During the drought, people are affected by shortage of clean drinking water, shortage of fodder for livestock and scarcity of food in the absence of employment. Therefore, it is necessary to address these problems through suitable policies and support systems to enable the local communities to face the drought bravely.

Policy Support

Suitable policies and support services are the need of the hour in the areas, namely water scarcity, fodder supply, food security and rural employment.

Water Scarcity

The major sources of water during the drought are open wells and bore wells which are mostly owned by individuals. These water sources are generally used indiscriminately and wasted by the owners during good and bad times, while the others suffer from shortage.

Water reserves for emergencies

Use of bore-well water for cultivation by bore well owners to irrigate crops like pearl, millet and sorghum during summer, while most of the villagers are unable to fetch adequate water even for drinking. Indeed, though these precious groundwater reserves belong to the entire community, the ownership is concentrated among a few rich, who are capable of investing in wells. Misuse of such water further depletes the groundwater-table and causes water shortage for the poor and the middle class people. It is therefore necessary to introduce a suitable policy to control the use of ground water for irrigating seasonal crops during the drought.

Furthermore, the government in association with the local communities should identify reliable groundwater resources in the region, which need to be kept in reserve. Digging of bore wells for private use should be prohibited in these reserved areas and restricted number of bore wells, adequate to meet the drinking water needs should be drilled and maintained by the local authorities. The water from these reserves should be used only during emergencies and drought period to meet the water requirement of human beings and livestock. A policy decision should be taken to identify the emergency water reserves, at least for every village in the drought-prone Rayalaseema region. Subsequent efforts should also be made to recharge the groundwater around these reserves by giving priority to various watershed development and conservation programmes. Water reserves should be under the joint ownership of the village community and the local government and equitable distribution of 'water from these reserves can be organized through the peoples' organization. Conservation of such water storages can avoid transportation of water from long distance during the drought. Such practice of maintaining deep bore-wells by the Government is common in many African countries.

Water Storage and Transportation

Water shortage is often aggravated due to the inability of poor families to transport water from the sources and to store it in bulk. Therefore, it may be an ideal practice to promote the maintenance of water storage structures in every household, which can also be linked with roof top harvesting of water. A family having storage capacity of 1000-2000 litres should be able to meet their emergency water needs for 2-3 weeks. The families having such storage facilities can plan to store water well before severe water crisis. The government can formulate a policy to include water storage structures as part of the rural housing and sanitation schemes launched in the Rayalaseema region.

Transportation of water from the source of water to the residence is another important problem which not only takes a lot of time and energy but also affects the quality of water. In this process of water transportation, several vested interests having transportation facilities exploit the poor. Therefore, it is recommended to maintain water transport facilities by the community or the Gram Panchayat.

Remedial measures

1. Both traditional and modern local level practices of the preservation of water, soil, vegetation and environment need to be practiced and promoted.
2. Follow up activities to earth works during post implementation phase is crucial for sustainable development of natural resources.
3. Research efforts to focus on new areas of watershed development practices and follow up measures are essential for ensuring sustainability.
4. Crop combinations to improve soil and better productivity with optimum use of water, need be promoted.
5. Data on ground water and surface water from various sources need be considered in planning watershed projects.
6. Sprinkler and drip irrigation to be promoted over conventional irrigation practices.
7. Mapping for soil, slope, ground water etc., for optimum use of land to be prepared.
8. Best practices in optimum land use practices to be compiled.
9. Joint Forest Management to be integrated with watershed development.
10. Alternative cropping pattern, other than paddy and sugarcane to be promoted.
11. Water harvesting structures suitable to local areas need to be promoted.
12. Existing data basis i.e., maps from Survey of India, soil classification, census data, satellite imagery etc to be used for watershed development.
13. Medicinal and aromatic plants should be promoted on watersheds.

14. Mass value education and motivation programme are needed to promote socially and ecologically conducive patterns of consumption, production and life styles for farmers who are taking up agriculture.

31

Gandhian Philosophy for Rural Reconstruction

Gandhi came to be known as 'Mahatma' to the people of his country and to the world. Indians gave him the name "Mahatma", the great soul. This was not because of his fame, nor because of remarkable position, but because he was recognized to be spiritually matured. Many a Indians thought that he lived nearer to the truth, understood the meaning of life more profoundly than others and as a result was able to act as leader of his people.

He was a dominant figure on the Indian socio-political scene for nearly three and half decades that are from 1914 till his death in 1948. During this period, through his ideas and action, he played the multiple roles of, a leader of a mass movement for political freedom, reformer for equality of women, crusader against untouchability, promoter of Hindu-Muslim unity, organizer and thinker of rural reconstruction programmes and champions of non-violence, peace and human rights.

Rural Reconstruction

Gandhi's idea to develop the Indian society was based on his understanding of the society and hence based on the village system. Talking about the importance of village, he wrote in 1936, "I would say if the village perishes, India will perish, too. It will be no more India. His one mission in the world will get lost" (Harijan, 29.8.36).

He was aware of the realities of village life and knew the plight of the half starved masses of India. He often acknowledged the same in his vivid descriptions of Indian villages. He wrote "Instead of having graceful hamlets dotted the lands, we have dung-heaps. The approach to many villages is not a refreshing experience. Often one would like to shut one's eyes and stuff one's nose, such is the surrounding dirt and offending smell," (Gandhi: Constructive programmes -its meaning and place, page-2). His understanding of the plight of the people has been extremely well brought out in his writings, identifying his emphasis on removal of poverty over asthetics.

Concept: His concept of rural reconstruction is a comprehensive one, emphasizing on the economic, political, social, educational and ecological and spiritual dimensions. He ceaselessly insisted on a pattern of village life, which will be man centered and non-exploiting. The decentralized village economy should provide full-employment to all on the basis of voluntary cooperation and work for achieving self-sufficiency in its basic requirements of food, clothing and shelter (Gandhi: Hind Swaraj, Page 6). In short, it can be said that rural reconstruction, according to Gandhi should not be merely concerned with raising the standard of living of village folk, thought that was important but with the laying of the basis for peace, justice and freedom for all becomes important. Talking specifically about an ideal village, wherein he outlined the objective of rural reconstruction, he said:

"My idea of an ideal village is that of a complete republic, independent of its neighbour for its own vital wants, and yet dependent for many others in which dependence is a necessity. Such a village will contain intelligent people. First concern of the village should be to grow its won food. Then only, all communities will live together in harmony."

The curse of untouchability, intoxicating drinks and drugs will not exist. Women will enjoy the same rights as men. People in villages will not live in dirt and darkness as animals. No one will allow in luxury. The village community should take up the responsibility for providing work to all able bodied people and every one will have to contribute his quota of manual labour.

It is significant to note that while talking about rural reconstruction and emphasizing on the quality life and interdependence of individuals, Gandhi never ignored the possibility of conflict arising out of opposite interests in the individuals and collective goals or between the present and future welfare or the local and universal welfare even in rural reconstruction work. He accepted the possibilities of existence of such conflicts and believed that they can be resolved through peaceful, non-violent means. Truth, non-violence, freedom, equality, full employment, bread labour, trusteeship, decentralization, Swadesh and co-operation were perceived as cardinal principles for rural reconstruction.

Values

Of these, the first four are universal or core values, the remaining, flowing mostly from them and are linked with his economic ideas. They were formulated by Gandhi to regulate initially the conduct of inmates of Satyagraha Ashrams in 1930 and latter extended to the work for rural reconstruction. These were not intended to be mechanical formulae, but as practical aides to moral and spiritual growth. A brief elaboration of some of these principles, like truth, non-violence, freedom and equality will be useful to understand them and their importance in the context of initiating action for rural reconstruction.

(a) **Truth:** He regarded truth as the source of Dharma. Hence there should be truth in thought, speech and action. The man who has realized truth completely has nothing else to know, because all knowledge is necessarily included in it. And that is why truth is perhaps the most importance name of God. In fact, it is better to say that truth is God, than to say God is truth.

His concept of truth involves complete tolerance to those who differ. According to him, the aim of human life is to attain truth and non-violence. Truth is of two types, ultimate and relative. It is comparatively easy to achieve relative truth. However, the endeavour should be know the ultimate truth, because this results in realization of God.

(b) **Non-Violence:** Gandhi considered non-violence, besides truth, as synonymous with God. He believed that non-violence has its own relevance in resolving conflict and is also related to the reconstruction of the society. Non-violent resolution of conflicts is in accordance with the dignity of man's spirit. He can save his spirit by observing non-violence, which is the tune with his spirituality. Another aspect of Non-violence is progress. It binds people together, promoting cooperation, harmony and unity, and preventing destruction, contributes to development.

(c) **Freedom:** Closely linked with truth and non-violence is freedom, without the freedom of body, mind and soul, individual can not attain perfection. It is used to indicate freedom to make a choice and to take a decision without which development of individual is not possible. This freedom can be achieved by acquisition of the capacity by all to resist authority, when it is misused. It makes people tolerant to the other ideas.

(d) Equality: Flows logically from the concept of non-violence, since non-violence and non-exploitation is impossible without equality.

Programme for Rural Reconstruction

The constructive programme, as suggested by Gandhi, for rural reconstruction has been summarized below:

(1) Establishing communal unity by promoting better understanding especially between the Hindus and Muslims.

(2) Abolition of untouchability.

(3) Introducing prohibition through the efforts of doctors, women and students and by promoting recreational facilities.

(4) Establishing economic equality.

(5) Establishing Khadi production centers in each of the 6,00,000 villages of India, covering every family and every aspect of the production of distribution processes, from growing the cotton to the marketing of the finished products.

(6) Improving traditional village skills and development of other village agro and animal, based industries, hand grinding, hand pounding, soap making, paper making, match box making, tanning and oil pressing on mutual help basis to attain self-sufficiency in food and clothing.

(7) Improving livestock along with the development of agriculture.

(8) Introducing new or basic education in every Indian village, to transform village children, into model villagers as well as to change the attitude of the people towards physical labour etc.

(9) Organising adult education.

(10) Promoting the education, health and hygiene. This involves a detailed programme including thinking of the purest thoughts, breathing the freshest air, establishing a balance between physical and mental work standing and sitting erect, being neat and clean, and control over the quality and quantity of food. Such education should be imparted independent of the government by the family and the village community.

(11) Improving village sanitation.

(12) Emancipating women.

(13) Organizing the peasantry for the improvement of their condition and the achievement of their rights through non-violent means.

(14) Organising labour with a non-political purpose on a local basis. This is important because labourers are trustees of labour force, which is a great wealth.

(15) Uplifting the adivasis or aboriginal tribes.

(16) Organising student services on a non-political basis.

(17) Caring and rehabilitation for the lepers.

(18) Promoting Panchayati Raj. Gandhi strongly advocated the decentralization of political ad economic power in favour of more or less self-sufficient and self-governing village panchayat.

Agencies for Rural Reconstruction: Voluntary actions formed the key in Gandhi's idea of rural reconstruction. He believed that efforts for rural reconstruction should come from within the people and should be independent of the government, otherwise it will result in perpetual dependence. Consequently, the efforts for rural upliftment should be initiated, managed and organized by the people themselves.

Realizing the importance of voluntary action for rural reconstruction work, he appealed to his admirers and followers to settle in villages and initiate the above-mentioned programmes. Tin response to his call, a large number of people settled in villages by forming groups and devoted their might for the reconstruction of society. These workers in course of time came to be known as "Constructive Programme Workers". The number of these workers now will be about few thousands considering the number of organizations engaged in Gandhian constructive programme including the organizations working for khadi and village industries.

Conclusion

About 85 years have passed since Gandhi was exposed to rural problem and then expressed his views on rural reconstruction. 12 five-year plans have been formulated; including eleven plans have been implemented after 1950. Lot of changes has taken place in the socio-economic and political life of the people even in the villages.

But, despite all this, development has remained a key concern in the conduct of country's development. Efforts for rural development till now are centered round the problems of poverty, ignorance, illiteracy, ill health and exploitations. This is even after the government and non-governmental organizations have put in their might in dealing in the problems. This raises questions about the problems and ways and means adopted to deal with them. In this context Gandhi's ideas and action for rural reconstruction has its importance and relevance to deal with the myriad problem of the people living in villages. What is important is to examine the ideas and action in the light of changes that have affected the life and living condition of the people and initiating action at the level of the people through people's groups based on a determined political, administrative and peoples' will.

32

Value Oriented Education for Social Reconstruction*

Value Oriented Education

A value can itself be defined as a belief, which guides human behaviour and helps in making decisions about choices. Faced with many choices, man makes his decisions, based upon his personal values. In this process, value education has a very crucial role to play. Besides creating awareness, value education helps an individual to opt for choices, which would contribute towards integral growth and ultimate happiness of the individual and the society.

Any worthwhile attempts to discuss "value education" cannot ignore the issue of 'value in education'. Value in education proposes that there is a basic difference between 'teaching a subject' and 'educating an individual', between being 'subject/ discipline-oriented' and 'pupil-centered': and that the true vocation of education is the latter. To recognise this distinction is to recognise the fact that there is no such thing as a neutral educational process. All education - no matter what the topic, no -matter what form of presentation - carries a predisposition, a specific inclination, a value. There is no such thing as an 'unbiased education'.

Value Education should focus on the following areas:

1. To contribute intellectual, moral, physical and overall personality development.
2. To make an individual to be a responsible citizen, their role and sense of responsibility towards society, family and the world around him.

---

*Paper presented at UGC National Seminar on "Value Oriented Education" organized by Department of Education on 22-23 November 2004, S.V. University, Tirupati - 517 502.

3. To develop the ability to distinguish between the right and wrong.
4. To live in harmony with nature and the world.
5. To create an attitude of genuine appreciation for the value and respect for all forms of life.
6. To be aware of social problems.
7. To be ready to accept leadership.
8. To become human and learn to give more, than to take.
9. To create environmental awareness cultural heritage and ethics in personal and social life.
10. To promote the concept of equality of sex through elimination of sexual bias and ensuring equal participation of women in all walks of life.

Philosophy of Value-Oriented Education

Value-oriented education is inherent in the concept of education. There are at least three assumptions of the educational process.

1. There is first, the pursuit of man to know himself and the Universe and to relate himself with the Universe as harmoniously as possible. This pursuit constitutes the very theme of human culture. And education derives its fundamental thrust from the cultural setting at a given point of time.
2. Secondly, there is a process of transmission of the accumulated results of the past to the grouping generation so as to enable it to carry forward the cultural heritage and to build the gates and the paths of the future.
3. And thirdly, there is in the process of transmission, a deliberate attempt to accelerate as far as possible the process of human progress.

In its very nature, education is a normative endeavour. Being at once a product or instrument of culture, education tends to promote the highest aims of culture. Hence, education tends to be a process of training where by individuals in the society are enabled to embody progressively those values, which we in our highest thought and aspiration come to regard as something most desirable. It is in this context that education encourages and fosters the arts and sciences as well as technologies whereby man and the Universe can be ideally interrelated. At the same time, the idea of human progress is built up, and education endeavours to discover and apply efficient means of the right rhythms of acceleration of individual and social progress in general.

Education is thus in its nature value-oriented. The conditions through which human culture is passing today provide additional reasons for value-oriented education.

(a) An increasing number of people of thought and action feel that humanity has been gripped by serious maladies and that these maladies are the result of our disequilibrium between the ideals that mankind is labouring to realise during the recent centuries and the disconcerting actualities which refuse obstinately to change. With the passing of every decade, humanity seems to feel more and more acutely that the realisation of its ideals has become imperative, while at the same time, it seems almost impossible to accomplish this realisation. It is, therefore, felt that humanity is passing through an acute crisis.

(b) A huge structure is being built up with an increasing insistence on efficiency needed for industrialised society, leaving practically no room for the growth of profounder wisdom which can rightly guide human progress in the critical times through which we are passing today.

(c) As never before, humanity is able to envisage several alternative possibilities of the imminent future. As never before, it is felt that human volition can play a decisive role in selecting, planning, designing and actualising these possibilities. As never before, humanity is convinced that the most desirable course for the human race is to strive with fixed determination for human unity, global peace and for the advancing of the three great ideals of progress, namely, liberty, equality and fraternity. As never before, there has been an increasing perception that the most effective means for achieving these desirable objectives is value-oriented education.

(d) This feeling is reinforced by the fact that under the pressure of technology development, the world is shrinking, and we are dreaming of the possibility of a planetary civilization, for which we have not yet secured a corresponding psychological development, which could enable human consciousness to sustain such a planetary civilisation. On the contrary, there is a growing preponderance of those impulses which can thrive only in ignorance, fragmentation, discord and violence.

(e) In India, there is a feeling that the country is sinking under the weight of problems such as those of terrorism, corruption, and plutocracy, and it is realised that solutions need to be sought at a level that is far deeper than the level at which we are now thinking and acting and that special attention has to be paid to the promotion of values that can counteract the increasing destruction of the country and its culture.

Against this background, both from the global point of view and from the Indian point of view we need to develop and practice value-oriented education.

Integral Value-Oriented Education

In our present system of education, we are too occupied with mental development, and we give preponderant importance to those qualities which are relevant to subject-oriented, book-oriented, and examination oriented systems. In contrast, the concept of integral education implies a simultaneous integrated process of development of the qualities and values relevant to physical education, vital education, mental education, physic and spiritual education.

Integral value-oriented education is a matter of research, and the results of this research indicate the need to simultaneously develop knowledge, will, harmony and skill, and that this development should be for each individual a system of natural organization of the highest processes and movements of which he or she is capable.

Morality and Spirituality

In any sound philosophy of value-oriented education, an effort should be made to arrive at clear conceptions of morality and spirituality, since both are distinct and yet related, and since both need to be distinguished from religion. Again, this matter is very important in the context of the Indian system of education, since the Indian Constitution clearly states that "No religious instruction shall be provided in educational institutions wholly maintained out of the State Funds", and that "No person attending any educational institution recognized by the state and receiving aid out of State Funds shall be required to take part in any religious instruction that may be imparted in such institutions or to attend any religious worship that may be conducted in such institutions or in premises attached to these unless such person or, if such a person is a minor, his guardian has given his consent there to".

As far as the distinction between morality and spirituality is concerned, it may be said that much depends upon what we intend to include in our definition of the word "morality" or in the word "spirituality". In Indian thought the distinction between morality and spirituality has been clearly made and we have two definite terms, 'naitik' and 'adhyatmik' each having its own specific and distinguishing connotation.

Value-Education and Ethics

Ethics have been described in the Oxford Dictionary as "a set of principles of morals, science of morals, moral principles, rules of conduct of a group, organization or an individual". Values have been described as "one's principles and standards, one's judgements what is valuable or important in life".

Contribution to a healthy society is an enterprise in which value education in our schools and colleges has a crucial role to play. These basic values and ethics can be derived by each of us from our experiences as human beings by using our common sense and intelligence, values which are positive when they promote justice, bliss, happiness, dignity and beauty. And negative when our actions result in war, injustice, sorrow and loss of dignity of fellow human beings. Our values are based on our interaction with others. Distilled from clashes of paradigms between individuals, groups and different members of our society, our teaching institutions must define, and teach values the practice of which makes students respected in their own eyes and also those of others, not as just ordinary citizens but as the best among them.

Physical values

Next to intellectual values are come across physical values. It might be recalled that it were the Greeks who made the greater advances in the realm of knowledge, who laid great stress and contributed to intellectual development. They simultaneously realized the critical importance of nurturing physical values. The truth of the adage "a healthy mind in a healthy body" can hardly be gain said. Teachers can create in the child a keen interest in physical fitness, health and games and sports.

Cultural Heritage and Value Education

Technology today is the foremost source to bring social value changes and motivates economic value system. But technology is also banishing the traditional boundaries and concepts. It is bringing forth the desperate need for enduring relationships, not only between human beings but also between our environment and society.

Today the young are confused and bewildered by the intellectual problems of the day; they are eager to find a way out of these problems and to achieve understanding amidst the conflict of cultures and the clash of civilizations. However the profound but paradoxical trend is that science and technology seem to be calling to humanity to eschew the concept of secularism and for the sake of survival or better living to look forward towards spiritual concepts. If this is taken seriously and if we can accept science and technology concepts of values, then our whole outlook opens up to the grand convergence of metaphysics and physics.

Teachers inculcate a fundamental understanding on learning process leading to conceptions of citizenship, privileges and responsibilities involved in being citizens of a great nation. They also implant the meaning of individual freedom and the rights occurring from it along with its inseparable counterparts, of social responsibilities and duties flowing from individual freedom.

The process of education system will not be complete without value content

In a value-oriented system of education values should be its centre, and they should constitute a centrifugal force with full control over the objectives, content, methodology and management of education. Further, in such a system, the benefits of education should reach beyond the four walls of the classroom to the population. It is important particularly in the context when only 65.38 per cent of adults are literate (2001 census). It implies that in a value-oriented education, non-formal system should supplement the formal system. Once this concept is accepted needless to say that, there is an urgent need to revamp the entire system of education.

Education is thus the means to achieve the goals of progress and prosperity. Thomas Jefferson, former U.S. President once remarked; that "Education alone can erode ignorance". One will, however have to be very cautious and ensure that the content and process of education is strong enough to achieve its objectives.

Education is an Instrument for Poverty Eradication

The relationship between education and poverty reduction is quite straight and linear as education is empowering. It enables the person to participate in the development process. It inculcates the knowledge and skills needed to improve the income earning potential and intern the quality of life. Moreover, education of girls and women helps in improving the number of other indicators of human development.

Education helps to lay the foundation for the following pillars of poverty reduction: Empowerment, human development, social development and good governance. Basic education empowers individuals as:

- It opens up avenues of communication that would otherwise be closed, expands personal choice and control over one's environment, and is necessary for the acquisition of many other skills.
- It gives people access to information through both print and electronic media, equips them to cope better with work and family responsibilities, and changes the image they have of themselves.
- It strengthens their self-confidence to participate in community affairs and influence political issues.

- It gives disadvantaged people the tools they need to move from exclusion to full participation in their society.
- It empowers entire nation because educated citizens and workers have the skills to make democratic institutions function effectively, to meet the demands for a more sophisticated workforce, to work for a cleaner environment, and to meet their obligations as parents and citizens.

Social and Economic Gains

Investing in women's education results in substantial social and economic gains.

- Educated women have fewer children. In South Asia, women with no education have seven children on average; women with at least seven years of education have fewer than four children.

- Educated women have healthier children in Africa, one out of five children dies before the age of five if the mother has no education; the probability is more than halved for children whose mothers have seven years of education. Educated women has a stronger positive effect on children's health than educated men.

- Mothers are also much more closely involved in the immediate care of children and in the critical decisions about food, sanitation and general nurturing, all of which influence children's health and development. Longer spacing between births leads to healthier children.

- Education provides women with greater opportunities for employment and income, and raises the opportunity cost of their time in economic activities compared to child rearing. Such economic gains motivate families to have fewer children.

- The vicious cycle of high birth rates, high maternal and infant mortality and endemic poverty has been transformed into a virtuous circle through investment in human capital-enhancing labour productivity, reducing fertility and mortality, raising further investments in people.

Social Development

- Education is an important means of facilitating and directing social change. Children (and adults) who attend school are exposed to new ideas and concepts and attitudes that form part of the basis for social change.
- The socialization obtained by attending school includes such values as punctuality, following instructions, managing time, planning work, focusing attention, adhering to rules and receptivity to new concepts, thus helping to develop persons better suited, function effectively in a changing society.
- Education also plays an important role in cultural transmission. Transmission of culture, appreciation of cultural heritage, understanding of national history, inculcation of cultural values are all increasingly left to the schooling process as traditional societies change.

The continuing challenge for education is to ensure that all people have the knowledge and skills necessary for continuing human and economic development and for breaking the poverty cycle. The linear relationship between education, poverty and empowerment is, however, governed by the circumstances of a country and within a country in a particular region. Education, thus, influences and is influenced by the context in which it is developed. This synergistic relationship implies that education must be in a constant state of change as it responds to changing social and economic needs and that education in itself is a force for social and economic change as people become more empowered and more productive.

Education and Human Value

Human value should be the major objective of education at all levels; and all other objectives of personality development, economic development, total employment etc.

The close relationship between society and the family, results in certain norms, values and rules of behaviour, which are required to be observed in all roles and relationships. This can result in either equity or inequity and affect, especially, the vulnerable groups in the family such as women and children particularly the girl child. Thus, the problems of our society, such as patriarchy, have had an inexorable effect on the girl child, and consequently, not only on women but on women's role and function as decision makers and influences in the family. The status of women in the society can be measured from the importance given to women's education.

Conclusion

Education has a vital role to play in increasing the capacity of the family and the community for a better quality of life through the competencies they develop. Not only are they empowered through such competency based career development but, intern, they can extend it through their work to the community and vulnerable groups, thus leading to the social development, and particularly to the development of women through self-awareness and acquiring skills. It is worthwhile to create the awakening among the people, so that they can come up by taking care of themselves for social reconstruction.

REFERENCES

S. Parvathi and C. Karthikeyan, "Empowering the Status of Women" *Social Welfare*, Vol. 49, No. 5, August, 2002, Central Social Welfare Board, New Delhi.

Dr. Karan Singh, "Education in the Twenty-First Century" *Yojana*, Vol. 46, September 2002, Publication Division, New Delhi.

Dr. Anil Wilson, "Value-Education or Value-in-Education", *Ibid*, p. 10.

Dr. Kireet Joshi, "Philosophy of Value-Oriented Education", *Ibid*, p. 12.

M.M. Luther, "Implementation of Value Education Programmes in the Indian Context", *Ibid*, p. 19.

Dr. Saiyid Hamid, "Role of the Teacher in Promoting Value Education", *Ibid*, p. 25.

Swami Gokulananda, "Cultural Heritage and Value Education", *Ibid*, p. 28.

K. Venkatasubramanian, "Education and Poverty", The Supreme Saviour, Vol. No. 109, 16-31 January 2002, New Delhi.

Index